QUESTIONS WOMEN ASK IN PRIVATE

H. NORMAN WRIGHT

Trusted Counsel on the Most Compelling Issues Women Face Today

QUESTIONS WOMEN ASK IN PRIVATE

Regal Books
A Division of Gospel Light
Ventura, California, U.S.A.

Published by Regal Books
A Division of Gospel Light
Ventura, California, U.S.A.
Printed in U.S.A.

Library of Congress Cataloging-in-Publication Data
Wright, H. Norman.
Questions women ask in private: counsel on the most compelling issues women face today/ H. Norman Wright.
p. cm.
Includes bibliographical references.
ISBN 0-8307-1522-3 (hard cover)
1. Women—Psychology. 2. Women—Conduct of life. 3. Women—Religious life. I. Title.
HQ1206.W953 1993   93-913
305.4—dc20   CIP

4 5 6 7 8 9 10 11 12 13 14 15 16 17 18 19 20 / 03 02 01 00 99 98 97

Rights for publishing this book in other languages are contracted by Gospel Literature International (GLINT). GLINT also provides technical help for the adaptation, translation, and publishing of Bible study resources and books in scores of languages worldwide. For further information, contact GLINT, Post Office Box 4060, Ontario, California, 91761-1003, U.S.A., or the publisher.

CONTENTS

Section Two
MARRIAGE ISSUES

Section Three
FAMILY ISSUES

Section Four

PARENTING ISSUES

DIVORCE AND REMARRIAGE

INTRODUCTION

The phone rings. An appointment is made. Thousands of times a day it happens throughout our country. It could be a friend of yours, your adult child, a relative or...you. Every day, scores of women make calls to professional counselors or ministers with questions and issues that have been festering for months or years. Or they call because they have been plunged into a severe and immediate crisis. But whatever the reason and motivation, they are seeking answers and solutions.

Many more women than men seek help from a counselor. Women are much more prone to want to find solutions and are more willing to admit they need someone else's help than are men. I see this all the time in my own practice and in our clinic. I listen to women discuss many issues and concerns; some are solved quickly while others take many months. And the issues cover a broad spectrum.

I listen to some women who feel hopeless, purposeless and unfulfilled in their lives. I hear others who just want to improve what appears to be a fairly well-functioning life. Their outward appearance is sometimes deceiving. They often appear healthy, strong and as though they have it all together. Most have families, careers, homes or apartments and attend evangelical churches in Southern California. But a woman's interior does not always match what I see on the exterior. In spite of appearances, many of these women feel empty.

I remember one middle-aged woman who sat in my office and said, "Norm, I just don't understand it. I feel like God has forgotten that I exist. If God is there, why did He check out on me? Everything that I try is a waste. Nothing clicks. I gave and gave to my children and they didn't turn out right. I failed as a parent, as a wife and as a real estate agent. I've worked hard, tried to live according to the Scriptures, but God didn't come through. Don't try to tell ME that He loves me!"

Another woman told me, "I feel so unfulfilled in my marriage. There's nothing there. There is no excitement, no communication. In fact at times I wonder if he is aware that I even exist! I thought we knew one another when we were married, but now I don't know....We were one of the few that had a pure relationship while we dated. We were seen as the ideal Christian couple. We pray together—or at least, we *did.* Now it's not much. Even sex isn't much. I guess I've sort of given up on us. I'm sure God has. What do I do now?"

These women are asking honest questions and are searching for a way to fill the emptiness in their lives.

What about you? Have you ever gone for counseling? Have you ever wanted to sit down with someone to find help with a problem? Have you ever wondered what women ask in counseling sessions? From time to time people ask me what others talk about and why they would seek out and open their lives to a complete stranger.

How This Book Began

What *do* women ask in counseling?

We posed that question by mail survey to 700 professional counselors, ministers, lay counselors and social workers in 1992. Amazingly, we received more than 700 responses—an incredible response rate.

We asked them: "What are five frequently asked questions posed by your female clients, indicating the troubling or sensitive issues they are struggling with in counseling?"

We received more than 3,500 questions. But remember, each question asked could reflect scores or hundreds of counselees who have asked this question over the years. Each question was carefully considered and the most frequently asked questions were selected to serve as the basis for this book. (We posed the same question to the respondents concerning the questions men asked in counseling. Appendix 2 of this book will introduce you to some of the men's questions.)

From the data collected, we now have the most significant and most asked questions women ask of those whom they see as being able to assist them. The questions include the issues of submission, anger, abuse, divorce, affairs, self-esteem, intimacy, sex, romance, how to change a husband, communication, parenting, finances, home versus work, stress, addictions, grief, abandonment, stepparenting and many more.

For some of those who seek counseling, the issues they raise are out of a sense of desperation. They try on their own for some time to resolve these issues but each time face a dead end. They realize that someone else needs to work with them. Most likely some of the counselees seek help at the early stages of their concern. They want to resolve the issue before they reach the desperation stage.

You may find yourself identifying with some of the questions asked in this book. You may have had some of these same concerns in the past or may be facing them now.

The Counselor

Sometimes people wonder what actually takes place in counseling. How does it work? How long does it take? Who does all the talking and the work? What should a woman expect when she sits down and talks with someone who is skilled in counseling?

The person you meet with when you go for counseling is trying to work himself or herself out of a job. In other words, they want you to grow and improve as rapidly as possible so you will no longer need their expertise. Their hope is for you to learn from the experience so that when you confront other issues in your life you will be able to draw upon the new knowledge and resources you have accumulated.

Your counselor, whether it be a psychologist, marriage counselor, minister or lay counselor will not be doing all of the work. Their role is to enable you to make healthy decisions, discover information you were lacking and move ahead in your life. A counselor functions as a resource, a guide, someone who helps you apply what you have learned. A counselor is someone who encourages and believes in you as a person.

The Christian counselor also guides you to discover the riches and abundance you have through knowing Jesus Christ and helps you apply God's Word to your life and circumstances in a new way.

Do not expect your counselor to solve all your difficulties for you or tell you, "Now, this is exactly what you need to do." Sometimes I have heard counselees say, "Yes, I know you're not going to give me a direct answer. You're going to say, 'What do you feel you could do about this situation?' or 'What are your options?'" Often this is true. But at other times a counselor will give definite direction but perhaps in a more indirect way such as, "Have you considered trying this...?"

It is better for you to make the decision rather than becoming dependent upon any counselor. Your ultimate source of authority, wisdom and guidance is Jesus Christ. Counselors can offer suggestions, opinions, guidance, assist you in exploring options and recommend new steps to take for yourself or for a relationship. But the final decision of what is done must be yours.

Perhaps one of the greatest frustrations counselors experience is that so many people wait so long to seek help, or they hesitate because of fear. Many women wonder, *What will others think about me if I go for counseling? Will they think less of me? Will they see me as sick? What will my counselor think about me after hearing all this garbage?*

A counselor is not there to sit in judgment. He or she is there to help you and minister to you, and it really does not matter what others think about you if you go for counseling. They are not experts on you nor your judge. Most would applaud you for having the courage to go. Do not let your fears paralyze you if you feel you need help.

Benefits of This Book

Resource Guide

This book reflects questions that thousands of women have asked. And because we are not in the actual counseling office with the usual amount of time to dissect the issue and work together to discover a problem and solution, the answers will be a bit more direct than you might hear in counseling. I will attempt to offer my opinion and give suggestions based upon what I have learned in more than 25 years of counseling, from teaching, study and from counselees. Additional resource helps are given for some of the questions for your own in-depth study. One of the benefits of this book is that it is a resource to guide you in seeking solutions for your own questions and issues.

This book could be considered similar to an employment agency, only instead of helping you find the right vocation for your ability, it will point you to the right resource that will assist you in discovering a much more in-depth approach to each problem or situation.

A New Perspective

This book does not contain the final answer on any subject. Rather, it is designed to offer suggestions and help you discover a new perspective on an issue, or new alternatives. Consider this a beginning point in your journey. You may discover an identical or similar situation to your own and be able to apply the principles and suggestions.

You may find yourself responding with the feeling, "So I'm not the only one with that concern or that experience!" Time and time again in the counseling office people will exclaim, "You mean this is not that unusual? Others have experienced this? I'm not the only one and perhaps that means I'm not crazy! What a relief!"

Do not be surprised if the answer to the issue or question you are personally seeking is not found in the section you are looking under. You may discover it elsewhere, which is why it is important for you to read all the questions and answers. The chapters contain some overlap; an answer to a question that is not an issue for you may provide the help you are seeking. What you discover may not fit exactly, but you may find a principle, idea or concept that you can expand, make your own, and apply to your area of concern. Read thoughtfully, for out of your thought process creativity will emerge.

Source of Hope

If anything is accomplished by this book, however, I would like it to be a source of hope for you that there *are* answers, there *is* hope, there *can be* new beginnings in life regardless of what has taken place in your background or in a current situation. Many who come for counseling feel stuck, mired in place by a nongiving cement. I talk to people all the time who are functioning physically but appear to be crippled emotionally and spiritually by past experiences.

Self-help

It would be difficult to recount the number of people I have counseled since beginning my practice in 1967. Many of my counselees gain new insights and information and are able to break free from the effects of the past and move forward with their lives. You may be able to do this on your own by your own study. Others cannot. They struggle and struggle and progress is limited. They need the assistance of an actual counselor who can walk with them and loan them faith and hope until their own is activated. If you are dealing with past issues that trouble you I hope this book will help you.

Feeling Stuck?

I do not know why you are reading this book or what issues you are struggling with at this time. Perhaps you need to let go of regrets you may be carrying from lost opportunities or relationships.

Perhaps you need to let loose of blame or resentment you harbor from hurts inflicted upon you by others.

Perhaps you need to let go of buried memories that have been repressed and seared over because of the pain and damage experienced. Remember, when memories have been buried, they have been buried alive. Someday they will resurrect and you probably will not be in charge of them when they emerge.

When any of us carry this unnecessary baggage with us we are limited and actually stuck. Do you understand the feeling of being stuck? I do. I have been there.

My Snake River Episode

I remember a time when I was fishing the Snake River with a friend. We had been walking the river for about an hour when we found a place where two channels of the river converged—an ideal spot to fish. Because both my friend and I had waders on, we could walk through the water to any spot we chose. He chose to stand near the bank, and I headed out to a spot where the two channels came together.

As I stood there casting into the frothy water, I noticed that my feet were settling a bit deeper into the mud and sand. I did not think much about it, but every time I cast and shifted my weight, I sank a little deeper into the riverbed. But when I decided to move to another spot in the river, I could not move my feet. I tried lifting one leg and then the other, but both feet felt encased in cement, and nothing I tried seemed to work. I was stuck and stuck good.

The more I tried to extract my feet, the more I sank. Finally, in desperation I hit upon the idea of lifting my feet out of the waders, then pulling the waders out of the mud. If I had not thought of taking my feet out of the boots first, I might still be stuck there!

Reflect on Your Needs

You have probably experienced being stuck, but perhaps in different ways. You may be feeling stuck in your life now, wanting more but unable to move ahead. When you are stuck in the past, the rest of the world passes you by, and all you can do is wave. You are not in the flow and you are not being blessed.

Before you read on, take a minute and reflect on your own personal life. Ask yourself these questions: "What do I want from this book?" "What is there in my own life that I would like to change?" "In what area do I need help?" "How do I want to be different?" "Do I believe that help is possible and am I willing to submit to God's solution rather than attempting to force my own desires upon Him?"

Whoa! You may be thinking, *Where did that last question come from?* Too often as we seek solutions for our difficulties we have the outcome mapped out. It is good to have a goal in mind but we must also have a willingness to seek the face of God and His solution for our lives. The end result and timing may be different than we anticipate.

God's Solutions

You may think that God has let you down. You may feel you have tried everything possible and nothing has or will work. You may think that because a man is authoring and compiling this book he has nothing to say to you, as you have been abused much of your life by men. You may believe that what you have experienced has been so devastating, very little change is possible. You may also think God does not exist for you.

I hear your statements. They are honest thoughts that describe where a hurt person is at that moment. I would like to encourage you with one suggestion.

Change and Grow

Be open for change and growth in your life. The longer we live with a problem or intolerable situation the more our vision of change becomes defective. We see only our current situation and stay rooted in place while life and the world around us continues moving ahead. We become locked into the past and present rather than looking to the future. The more this occurs, the more the future appears like some unattainable, ethereal, unrealistic dreamworld.

Have Vision

One of my favorite Bible verses is in the book of Joel, "Your old men will dream dreams, your young men will see visions" (2:28). When you have a vision for what you want to become, as well as for the future, you are able to move upstream against the difficult currents that hit you in the face again and again. When you see things as they could be, you need not let the odds overwhelm you. You will still recognize obstacles but you won't dwell upon them.

Do you know what one of my hopes and dreams is for every counselee? I hope she will be able to see the potential for her future as God sees it. I want her to become a risk-taking visionary. I know it is scary to keep trying and running the risk of heartache or disappointment. But what potential. I love what Chuck Swindoll says about vision:

> Vision is the ability to see God's presence, to perceive God's power, to focus on God's plan in spite of the obstacles....Vision is the ability to see above and beyond the majority. Vision is perception—reading the presence and power of God into one's circumstances. I sometimes think of vision as looking at life through the lens of God's eyes, seeing situations as He sees them. Too often we see things not as they are, but as we are. Think about that. Vision has to do with looking at life with a divine perspective, reading the scene with God in clear focus.
>
> Whoever wants to live differently in "the system" must correct his or her vision.[1]

A common illustration of creating a vision for what you want occurs when both wives and husbands come separately for counseling. Their issue is the same. They feel they do not love their partner and somewhere they gained the misbelief that it is impossible to learn to love their spouse again. Some do not even want to try. Others do but are confused about how to accomplish this. Many times I have suggested, "Could you imagine what it would be like if you did love your spouse. Describe for me what it would be like. Describe how you would feel about him, how you would treat him, think about him, support him, encourage him, pray for him, talk about him to others and so on." We talk about this and refine it so that it is realistic and attainable.

My final suggestion to them is this: "Please take what we have talked about and write out in detail this vision you have created for loving your spouse. Read it out loud several times a day and write it out several times as well. Pray over each facet of this vision out loud and ask God to make this love come alive within you. And then behave toward your spouse as though you actually did love him. Do this for a month and let's discover what happens."

Perhaps you know the rest. Yes, it takes work, commitment and effort. And above all, it takes a willingness to change and be open to

God's direction in our lives. Can you imagine what would happen if you would apply this same procedure to someone you resent and with whom you want to move toward forgiveness? It can happen.

Have Hope

Do you use the words "impossible," "can't," "never" or any other limiting words when you confront whatever it is in your life you would like to change? It is a strange mixture, wanting to change but being immobilized by words of defeat.

Become a person of hope. When you look at your situation, can you envision what it would be like if it were different? Do you see several variations of how it could be different? I think we need several options because we cannot predict in advance the final outcome. We might be surprised by the outcome. At times, what I wanted and felt was best never turned out that way, but I discovered I was able to gain insights and strength and not just exist but live abundantly with the situation. At other times, the final outcome was totally different from what I wanted or predicted and I discovered that it was fulfilling; though you would never have convinced me of this beforehand.

Fear

If you came to me for counseling, one of the questions you would probably hear me asking you is, "What is the fear in your life that drives you?" Strange? Perhaps, especially if you had said nothing about being fearful. But over the years I have discovered time and time again that most people are driven more by fear than drawn by hope. Think about it for a moment. What does motivate you? If you have thought of counseling but have not taken that step, what has stopped you? What has stopped you in other areas of your life? Have you ever listed your fears? Is your life characterized by faith more than fear? It is something to consider.

Our fears cripple us from moving ahead and we end up walking with a crutch. And fear clouds our vision as well. Fear hinders relationships from developing and blocks a full relationship with God.

Fear is a protective device to keep us from hurt but has its own dire consequences that are even worse. Fear actually limits our vocabulary. Phrases such as "I can"; "I will"; "I'm able"; "With God's help and guidance" are missing because of fear. Learning to live with faith and hope, however, can evict the fears in our lives. But it is a slow-growing learning process. Faith is stepping out without the knowledge that there is firm footing in front of us. People keep from seeking counseling because of their fear. I have heard many say, "You don't know how scary it was calling to make this appointment and coming here. I almost called and canceled several times because of my fear." But soon their fear dissolves and they begin to grow.

One of the fears that can immobilize us is the feeling that in spite of a desire to change our lives, the cost will be too much or the pain too much or all of our efforts will be wasted. Your situation or your friend's may seem impossible. I have felt that way as I have sat and listened to some personal or marital situations. My humanity almost got in the way of relying upon the grace and power of God. From time to time I need to read a statement by Oswald Chambers *(My Utmost for His Highest)* as quoted in Lloyd Ogilvie's book, *Lord of the Impossible.* Here's what Chambers says about our impossibilities:

> [They] provide a platform for the display of His almighty grace and power. He will not only deliver us, but in doing so, He will give us a lesson we will never forget; and to which we will return with joyous reflection. We will never be able to thank God enough for having done exactly what He did.[2]

Reach Out

Are you hesitating to reach out to someone for guidance and counsel? Are you limiting your future and growth because of a fear or a resentment? If you have been doing this for some time you know what that is accomplishing. So why not try something different! Reach out. Look for answers in this book. Use them as a beginning for your healing process. Use them to share with others and become a source of healing in their lives.

To help you move toward the future, I would like you to consider the words that helped me during 1991. Roger Palms wrote a penetrating devotional book entitled, *Enjoying the Closeness of God.* He said:

> In Christ I am free to live, free to be flexible, free to move, free to fail, free to succeed. I can confidently know that there are things I will do well and things that I will not be able to do at all. I don't have to try to prove to myself or to others that somehow I can be what I am not. God made me; God owns me.
>
> And as I relax in Christ, I begin to see that there have always been people like me. This reinforces my certainty. I meet people in Scripture—people like Abraham, Moses, Stephen—who did not fully understand themselves or their purpose, but they knew that God understood them. They did not always feel strong or healthy or wise. They wondered at God's commands as sometimes I do. Even the disciple who loved Jesus most didn't always understand everything he did or taught. Realizing this allows me to have moments of depression; it allows me to cry and pound my fists on God's chest. It allows me to be the person I am because I am God's person. I can look to my Creator because I am his. I can look to my Redeemer; I can look ahead to fulfillment and to deliverance. And I can be happy even in my "failures," waiting to see how these too will be used because I am secure in the One who made me and owns me.
>
> I know that there is a tomorrow.[3]

Now, let's consider the questions most often asked by women in counseling and the problems—and solutions—these questions reflect.

Notes

1. Chuck Swindoll, *Living Above the Level of Mediocrity* (Dallas, TX: WORD, Inc., 1987), pp. 94,95.
2. Lloyd John Ogilvie, *Lord of the Impossible* (Nashville, TN: Abingdon Press, 1984), pp. 17,18.
3. Roger C. Palms, *Enjoying the Closeness of God* (Minneapolis, MN: World Wide Publications, 1989), p. 246.

Chapter 1

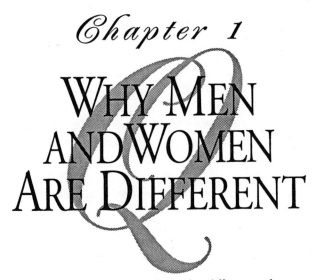

WHY MEN AND WOMEN ARE DIFFERENT

I have been tackling questions about the differences between men and women each week for the past 25 years with women in counseling, and these questions will be asked in the next century as well. To illustrate the problem let's look at some common comments.

A woman shared the struggle she is having with her husband: "I don't think men understand the difference between sharing their feelings and what they *think* about their feelings. They tend to intellectualize so much of the time. Why do men have to think about how they feel? He doesn't have to respond like a textbook or edit everything he shares. I wonder if his emotional side threatens him? Of course, you can't always control your emotional responses."

This comment points to the differences between men and women as well as to personality types. Remember, some gender differences are innate, while others result from cultural conditioning or environmental influences. The concern here is not "why men are the way they are." Rather, it is to identify the differences between men and women. These differences vary in intensity, and some men reflect what we call "feminine characteristics."

Have you ever felt like this wife? "I wish he didn't think he always had to define everything. I feel as if I've been talking to a dictionary. Every week for the past year my husband has said, 'What do you mean? I can't talk to you if I don't understand your words. Give me some facts, not those darn feelings!' Well, sometimes I can't give him facts and definitions."

Again, we have male/female differences but also differences in personality types.

Another woman told me, "My husband is an engineer and you ought to be around when his engineer friends come over. The house is like a cerebral, cognitive conference! All logical facts. They walk in with their slide rules and calculators, and it's as though the house were swept clean of any emotional response. They talk but don't disclose. They share, but on the surface."

This is definitely a combination of male/female differences and personality type distinctives.

A Man's Communication Style

Q. MY HUSBAND IS INSENSITIVE; HE DOES NOT UNDERSTAND MY FEELINGS NOR SHARE HIS FEELINGS WITH ME. ARE MOST MEN LIKE THAT?

A. Men follow a distinct pattern in their communication style. First of all, they mull over the problem. It is put on the back burner to see if the issue will go away on its own and gets resolved with as little effort as possible. During this stage of letting the issues simmer, they may feel it is unnecessary to talk. But if mulling does not work, storing the issue deep inside is the next phase. To many men, this is the easiest solution of all. But if this does not work, he will talk about it. It could be with a sigh of resignation or—with an explosion. This is a gender distinction but varies in intensity depending upon cultural conditioning and personality type.

Often men will say, "She expects me to have all these reactions right at my fingertips and be able to call them up on the spot. Well, I don't operate the way she does. I need a little more time to think things through. Somehow she has the idea that wanting time to think is not being open and honest with her. That's ridiculous. I'm not trying to hide anything, I'm just trying to be sure in my own mind before I talk to her about it. What's wrong with that?" This is not a male/female difference but a personality type distinction!

Remember, men tend to communicate to resolve. They want the bottom line so they can "fix it." Sometimes you may not know if you want an issue resolved until you have talked about it. Many women want to express themselves because it is their way of interfacing with the world; they enjoy self-expression.

I also hear men saying, "I understand her need to talk about us and our relationship. I happen to think that there is a right and a wrong way to talk about those things. If you're not careful, the whole thing can get out of hand. It's best to be as rational as possible. If you let it get too emotional, you never can make any good decisions, and if it gets too personal, someone could get hurt. A little bit of distance goes a long way."

This is both a male/female difference as well as personality type.[1]

The Right Brain/ Left Brain Difference

Q. HOW CAN I GET MY HUSBAND TO RELATE
TO ME EMOTIONALLY? WHY IS HE SO MYSTERIOUS?

A. Biology plays into the gender-related communication gap. Some of the differences between men and women have a physical basis. It is vital for you (and your husband) to understand that men cannot change their physical makeup.

A genetic right-brain/left-brain difference exists between men and women. This is part of the reason why men are the way they are and why you have difficulty communicating with them. At birth the cortex of the brain is more highly developed in women than in men. As infants, women respond more to the sound of the human voice than do men. Women are left-brain oriented and tend to be more verbally skilled. Men are not. The left side controls their language and reading skills. It collects data and puts it together in step-by-step fashion.

A woman's left brain develops earlier than a man's, which gives her an edge in writing and reading. This is why many little boys do not read or write as well as little girls. Oftentimes a boy can build a complicated model but cannot read as well as the girl who is a year younger. The male's right brain develops earlier than the female's and all through life men tend to use this side of their brain more skillfully in the spatial area but not the emotional. Please remember that!

For the most part, men use the right side of their brains more efficiently than women. And a man's brain is more highly specialized, which comes into play in working a jigsaw puzzle, looking at a road map, designing a new office, planning a room arrangement, solving a geometrical problem or listening to musical selections on the stereo. The right half of the brain does not process information step-by-step like the left portion. Instead, it processes patterns of information. It plays host to our emotions. It has been called the intuitive side of the brain. It will link facts together and come up with a concept. It looks at the whole situation and, as though by magic, the solution appears.

If I am a typical man, I will use the left side of my brain for verbal problems and the right side for spatial tasks. If I am putting together a new table that came in several pieces, I use my right brain to visualize the end result. Thus I shift from one side to the other. I am seeing how it fits together in my mind. If my wife, Joyce, comes out to discuss who we are having over for dinner, I am responding out of my verbal side, the left.

Most men do not use all the abilities of the right side of their brains as well as they could. I know *I* don't.

On average, a woman is different from a man in the way she uses her brain. And it gives her an advantage over men! But this can also frustrate a man in relating to a woman.

A woman's brain is not specialized. It operates holistically. Women have thousands of additional nerve connectors between the left and right side of the brain. A man shifts back and forth between the sides of his brain. He can give more focused attention to what he is doing.

But a woman uses both sides of her brain simultaneously to work on a problem. The two parts work in cooperation. Why? Because some of the left-brain abilities are duplicated in her right brain and some of the right brain in the left.

Women have larger connectors between the two sides of the brain even as infants and thus can integrate information more skillfully. They can tune in to everything going on around them. A wife may be handling five hectic activities at one time while her husband is reading a magazine, totally oblivious to the various problems going on right under his nose. The result causes women to be more perceptive about people than men are.

Most women have greater ability to pick up feelings and sense the difference between what people say and what they mean. This fact should temper a woman's expectation of a man's perceptual ability. A man does not pick up on all the sensory data that a woman does.

This is why a woman may recover some of her functions following a stroke whereas a man is limited. Her ability to use both sides of the brain means that the undamaged side can step in and begin to fill the void left by the other.

Both men and women have a tendency to prefer one side of the brain or the other, and this affects a person's approach to life and work. Men do not change their preference or dominance throughout their lifetime, but they can develop the skills of the less-preferred side of the brain.[2] And remember, our culture tends to reinforce these bents and inclinations. Much of the difference is cultural reinforcement, expectations and perpetuation of stereotypes.

Expectations of Men

Q. HOW CAN I GET MY HUSBAND TO PAY MORE
ATTENTION TO ME AND RELATE TO ME AT A
MORE PERSONAL LEVEL? AM I EXPECTING
TOO MUCH FROM HIM?

A. Let's consider what our culture expects of men. A man in our United States society is expected to:

- Be in control.
- Be confident.
- Be more concerned with thinking than feeling.
- Be rational and analytical.
- Be assertive.
- Be courageous.
- Be competitive and rivalrous.
- Accomplish tasks and achieve goals.
- Be knowledgeable about how mechanical things work.
- Endure stress without giving up or giving in.
- Express anger.
- Be able to bear pain.
- Be sexually potent.
- Be able to "hold his liquor."
- "Settle down" at an appropriate age to be a devoted husband and father.
- Be a provider.

A man is not expected to:

- Lose control over a situation, or lose control of himself.
- Openly cry.
- Be afraid.
- Be dependent.
- Be insecure or anxious.
- Be passive.
- Express loneliness, sadness, or depression.
- Express the need for love or affection.
- Exhibit typically "feminine" characteristics.

- Be playful.

- Touch other men.

- Be impotent (sexually or otherwise).

So what happens? Women want men to be different and men spend time and energy guarding themselves against what they *think* must not be. Their energy often goes into keeping themselves from responding in a way that would actually benefit male/female relationships.

I have seen this difference in men and women regarding grief responses. Most men find it easier to mourn alone. When they experience a loss they either initiate some action or engage in action immediately afterward. These actions indicate a man's need to be in control.

Women tend to want men to be competent in areas they themselves are proficient in, such as expressing their feelings, demonstrating love, and nurturing and being intimate. But here we have a problem. You are asking something of a man for which he has had no training!

- You ask a man to be trusting and open but he has been *trained* to be defensive and suspicious.

- You ask a man to show his feelings but he has been *trained* to hide them. Most men have never learned a feeling vocabulary so how can they express what they cannot verbalize? I have worked with many men and asked them to memorize a list of feeling words and to begin using a thesaurus and synonym finder to expand their ability.

- You ask a man to be vulnerable but he has been *taught* to be strong, in control, and able to conquer all.

- You ask him to feel a need for you but he has been *taught* to be independent and self-sufficient.

- You ask him to let himself go but he has been *taught* he must be in control.

When you ask a man to move into his feelings, it is like sending him into a foreign country without a passport. He feels totally out of control.

A Man's Need to Control Emotions

Dr. Ken Druck has suggested some ways men tend to appear emotionally unaffected and in control of their lives.

- Men rationalize a course of inaction by telling themselves, "What good is it going to do to talk about it? That's not going to change anything!"
- Men worry internally, but rarely face what they really feel.
- Men escape into new roles or hide behind old ones.
- Men take the attitude that the "feelings" will pass and shrug them off as unimportant.
- Men keep busy, especially with work.
- Men change one feeling into another—becoming angry instead of experiencing hurt or fear.
- Men deny the feeling outright.
- Men put feelings on hold—put them in the file drawer and tend to forget what they were classified under.
- Feelings are confronted with drugs and alcohol.
- Men are excellent surgeons. They create a "thinking bypass" to replace feelings with thought and logic.
- Men tend to let women do their feeling for them.
- Men sometimes avoid situations and people who elicit certain feelings in them.
- Some men get sick or behave carelessly and hurt themselves so they have a reason to justify their feelings.[3]

Many men are threatened by your expression of emotions or when you get "emotional." But do you know why? Most men are raised to feel they are responsible for fixing things—but how do they fix your "feelings"? It is hard to be solution-oriented with feelings. Often when a man sees his wife upset, he may blame himself for being the cause of her pain. But instead of being compassionate and tender toward her he may become angry at her for making him feel so bad about himself! Men have a fear that once you become "emotional" you will go on forever and he won't be able to do anything to get you to stop. And remember, when they are unable to express their feelings, many men prefer to express themselves sexually.

The Importance of Trust

Unfortunately, I have seen women block their husbands from sharing. If a husband finally opens up to a woman and what he says is discounted, shared with others, ridiculed or rejected, he will clam up. Safety, acceptance and support are essential if a man is going to open up. He wants what he shares to be used for his welfare, not against him. Trust is a major issue.

Distance occurs between a husband and wife when wives openly discuss with others (1) the personal things that go on between them and their husbands; (2) finances; (3) how he feels about his parents; and (4) what he is concerned about at work. If a husband shares, do not broadcast it to the whole world.

I remember one husband told me, "I was at a gathering with my wife and she shared something it took me weeks to tell her. She was angry with me that night and she shared this as a joke. I was so embarrassed. I was hurt and angry at her. If she shared this, what would happen if I really opened up? I don't want it used against me. Never again."

You do not have to resign yourself to living with an unexpressive man. Becoming fatalistic is not the answer. I am not talking about divorcing him either.

"Don't be so concerned about men not expressing their feelings. That's just the way they are!" If you hear that excuse, do not listen. Men tend to be that way, but they can change. Challenges or reproaches do not work. Carefully worded invitations do work. Men do respond initially to questions that elicit factual responses. It is easier for a man to tell his wife what he does at work than how he feels about it. He can tell her how he did at sports or school when he was growing up easier than how he feels about what he does now. *But starting with the facts is an introduction to his feelings.*

A man needs you to help him in the process of opening up. A man needs to see your requests for sharing as a participation in his life, not an intrusion. He needs to see that you do not want to know his feelings so you can use them against him, but rather to become more intimately involved with him. He needs to see that your desire is not to control him but to share with him. He needs to know about the extent of your caring and that you will support him and keep it to yourself.[4]

Help Him Express Himself

Remember these points:

Do not label your man's resistance to showing his feelings as being insensitive and uncaring. You are asking him to express something he has not been trained to express. He does have feelings and is not insensitive. Just because he is conversant with thoughts and ideas does not mean he is this way with his emotions.

For some men, the word "feelings" is a gunpowder word. It sets them off and their defenses intensify. They have either heard women talking about their feelings or have been pressured to share them with limited results.

Choose a time you feel is good for both of you. Tell him there is something you want to learn about yourself and you need his help with it for just a few minutes. Ask him to recall something interesting that happened recently and have him tell you about it. Let him know that you want to see how close you can come to describing his internal reaction to that situation. When you describe back what you think he felt, use a word picture or emotional analogy. "I bet you felt like an elephant had jumped all over you," or "I bet you felt like someone had been tailgating you all day on the freeway," or "I bet you felt all wrung out like a wet towel!"

Ask him if you came close to describing his internal reaction. You may want to ask him to use his own analogy to clarify what happened. The phrase "internal reaction" is less threatening and appeals to his cognitive mind. It could be much easier for him to express what did occur internally.[5]

Do not pressure him to respond immediately. He probably has to think his way into his feelings first. Encourage him to take a few minutes to "think" about what his "inner reaction or response" is. If he is an introvert, he definitely needs time to think it through first.

Avoid being vague when you share your feelings. He likes specifics, a goal and an agenda. Let him know that you are more process-oriented and you either need him to hear your feelings or give an opinion. Do not think out loud. As most men are single-minded, this will distract him and prevent him from concentrating. Let him know your style of communicating and affirm his style. Affirm any attempt on his part.

Never, but never, interrupt him when he is expressing a thought or feeling. Stick to the subject; most men are not tangented thinkers. They think in a straight line and when talking to another person, man or woman, get upset if that person shifts from one topic to another. If you interrupt him, he interprets it as though he is doing it wrong. Never make a value judgment on his feelings when he does share.

If your husband is struggling to share what he is feeling, ask him, "Would it be all right if I asked you some questions to help me understand what's going on?" Usually he will say yes.

You could use such questions as:

"Is there something you're disappointed about at this time?"

"Is there something you're afraid of at this time and it's difficult to admit?"

"Is there something you're frustrated or angry at right now?"

"Did someone do something to hurt you in some way?"

What if you ask him to share more of his feelings and he responds with, "I just don't know how. If I knew how then I would"? If you say, "Well, it's not so hard. Just start sharing them," do not expect much of a response. He does not know how and he needs some help. A better response would be, "I appreciate you letting me know this. I can understand how frustrating that could be. If you'd like some suggestions, let me know." And wait to see if he responds. Allow him to share his feelings in his own manner and to feel in charge of how he shares his feelings.

One wife said, "When I wanted John to share, I wanted his feelings when I wanted them. My requests came across as demands. And one day he told me so. I learned to be sensitive to his days and moods, and whenever he began to share some of his frustrations I listened and listened well. He didn't want a dialogue or someone to solve his problems. He wanted to vent, and I wanted to hear!"

After he shares, thank him. Let him know how much it means to you and ask if there is anything you can do to make it easier for him. Before he leaves for work in the morning, ask what you can pray about for him that day. This gives you something specific to talk about at the end of the day.

Personality Traits

I have talked to some women who say, "But, I've met a number of men who are emotionally oriented. They talk about feelings and seem to respond to life with their emotions. Why can't my husband be like this?" The answer is simple. You are responding to what we call a personality type rather than gender difference.

Let me explain. One of the most accurate tools to help us identify our personalities is the Myers Briggs Type Indicator (MBTI). It is a descriptive test that defines eight basic personality traits that will affect us in our relationships. You cannot fail the test nor can you get a poor score because everyone has all eight traits in their personalities. The eight traits form four pairs of opposites. We all prefer to use one pair over another.

The eight traits are as follows:

Extrovert or **Introvert**—This is the way people prefer to interact with the world and the way they prefer to be stimulated and energized.

Sensor or **Intuitive**—This preference describes the way people prefer to gather information.

Thinker or **Feeler**—This describes how people prefer to make decisions.

Judging or **Perceiving**—This describes how you prefer to orient your life, whether structured and organized or spontaneous and adaptive.

These traits are thought to be inherited from our families. We do not learn them, although our preference can be strengthened or weakened by our environment and experiences.

You are born with a predisposition and each trait is a preference. It is like being right-handed. It does not mean you never use your left hand, you just prefer the right hand and it is the strongest. The more you use it the more you rely upon it. If you were born an introvert, you will always be an introvert no matter how much you practice being an extrovert.

The Extrovert-Introvert difference may be part of the problem you are struggling with if your husband is unexpressive with his feelings.

Extroverts tends to talk first and think later. They brainstorm their ideas and thinking processes out in the open for everyone to hear. They prefer talking over listening and are energized by their interaction with people.

Introverts rehearse things thoroughly before expressing and will often respond to a question with, "Let me think about that." They freeze if you pressure them for an immediate response. They prefer their peace and quiet and feel drained after a great deal of interaction with others. They are good listeners and prefer a few close friends rather than a crowd. They do not care to be around excessive talkers, although they develop a high level of concentration and can tune out noise.

Let's consider another pair of traits that relate to what we have been discussing. Consider the characteristics of a Thinker and a Feeler:

A Thinker tends to:

- stay cool, calm, and objective in situations when everyone else is upset.

- settle disputes based on what is fair and truthful rather than what makes people happy.
- enjoy proving a point for the sake of clarity; they might argue both sides in a discussion simply to expand intellectual horizons.
- be more firm-minded than gentle-hearted; if they disagree with people, they would rather tell them than say nothing and let them think they're right.
- pride themselves on their objectivity despite the fact that some people accuse them of being cold and uncaring.
- not mind making difficult decisions. They can't understand why so many people get upset about things that aren't relevant to the issue at hand.
- think it's more important to be right than liked; it's not necessary to like people in order to be able to work with them and do a good job.
- be impressed with and lend more credence to things that are logical and scientific.
- remember numbers and figures more readily than faces and names.

A Feeler tends to:

- take others' feelings into account when making a decision.
- feel that "love" cannot be defined and thus takes great offense at those who try to do so.
- overextend themselves in meeting other people's needs; they will do almost anything to accommodate others.
- put themselves in other people's moccasins. They're concerned with, "How will this affect people?"
- enjoy providing needed services to people.
- wonder, "Doesn't anyone care about what I want?" although they may have difficulty actually saying this to anyone.

- prefer harmony over clarity; and is embarrassed by conflict in groups or family gatherings and will try to avoid it.
- often be accused of taking things too personally.

A person can be a Feeler and still not *talk* about his feelings. He can also relate to others in a thinking mode when he feels it is best.

Interestingly enough, thinking and feeling are the only two preferences that have gender-related issues. About two-thirds of Feelers are women and the same proportion of men are Thinkers.[6]

Dr. Dave Stoop describes the difference in this way:

The thinking person uses pro-and-con lists of facts in order to arrive at the best decision. The feeling person will probably make a bad decision if he or she relies only on factual information. The feeling person needs to look at the values and emotions involved in order to make a good decision.

The way we handle our emotions is related to our preference on this trait, even though the trait has nothing directly to do with emotions. Those who score on the thinking side are often uncomfortable talking about the area of feelings. They may also not be as comfortable in the area of aesthetics and the cultivation of relationships. To others, they appear cool and aloof; sometimes they are accused of having ice in their veins, even though they are very sensitive.

Feeling persons, on the other hand, can be quite comfortable in the area of emotions. They are usually aware of what they are feeling and can tune in to what others around them are feeling as well. When they make a decision, they are concerned about how it will affect the others involved.[7]

If you are married to an Extrovert-Feeler (EF) you will be hearing about your husband's emotions because he will share them outwardly. But if you are married to an Introvert-Feeler (IF) you have a husband who is the same as an Extrovert-Feeler, but who keeps it inside. You end up believing he is insensitive and unfeeling. That is not true; you will just need to be more creative to discover what is inside of him.

Communication Suggestions

Q. DO MOST MEN HAVE TROUBLE COMMUNICATING THEIR INNER FEELINGS WITH THEIR SPOUSES? WHAT DO YOU SUGGEST TO HELP OUR COMMUNICATION PROBLEM?

A. One of the most common complaints I hear in counseling is the issue of the uncommunicative husband. And most wives either engage in a direct frontal attack, which does not work, or withdraw into resentment, which does little to encourage a partner to open up. What I suggest is a bit different but you have nothing to lose because what is being tried now is not working.

1. Accept his silence. Decide in your mind to give him permission to be silent and to respond the way he does. This will reduce the pressure and frustration you feel when you expect a response and do not get one. By inwardly accepting his silence, you will retain a sense of control over the interaction.

2. Avoid asking questions that can be answered yes or no. Use open-ended questions, those that require a full answer. For example, instead of asking, "Did you like the movie?" ask, "What did you like about the movie?" Another open-ended approach that will draw him out is, "I'm interested in your perception of this issue and I think you have something important to add. Tell me what you're thinking."

3. Allow him to be silent. Perhaps you tend to rescue him. A silent spouse is not always ready to give more than a yes or no response. One of your tendencies may be to "rescue" him by filling the uncomfortable silence with your own words. Do not feel you must ease the pressure by elaborating on or illustrating your question or by putting words in his mouth. You might say, "I'm interested in what you have to say, but you may need to think about it for a while. That's fine with me. Take your time. When you're ready to talk about it, let me know." Giving permission for silence will take the pressure off both of you.

4. *Address his silence using a direct approach.* Another way to invite your spouse to interact is to address his silence directly. You could say, "Honey, I'm looking for a response from you and you appear to be thinking about something. I'm curious what your silence means at this time." Then wait. Or say:

"You may be concerned about how I will respond if you share what's on your mind. I think I'm ready to listen."

One wife used the direct approach and said, "Sometimes when I want to talk with you, you seem preoccupied or hesitant. I wonder if it's the topic or if there is something I do that makes it difficult for you to respond. Maybe you could think about it and let me know later." Then she stood up and began to leave the room. But her quiet husband said, "Let's talk now. I'm ready to comment on your last statement."

The direct approach is most successful when you invite your partner to tell you how you have been making interaction difficult for him. But it is so important to listen to him and not become defensive, no matter what he says. What he shares may not be accurate from your perspective, but that is how he sees it. Be careful not to say anything that might cause him to retreat deeper into his shell.

You cannot change yourself or your partner. But—you can encourage and help him to develop the nonpreference side. I have seen this happen in the lives of many men. I have experienced it in my own life as well.

We can all learn and grow! I have seen amazing changes occur in couples of all ages when each has read and studied the book *Type Talk* and applied it to their lives. It could make a difference in your relationship, too.

Recommended Reading:

Druck, Ken. *The Secrets Men Keep.* New York: Ballantine Books, 1985.

Kroeger, Otto, and Thuesen, Janet M. *Type Talk.* New York: Delecorte Press, 1988.

Tannen, Deborah. *You Just Don't Understand: Women and Men in Conversation.* New York: William Morrow and Co., 1990.

Wright, H. Norman. *How to Speak Your Spouse's Language.* Tarrytown, NY: Fleming H. Revell Co., 1988.

Notes

1. H. Norman Wright, *Understanding the Man in Your Life* (Dallas: WORD Inc. 1987), pp. 93-95, adapted.
2. Joyce Brothers, *What Every Woman Should Know About Men* (New York: Ballantine Books, 1981), pp. 31-34, adapted. Jacquelyn Wonder and Priscilla Donovan, *Whole Brain Thinking* (New York: William Morrow and Co., 1984), pp. 18-34, adapted.
3. Ken Druck, *The Secrets Men Keep* (New York: Ballantine Books, 1984), pp. 27,28.
4. Wright, *Understanding the Man in Your Life,* pp. 100,101, adapted.
5. Dan Kiley, *What to Do When He Won't Change* (New York: Fawcett Crest, 1987), p. 140, adapted.
6. Otto Kroeger and Janet M. Thuesen, *Type Talk* (New York: Delecorte Press, 1988), pp. 18,19, adapted.
7. David Stoop and Jan Stoop, *The Intimacy Factor* (Nashville: Thomas Nelson, 1993), p. 90.

Section One

WOMEN'S
ISSUES

Chapter 2

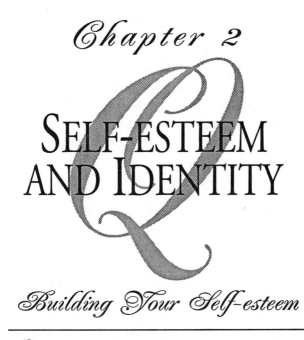

SELF-ESTEEM AND IDENTITY

Building Your Self-esteem

Q. MY SELF-ESTEEM IS SO LOW. HOW DO I BUILD
IT? HOW CAN I FEEL GOOD ABOUT MYSELF,
RESPECT, ACCEPT AND LOVE MYSELF?

A. One of the most frequently asked questions of counselors has to do with a woman's identity and self-esteem. Women of all ages struggle with this issue and in spite of all the teaching and resources available for help, the conflict still continues. The questions listed will give you a feel for the diversity of concern as well as perhaps connect with the thoughts and concerns raised. Answering questions such as these is not always easy because building one's identity and self-esteem is a process that takes time. I hope the information expressed will help to alleviate some of the confusion and point you in a direction in which the building process can begin and continue. You will need to apply it to your own situation.

Identity Based on False Foundations

What others say. Many women base their identities on false foundations. One such falsehood is what others have said about them in the past. A girl hears her parents say, "She never cleans her room," or hears her teachers say, "You're just one of those slow learners." So she grows up believing she is a sloppy, homely, stupid girl. Her identity is based on the comments of others. Did that happen to you? Those comments may not be true, but if you believed them they became true for you and you act them out as your identity.

If you have based your identity on what others have said about you, you have given those people tremendous power and control over your life. Are you sure their perceptions are accurate? Are there other people who can give you a more accurate picture of who you really are? How does their perception compare to God's?

Accomplishments. Some women base their identity on what they accomplish and how they perform. They believe that what they do earns them certain status ratings, which can increase based on the kinds of tasks or roles they become involved in. Do you?

Possessions. Some women base their identity on what they possess or own. They have an insatiable need to acquire things. When they do not feel good about themselves, they head for the mall. They struggle with the tendency to compare their possessions to what other women have. Do you?

Name-droppers. Still other women base their identity on who they know. Unfortunately, these women end up being name-droppers who tend to be threatened by the status of others, or who become a threat to others in their quest for status. Do you?

Appearance. Many women base their identity on how they feel about their appearance. They spend countless hours in front of a mirror. They change clothes several times a day and spend a lot of money on beauty aids. This type of woman's entire day or evening can be ruined if she feels unattractive. I emphasize her feelings about herself because her attractiveness is largely based on her perception of how she looks. Twenty-five people may rave about her appearance, but if she does not see herself as attractive, the compliments of others have no effect. Often her perceptions are based on the reactions of others. Are you like this?

I like what Jan Congo has said about these false foundations in her book *Free to Be God's Woman:*

When we contrast our appearance, our accomplishments, our friends or our possessions to others we are making a comparison based in large part on fantasy. We have never walked in the shoes of those women to whom we compare ourselves so we fantasize what it would be like. When we do this we compare our worst, of which we are most aware, to their best. And we're really comparing ourselves to a fantasy. Perhaps this is one of the reasons why soap operas and romance novels are so popular today. We are basically dissatisfied with our existence so we vicariously live our lives through other people.

When we believe we are only worthwhile if we are beautiful, if we use the right products, if we know the right people, if we are successful or if we are financially comfortable, we are building our self-image on faulty foundations. Subtly we find ourselves looking to other "significant" people to define for us what it means to be beautiful, what are the right products to use, who are the right people to associate with, and what it takes to be financially comfortable.

When we swallow these faddish opinions, society loves us because we fit its mold. But what happens when the mold changes?[1]

What Do You Believe?

What do you believe about yourself? Is your identity based on a faulty foundation? Answer these questions to help you know where you are at this time in your life.

1. Do you believe that there is something inherently wrong or bad about you?

2. Do you believe your adequacy is defined by the approval or disapproval of others? If so, who are these people? Did your father disapprove of you? If so, how does that make you feel?

3. Do you believe your adequacy is tied to how much money you make? Where did this belief originate?

4. Do you believe that you always must be right about everything to be adequate or feel good about yourself? Do you believe that if you are wrong, you will be disapproved of or rejected?

5. Do you believe that you are inadequate because you are overly sensitive?

6. Do you believe that you are helpless and powerless?

7. Do you believe that you must please everyone in order to be worthwhile?

8. Do you believe that your adequacy is tied to how much education you've had?

9. Do you believe that your adequacy and worth are tied to how you look? How tall or short you are? How fat or thin you are?[2]

Most of us have a critic residing within, which significantly influences what we believe about ourselves and how we respond to others. Your internal critic is like a condemning conscience. It operates on the basis of standards that were developed in response to the judgments and evaluations of your parents and other people you looked up to. Your internal critic is quick to point out that you do not measure up to these standards.

Why cling any longer to your low self-esteem and false identity when God has called you to something better? Consider God's alternative for your faulty beliefs about yourself and discover how to appropriate it.

I have talked with many women who say, "I really want to get rid of some of my old beliefs about myself. They do nothing but limit me. I really think it's time to clean house."

I usually answer, "That's a good beginning, but what about the rest of the work?"

"What other work?" they ask.

"House cleaning is only half of the job," I answer. "You also need to redecorate. Some of your deeply entrenched beliefs may not be that easy to dispose of. You will need to replace them with new, accurate and positive beliefs about yourself."

Let Go of Your Old Identity

It is important that you let go of your past identity (based on inaccurate messages about you), and build a new self-concept based on the unconditional love and acceptance of God. To do so, you need to decide which you value more: your old, false identity or your true, God-given identity. Once you decide which is of greater value (is there any question?), then you need to let go of one and grab for the other.

Dr. Paul Tournier compares Christian growth to the experience of swinging from a trapeze. The man on the trapeze clings to the bar because it is his security. When another trapeze bar swings into view, he must release his grip on one bar in order to leap to the other. It is a scary process. Similarly, God is swinging a new trapeze bar into your view. It is a positive, accurate, new identity based on God's Word. But in order to grasp the new, you must release the old. You may have difficulty relinquishing the familiarity and security of your old identity. But think of what you will gain.[3]

Dr. David Seamands describes it this way:

The primary sources of damage to our self-esteem need healing, repairing, and reprogramming. This is where healing grace is required. I want to make this as practical as possible, so let me make it personal and talk to you as if we were counseling together. Here are some of the questions I would ask:

Have you found and faced the painful places in your past which you feel are the chief sources of your low self-esteem? It is very important that you have the courage not only to honestly look at the people and incidents involved, but also to plug into the feelings which go along with them. Brain research proves conclusively that our memories store not only mental pictures from the past *but also the original emotions experienced at that time.* So when you feel you have discovered the hurts, humiliations, deprivations, or rejections, allow yourself to *feel their pain and also to feel your reactions to that pain.* This is not in order to *blame others* or to *escape responsibility.* It is done so that you can honestly face up to feelings you may have buried for years.

The best way to do this is by *sharing your feelings with God and with another person in prayer.* But you cannot confess to God what you will not first admit to yourself. When you also share with another person, this brings an even deeper level of openness and honesty with both yourself and God. This kind of openness can be very painful, and feelings may arise which will shock you. But grace is never shocked, never repulsed, and never withdrawn—whatever it is faced with. It is freely given, without any reference to our goodness or badness, worthiness or unworthiness.

The greatest manifestation of grace is the Cross, and the Cross means that when *God saw us at our worst, He loved us the most.* So armed with the courage grace can bring, look squarely at the worst, the most painful, the most humiliating, the most abusive, and the most devastating put-downs of your life. *Remember* them in your mind, and *relive* them in your motions, but don't stop there. *Relinquish* them to God in forgiving and surrendering prayer. It's doubtful you can do this by yourself, so get help from a close friend, pastor, or counselor.[4]

An Accurate View of God

An integral element in your positive self-identity is your perception of God. If your view of God is inaccurate, your view of yourself will also be inaccurate. Ideally, your overall response to God, based on a proper perception of Him, will be one of trust. But many women really struggle with accepting the fact that God loves them and that He is trustworthy. Instead, they are angry at God, feeling that He failed to protect them or that He let them down. Intellectually, they may acknowledge that God is the giver of good gifts. But emotionally they perceive Him as the giver of bad gifts. David Seamands describes the problem in this manner:

When we ask individuals to trust God and to surrender to Him, we are presuming they have concepts/feelings of a trustworthy God who has only their best interests at heart and in whose hands they can place their lives. But according to their deepest gut-level concept of God, they may hear us asking them to surrender to an unpredictable and fearful ogre, an all-powerful monster whose aim is to make them miserable and take from them the freedom to enjoy life.[5]

You and I need to know the God of the Bible and use His Word as our source of information.

Transfer the basis of your identity from your other beliefs to your infallible heavenly Father. He is the One who is consistent in His love and acceptance. Note what these paraphrased Scriptures say about Him and you!

1. He is the loving, concerned Father who is interested in the intimate details of our lives (Matt. 6:25-34).

2. He is the Father who never gives up on us (Luke 15:3-32).

3. He is the God who sent His Son to die for us though we were undeserving (Rom. 5:8).

4. He stands with us in good and bad circumstances (Heb. 13:5).

5. He is the ever-active Creator of our universe. He died to heal our sickness, pain and grief (Isa. 53:3-6).

6. He has broken the power of death (Luke 24:6,7).

7. He gives all races and sexes equal status (Gal. 3:28).

8. He is available to us through prayer (John 14:13,14).

9. He is aware of our needs (Isa. 65:24).

10. He created us for an eternal relationship with Him (John 3:16).

11. He values us (Luke 7:28).

12. He doesn't condemn us (Rom. 8:1).

13. God values and causes our growth (1 Cor. 3:7).

14. He comforts us (2 Cor. 1:3-5).

15. He strengthens us through His Spirit (Eph. 3:16).

16. He cleanses us from sin (Heb. 10:17-22).

17. He is for us (Rom 8:31).

18. He is always available to us (Rom. 8:38,39).

19. He is a God of hope (Rom. 15:13).

20. He helps us in temptation (Heb. 2:17,18).

21. He provides a way to escape temptation (1 Cor. 10:13).

22. He is at work in us (Phil. 2:13).

23. He wants us to be free (Gal. 5:1).

24. He is the Lord of time and eternity (Rev. 1:8).

Read these verses each day for a month. You will be amazed at how your perception of yourself will change.

Basis for a Healthy Self-image

Need to belong. Your self-image is established on several foundations. First, we all need to belong, to know and feel that we are wanted, accepted, cared for and enjoyed for who we are. God wants you, cares for you, accepts you and enjoys you.

Need to feel worthy. Second, we all need to feel worthy, able to say with confidence, "I'm good, I'm all right, I count." We feel worthy when we do what we think we should do or when we live up to our standards. We sense worthiness in being right and doing right in our eyes and the eyes of others. God is our primary source of worthiness. We do not need to keep striving in order to feel worthy. God declares us to be all right. As Jan Congo says, "Each of us is a divine original! We are the creative expression of a loving God."

Need to feel competent. Third, we all need to feel competent, knowing that we can do something and cope with life successfully. Again, God meets this need by declaring us to be competent. Philippians 4:13 is the new measuring rod by which we are assured competence: "I can do everything through him who gives me strength."

The point here is that your self-esteem and identity are gifts from God.

They cannot be earned through your achievements, nor are they based on what other people say about you, do to you or fail to do to you.

Steps Toward Healthy Behavior

Q. HOW DO I STOP COMPARING MYSELF WITH OTHER WOMEN AND FEELING INADEQUATE? WHAT STEPS DO I TAKE?

A. What can you do now? It is important to have the proper beliefs and a solid basis for your identity and self-esteem. But as you are establishing that solid foundation, it is also important to behave in a healthy new way. Here are several practical steps you can begin to take that will counter previous, unhealthy ways of viewing yourself. You may want to summarize these on a sheet of paper and post it where you will read it often.

1. Accept the fact that you are in process. You may be dissatisfied with certain features or characteristics about your life at the present. Realize that you are still the person God designed you to be. Yes, we have mental and physical weaknesses, we experience energy limitations, and we have needs and changing emotions. You may think you won't ever be what you want to be. But God has not completed implementing His design in you. You are still in the process of being shaped into a beautiful creation.

God knows what lies dormant within you, but He also loves you just as you are right now. He will also love you as you continue to grow and develop. Notice that I did not say He will love you more. You may think or feel that God does not love you as much today as He will when you "improve." Not true! God's love is unconditional. *He loves you!* And He wants you to cooperate with Him in bringing out the best in you. He wants you to cooperate in the creative process.

On one side of a 3×5-inch card, write the following:

Because of Christ and His redemption,
I am completely forgiven and fully pleasing to God.
I am totally accepted by God.

On the other side of the card write out Romans 5:1 and Colossians 1:21,22.

Carry this card with you for the next 28 days. Every time you get something to drink, look at the card and remind yourself of what Christ has done for you. If you do this consistently for 28 days, these truths will come to your mind for the rest of your life. As you read and memorize these statements and passages, think about how they apply to you. Memorization and application of these truths will have profound effects as your mind is transformed by God's Word.[6]

Another approach is to take a 3×5-inch card and on one side of the card write the word "STOP." On the other side write the following:

You are worth the precious blood of Jesus. [Write out] 1 Corinthians 6:19,20; 1 Peter 1:18,19 and Revelation 5:9.

Every time you find yourself thinking negatively about yourself take out the card and hold it in front of you with the word "STOP" facing you. Say the word "STOP" with emphasis and then turn the card over and read what it says. Do this as many times a day as you need to and in time these thoughts will become automatic for you.

You can hinder your growth by asking questions such as, "What will other people think?"; "Will they like me if I change?"; "What if I don't please them as much?" But you have not been called to make a good impression. Gauging your behavior by the reactions of others makes you their prisoner. It also robs you of your individuality and leads to "impression management." You end up saying what you think others want you to say, being what they want you to be and doing what they want you to do. It is all right to be you and to develop as God wants you to develop.

2. Affirm yourself instead of tearing yourself down. Listen again to Jan Congo:

You and I have unique talents and abilities, personalities, and opportunities. What joy are you missing in life because you aren't using the capabilities and potentials you have been given? Jesus wants you to be your own person. Do you feel that someone else is more attractive than you are, more naturally intelligent or better proportioned physically? Are you using that as your excuse for not appreciating what you have been given? Because others have attributes you don't have is no basis for your feeling inferior or their feeling superior. First Corinthians 4:7 *(NIV)* puts it this way, "For who makes you different from anyone else? What do you have that you did not receive? And if you did receive it, why do you boast as though you did not?"

All of our natural abilities have come from the hand of a loving God. What matters now is our faithfulness in developing what God has given us, rather than arguing with God about what we don't have or wish we had. The time has come to accept what we've been given. We can then be excited and not threatened when someone else excels.

When we begin with what we have, as opposed to what we don't have, we are often surprised at how very much God has given us with which to work. Take out a pen and paper and take some time to focus on your uniqueness.

A. Make a list of at least 10 things you like about yourself...20 things would be even better. No doubt the Lord has brought special people into your life who have helped you develop these characteristics and have affirmed your growth along the way. Put their names down beside your list.

B. Spend time in prayer. Thank God for the 10 (or 20) things you like about yourself. Do you realize you are praising God for His creation when you do this? Then thank God for the wonderful, affirming people He has brought into your life. Finally, thank God for creating you.

C. Next, make a list of the things you honestly don't like about yourself. Go back and put a check mark beside the things you could *change* if it was important to you. Please keep this list. We will refer to it later in the book.

D. The unchecked items on your list are the things about yourself which you cannot change. The time has come to thank the Lord for these and to verbalize to Him your acceptance of this "thorn in your flesh." Write out an acceptance prayer to the Lord.

E. After you have written out your prayer of acceptance, covenant with the Lord not to ever again bemoan the areas you are incapable of changing.

God is limitless but we definitely are not. By working through this exercise you choose the limitations you cannot change. You have also accepted them. This is a crucial step on your spiritual journey. Let's not waste any more time asking, "what if." If the limits on our ability can't be changed, let's accept them and accept ourselves as God does.[7]

3. Chart the consequences. Keep a record of what happens when you entertain negative feelings and thoughts about yourself, and when you behave negatively. Review those consequences and ask yourself, "Is this what I really want for my life? Could I possibly believe and do the opposite of what I've written here?" Instead of dwelling on your negative thoughts, feelings and behavior, focus on what God says about you and promises to you. For example, in the book of Jeremiah, God says, "Call to Me, and I will answer you, and I will tell you great and mighty things, which you do not know....For I know the plans that I have for you, ...plans for welfare and not for calamity to give you a future and a hope" (Jer. 33:3; 29:11, *NASB*).

4. Take new steps. Make a list of some special things you have always wanted to do and places you have wanted to go, activities you feel you did not deserve. Then ask someone to participate in these activities with you. Making such a request may be difficult for you at first because it goes against your feelings about what you deserve. But do not apologize, make excuses or give elaborate reasons. Just give it a try. After each activity, write down all your positive feelings and responses. Do not list any negative comments; only positive. Give yourself an opportunity to be and do something different.

5. *Believe what God believes about you.* Overcoming negative feelings, whether they stem from childhood or a current situation, will take time and effort, but change is possible. The main step you must take in this process is to accept what your heavenly Father believes about you.

In his unique book, *The Pleasures of God,* John Piper beautifully expresses how God desires to do good to all who hope in Him. Dr. Piper talks about God singing and asks, "What would it be like if God sang?"

> What do you hear when you imagine the voice of God singing? I hear the booming of Niagara Falls mingled with the trickle of a mossy mountain stream. I hear the blast of Mt. Saint Helens mingled with a kitten's purr. I hear the power of an East Coast hurricane and the barely audible puff of a night snow in the woods. And I hear the unimaginable roar of the sun, 865,000 miles thick, 1,300,000 times bigger than the earth, and nothing but fire, 1,000,000 degrees centigrade on the cooler surface of the corona. But I hear this unimaginable roar mingled with the tender, warm crackling of logs in the living room on a cozy winter's night.
>
> I stand dumbfounded, staggered, speechless that he is singing over me—one who has dishonored him so many times and in so many ways. It is almost too good to be true. He is rejoicing over my good with all his heart and all his soul. He virtually breaks forth into song when he hits upon a new way to do me good.[8]

Did you catch the significance of how God feels about you and what He wants for you?

Piper compares our relationship with God to a marriage. He goes on to talk about how the honeymoon ends for all married couples. Reality sets in and the level of honeymoon intensity and affection diminishes. The two people change, and defects become more apparent. But it is different with God.

God says his joy over his people is like a bridegroom over a bride. He is talking about honeymoon intensity and honeymoon pleasures and honeymoon energy and excitement and enthusiasm and enjoyment. He is trying to get into our hearts what he means when he says he rejoices over us with all his heart.

And to add to this, with God the honeymoon never ends. He is infinite in power and wisdom and creativity and love. And so he has no trouble sustaining a honeymoon level of intensity; he can foresee all the future quirks of our personality and has decided he will keep what's good for us and change what isn't.[9]

Does that say something to you about your value and worth? Does that fling open the doors of possibility for you? It can![10]

6. *Saturate yourself with the truth of your new identity in Christ.* Your old, strictly human identity was molded over time in figurative concrete with a great deal of reinforcement. But alterations can occur. When you soak up the truth of who God is, what He has done for you, and who you are as a result, you will begin to be different.

In war, saturation bombing is often used to totally obliterate enemy positions in certain areas. Planes continuously drop load after load of bombs in a back-and-forth, crisscross pattern until every inch of land has been covered. Similarly, you need to allow the Holy Spirit to saturate every inch of your heart and mind with the blessed truth of who you are and what you are becoming in Christ.

Action Steps

Years ago I was fishing in a lake with one of my shelties. He was perched on the bow of the boat riding along with his nose in the wind. I was headed into a cove at full speed, then I suddenly changed my mind about fishing there, swung the boat around, and reversed direction. The sudden course change caused my dog to lose his balance, and he went flying into the lake. I don't know who was more surprised, my sheltie or me!

I swung the boat around to where he was swimming (he was not too happy with me at that moment) and cut the engine. I picked him out of the water, but I did not put him into the boat right away because he was totally soaked. He did not have a dry spot of fur or skin on him. I held him away from the boat and gently squeezed his coat to eliminate most of the water.

My new dog is quite different. For one thing, he weighs three times as much as my sheltie did. And as my new dog is a golden retriever, he loves playing in the water, but he does not get soaked. His coat actually repels the water. When he comes out of the water he appears wet, but the water does not penetrate his thick coat. After a short time it does not even seem like he ever went swimming.

Some of us are thick-coated like my retriever, but in a negative way. God's truth has never thoroughly penetrated our outer layer and deeply influenced us. We have not been fully soaked. For growth to occur, you must saturate yourself in God's truth. How? Time and time again you will read the same instruction in this book: Take a Scripture verse or a thought I have been discussing, write it on an index card, and read it out loud to yourself morning and evening for three to four weeks. Spend time praying over the verse or thought, asking God to help you capture the vision of how it is to be manifested and reflected in your life. Envision yourself living out what you have read. Commit yourself by God's power to take steps to do what God's Word says. You will be different.[11]

Recommended Reading:

Congo, Jan. *Free to Be God's Woman.* Ventura, CA: Regal Books, 1988.

Seamands, David. *Freedom From the Performance Trap.* Wheaton, IL: Victor Books, 1988.

Wright, H. Norman. *Chosen for Blessing.* Eugene, OR: Harvest House, 1992.

Notes

1. Jan Congo, *Free to Be God's Woman* (Ventura, CA: Regal Books, 1988), p. 27.
2. Jordan and Margaret Paul, *If You Really Loved Me* (Minneapolis, MN: CompCare Publications, 1987), pp. 127,128, adapted.
3. Robert S. McGee, *The Search for Significance* (Houston, TX: Rapha Publishing, 1987), pp. 84,85, adapted.
4. David Seamands, *Freedom From the Performance Trap* (Wheaton, IL: Victor Books, 1988), p. 162.
5. David Seamands, *Healing of Memories* (Wheaton, IL: Victor Books, 1985), p. 11.
6. McGee, *The Search for Significance*, p. 66, adapted.
7. Congo, *Free to Be God's Woman*, pp. 96-98.
8. John Piper, *The Pleasures of God* (Portland, OR: Multnomah, 1991), p. 188.
9. Ibid., p. 195.
10. H. Norman Wright, *Chosen for Blessing* (Eugene, OR: Harvest House, 1992), pp. 14,15, adapted.
11. Ibid., pp. 43,44.

Chapter 3

SELF-IMPROVEMENT

Interdependence

Q. HOW CAN I BE HEALTHILY INDEPENDENT AND
ALSO HEALTHY IN A RELATIONSHIP?

A. Without seeming trite, the best way to be healthy in a relationship is to be healthily independent or "interdependent." The person whose identity is found through others often ends up with relationships that are addictive.

Dependency in relationships is not a Christian calling except for being dependent upon God, which all men and women are called to be.

An *independent* woman thrives on individuality, few restrictions and self-gratification. She finds her identity through herself.

But there is a third option and this is called *interdependence.* The interdependent woman has a strong sense of personhood and bases this upon being affirmed by God. She knows she has been given gifts and is willing to use them, but she can also rely upon others. This woman views others as her equal and also values herself. *Does this reflect you?*

In *Free to Be God's Woman,* Jan Congo gives four options in which to view ourselves and others. A *dependent* woman says, (1) "I am nothing and you are nothing," or (2) "I am nothing but you are a person of worth and dignity." The *independent* woman says, (3) "I am a person of worth and dignity but you are expendable." The *interdependent* woman says, (4) "I am a person of worth and dignity and you are a person of worth and dignity."[1]

In this last option, competition does not exist. Competition between women is a reflection of insecurity.

The interdependent woman allows herself and others the freedom to grow and be in process. She has role flexibility. She is relying on God's expectations for herself rather than others. *Does this reflect you?*

This style of living neither intimidates knowingly nor is intimidated. The interdependent woman does not try to prove she is superior to others nor does she attempt to live the way the world values people. *Does this reflect you?*

One final thought: An interdependent woman has balance in her relationships. She enters into relationships with others but she does not restrict them nor is she responsible for them either. She discovers the value of commitment.[2]

This is best summarized as Jan Congo says:

> Now we, as Christ's followers, find ourselves growing through healthy relationships. In 1 John 4:12 *(NASB)* it says, "No one has beheld God at any time; if we love one another, God abides in us, and His love is perfected in us." The Christian life was not meant to be lived in a vacuum. We are encouraged to be involved in relationships.
>
> As we rub shoulders with each other we see the need to be committed to one another. Only in commitment to imperfect human beings can we follow in our Master's footsteps.
>
> The very word "commitment" grinds on many eardrums today in this independent, self-centered society of ours. Yet it is only after we have committed ourselves to the God of love that we can commit ourselves to care for others and identify with them in their various stages of growth. We refuse to make others either our projects or our heroes. Instead we choose to walk, as much as is humanly possible, where they have

walked, to laugh and weep with them, to be available to them, to be as gentle with them as Jesus Christ is with us and to be vulnerable to them, demonstrated by our willingness to speak the truth in love about ourselves when we are with them. I choose to back up my words with an authentic lifestyle. In relationships I am willing not only to give but also to express my needs honestly and receive from others.

We are one of the best means of getting God's life and love to others. Jesus is our source of strength so never do we purposely choose to have others become dependent on us. In all of our relating, we must remember that the purpose is for Christ to be formed in you and in me (Gal. 4:19). If we find ourselves imitating anyone but Christ or pressuring someone else to imitate us then we need to confess and readjust. We need to honestly share, with no inhibitions, what we see happening and together we need to get our friendship back to its original purpose—that Christ will be formed in both of us.

Love is the evidence that I am Christ's woman. Only through dependence on Christ alone will I find myself freed to be a most courageous lover who will not lose her identity through loving but will find her God-given purpose in loving.[3]

Fulfillment

Q. HOW CAN I BE FULFILLED AS A WOMAN
IN TODAY'S SOCIETY?

A. I am not hedging in answering this question, but I will respond first with more questions.

What is fulfillment to you? What is happiness to you? Have you experienced a time in your life when you were fulfilled? What was that like? What have you tried recently in order to find fulfillment?

Often I hear people interchanging the word "happiness" for "fulfillment." But whatever you want to call it, fulfillment is possible for each of us. For us to be fulfilled, we need to be biblical-centered and not society-centered. We in a sense are to be counter-culture people. Romans 12:2 *(AMP)* tells us:

> Do not be conformed to this world—this age, fashioned after and adapted to its external, superficial customs. But be transformed (changed) by the [entire] renewal of your mind—by its new ideals and its new attitude—so that you may prove [for yourselves] what is the good and acceptable and perfect will of God, even the thing which is good and acceptable and perfect [in His sight of you].

Fulfillment comes when, no matter what our age, station in life, race, or socioeconomic class, our hearts and minds are focused on Scripture. We can learn to dwell on what we have rather than on what we do not have. Fulfillment is a choice in life. And more important than seeking after happiness and fulfillment in life is seeking joy. You can be fulfilled one day and feel empty the next day, whereas joy can be long lasting. It too is a choice, as it says in James 1:2,3 *(NASB)*, "Consider it all joy." It is a state of being more than a reaction to some experience or circumstance. And it occurs because of the promises of Scripture. Our lives in Christ give joy:

> I have told you these things that My joy and delight may be in you, and that your joy and gladness may be full measure and complete and overflowing (John 15:11, *AMP)*.

Joy is one of the fruits of the Spirit (see Gal. 5:22). Fulfillment comes by experiencing joy in our lives.

Criticism

Q. HOW DO I DEAL WITH THE CRITICISM OF OTHERS, INCLUDING MY PARENTS AND OTHER SIBLINGS?

A. Critics come in many shapes, sizes and styles. Criticism is not pleasant and it is even more difficult when it comes from your family. You end up with a mixture of feelings including love, obligation, hurt, dislike, anger and even hate. Sometimes part of you wishes these so-called experts would disappear.

Some of these critics are people who always need to be right. They have to come out on top in every discussion. They devalue your beliefs and they do not listen to you.

Blamers always find someone or something else responsible for problems and mistakes; they will not look at their contribution to the issue.

Pickers criticize you, pick at you, negate you and do not know what the words "praise" and "encouragement" mean.

So what can you do?

First of all, disconnect their assessment and criticism of you from the way you perceive and value yourself. God's standard is the only fair and healthy one to use. Their problems do not have to become your problems. I have encouraged people to tell themselves, "I did not ask for this person's opinion and I am not going to accept their criticism if it is not valid. I will continue to pray for them that they find the peace and contentment they are seeking."

The second step is major. The critic needs to be taught by you that you will no longer tolerate their criticism. Describe how you *do* want them to respond toward you. Just recently I worked with a counselee to help her gain the courage and steps involved to do this with her mother and sisters. It gave her a new direction in life. You cannot avoid these people, and there is no guarantee they will change. But many do change.

Several ways you can approach your critic are as follows:

You can either talk directly with the critical person or put it in writing. You can carefully and calmly state what has occurred before (and be sure not to accept or debate their justifications or denials) and what you will appreciate and accept in the future. Focus more on what you want and will accept than what they have done previously. You need to be specific in terms of what is acceptable and what is not.

If the person denies their criticism you could respond as one of my counselees told me she responded by saying, "Well, that's good. Then

I guess I won't have to be concerned about that ever happening in the future. If for some reason it does, I will immediately call it to your attention."

Direct? Yes. But have other more subtle approaches worked? Probably not. By doing this you are helping and admonishing these unfair people to put into practice the teaching of God's Word:

> Do not judge and criticize and condemn others, so that you may not be judged and criticized and condemned yourselves.
>
> For just as you judge and criticize and condemn others you will be judged and criticized and condemned, and in accordance with the measure you deal out to others it will be dealt out again to you (Matt. 7:1,2, *AMP*).
>
> Then let us no more criticize and blame and pass judgment on one another, but rather decide and endeavor never to put a stumbling block or an obstacle or a hindrance in the way of a brother (Rom. 14:13, *AMP*).

Friendship

Q. HOW CAN I ESTABLISH ENOUGH MEANINGFUL RELATIONSHIPS TO MEET MY INNER NEED FOR INTIMACY, FRIENDSHIP AND AFFIRMATION?

A. Have you ever hit it off instantly with a person? You know, you just clicked immediately? Sometimes relationships and friendships start out that way; most of the time they do not. Friendships are cultivated and nurtured; they take time and energy.

Women seem to have deeper and closer friendships than men. They seem to be able to relate better. And though most women don't have an abundance of close friendships, they do have a few. In order to build such precious, close friendships, you must be able to risk and invest time—even though the relationship might not work out.

Years ago I read a statement in Father John Powell's book *Why Am I Afraid to Tell You Who I Am?* It went like this, "I'm afraid to tell you who I am because if I tell you who I am you might not like who I am and that's all I've got!"

Developing a close friendship means sharing, praying and non-judgmental listening. Instead of searching for the right people for friendship, concentrate on being the kind of person that will draw others to you. This includes being genuine. No facades, no pretense, no false fronts. It involves being sincere.

The word "sincere" comes from a Latin word meaning "without wax." In ancient times, fine, expensive porcelain pottery often developed tiny cracks when it was fired in the kiln. Dishonest merchants would smear pearly white wax over the cracks until they disappeared, then claim the pottery was unblemished. But when the pottery was held up to the sun, the light would reveal the cracks filled in with wax. So honest merchants marked their porcelain with the words *sine cera*—without wax. That is what is meant by genuine sincerity: no hidden cracks, no ulterior motives, no hidden agendas.[4]

Friendship involves empathy or feeling with another person. You see the other person's joys, perceive what underlies those joys, and you communicate this to your friend.

Weight and Body Image

Q. HOW CAN I BE WORTHWHILE WHEN I AM SO DISSATISFIED WITH MY WEIGHT AND APPEARANCE? WHY IS BODY IMAGE USED TO DEFINE ME AND WHAT CAN I DO ABOUT MY ANGER ABOUT IT?

A. Do others say you are not worthwhile because of your weight and appearance or are you saying this to yourself? If others are saying this, realize they are not experts on you; their values are messed up.

These critics are wrong and they are saying something contrary to the way God sees you. To whom do you want to listen? Others or God?

Much of the time we are our own worst enemy regarding our appearance. We feel worthless because of our weight and appearance. I have talked to very attractive, trim women who *felt* they were overweight and unattractive. That was far from the truth but they were locked into their feelings.

Many women evaluate their femininity based on the feedback they get from others. Often tremendous energy is put into attracting the opposite sex. They have an obsession to be a certain weight; it is an American pastime to lose weight and be fit. Self-improvement has become synonymous with self-acceptance and self-esteem. More than 90 percent of women try to change their appearance in some way. They believe their lives will be better by having increased beauty. I like what Mary Ann Mayo says:

> The god of physical perfection promises that the achievement of outer goals will fix what ails us inside. Happiness and success will inevitably follow when we become as "body beautiful" as possible. *Self-improvement has become synonymous with self-acceptance.*
>
> Our efforts at physical perfection offer us tangible solutions to fix what ails us—the newest gym, the latest diet, hip fashions, a nip or tuck here or there. These cures require effort, energy, and money, but actually enable us to avoid the tedious and scary prospect of searching inward. They make us feel alive and up-to-date, but keep us from looking into the recesses of our soul. Thus distracted, we can easily continue to deny the trouble inside.[5]

It is interesting and sad to see how women have become slaves to society's standards for being "physically all right." About one-tenth of all young women and one-fifth of female college students are struggling with some eating disorders. Women who are happiest with their weight are 10 pounds underweight. Unfortunately, those who are at their ideal medical weight want to be 8 pounds underweight.[6]

This issue has most likely been with you for a while. Consider these questions:

1. Were you ever pressured to look a certain way? If so, by whom?

2. How do you feel about your appearance now as compared to several years ago?

3. List five positive features about your physical appearance.

4. What would you like to change and why? Is it possible and reasonable? If so, what is your plan and timetable for making this a reality?

5. If you discovered that you would be the way you are today for the rest of your life, how would you handle it?

6. What do you think you would have that you don't have now if you looked different?

What can you do to accept how you look? Here are a few suggestions:

1. Take steps to realistically improve what you can, such as weight, hair, posture, exercise. Nothing is wrong in trying to look good unless you attach your value and worth to it.

2. Take an inventory of your thought life concerning the messages you say to yourself about how you look. Replace each negative, disparaging thought with an accepting, affirming thought. Remember, you are probably overly critical of yourself.

3. Dig deep to discover where you learned these beliefs about yourself.

4. Give yourself at least three compliments a day about how you look.

5. Occasionally go out without attempting to look your best.

6. If you are angry about the mixed-up standards that exist to determine your worth, use the energy of your anger to correct the problem rather than taking it out on yourself. Treat your

body well. Write letters to sponsors, health clubs, advertisers who are always using the most attractive, perfectly trim women. They are considered the ideal. But they are the odd ones. Suggest that they use more average-looking people for their ads. React to any messages or ads that state or teach a false basis for your worth and value. You and I have strengths. We also have weaknesses. But with these, we reflect God's image in our lives. I hope you rejoice in that.

You want to say, "This is me. This is the best I can be and I like me when I'm this way. When I'm not, I can accept me. My worth is not dependent on what others think and what society says. Thank God that His acceptance and love for me is not based upon my appearance."

Perfectionism

Q. I AM A PERFECTIONIST AND I AM NOT SURE I LIKE BEING ONE; BUT IT IS ALL I KNOW. AND EVEN IF I KNEW HOW TO CHANGE, I WONDER IF I CAN LET LOOSE OF THIS LIFE-STYLE.

A. You have asked a common question. Our society abounds with men and women who have perfectionist tendencies. Some of them are what I call "Pure Perfectionists." These are people who evaluate every area of their lives from a perfectionistic point of view. Others are "Pocket Perfectionists": they have certain areas of their lives controlled by their perfectionism. Think with me for a moment about both of their life-styles. Have you ever thought of perfectionism as a thief? Oh yes, it does give you some rewards but it robs you of joy and satisfaction. You have assigned yourself a list of rules and regulations and you probably expect the people around you to follow the same list. You probably procrastinate as well because you hesitate trying anything unless you know you will be successful.

I have never yet met a successful perfectionist; they just do not exist. Your thinking pattern probably goes something like this, "What I produce is a reflection of how much ability I have and how much worth I have. My level of ability determines my worth as a person. What I'm able to attain reflects my worth as a person. Failure means I'm not worth much." Sound familiar?

The facts are that you and I will fail. We are failures. But God accepts our imperfections and declares us to have value. Because of God's grace, we have value and worth and are seen as perfect in His sight. Striving for perfectionism means that we are still living under the law rather than by the grace of God. Think about it.

The Change Process

If you are willing to challenge the basis for your security, you can give up your striving. But it will take work, time and a willingness to attempt not to do things perfectly! Here are a few suggestions to begin the process of change:

1. Make a list of the advantages and disadvantages of being a perfectionist.

2. Make a list of 5 to 10 benefits of making mistakes. What can you learn from them?

3. Write out two paragraphs discussing why it is impossible for you to be perfect.

4. What are three of your recent successes and three of your failures? How did you feel about each?

5. What are you currently putting off doing because of your fear of failure? Decide when you will attempt it.

6. What are 10 of your strengths. What are 10 of your weaknesses? Share both lists with God in prayer and with 1 or 2 friends.

7. Purposely begin doing things and leaving some parts incomplete. Affirm yourself for what you have done.

These suggestions may sound strange but they are a beginning. Remember, striving to be a perfectionist is your attempt to feel secure and adequate. In reality, however, security and adequacy are a gift from God. They are free. They cannot be earned.

When you replace your drive toward perfectionism with striving for excellence, you will find balance in your life. Do what you do to the best of your ability, knowing when to stop, affirming yourself, leaving room in your life to grow, forgiving yourself for imperfections. That is healthy. One day you may look at a project and say, "Yes, I like it. I perhaps could have done better, but I feel good about stopping now. I can accept it and me."

To help you in your journey, read the recommended books on perfectionism.

Spending Money

Q. HOW CAN I RESIST THE TEMPTATION TO SPEND MONEY?

A. Spending money may not be the real problem although it does have its own set of consequences. Recently I found a book titled *When Spending Takes the Place of Feeling: Women Who Spend Too Much and Don't Know Why* by Karen O'Connor, which clearly and helpfully covers the problem of overspending. Many women struggle with misusing money (as do men!) and it is important to discover the set of beliefs that support the problem behavior. Many overspenders have difficulty with self-esteem, setting healthy boundaries, knowing their own sense of reality and acknowledging and meeting their needs and wants.

Perhaps it would be helpful to keep track of when you spend, what is going on in your life at that time, how you feel after you spend and how you feel when you do not spend. If you were not able to spend at all during the time you feel compelled to, what else would you do to replace your spending? Karen O'Connor has several helpful guidelines to determine if you are an overspender. She says that women who are overspenders answer "often" or "very often" to many of the following statements.

1. I buy things I don't really need or want.
2. If I have money in my purse I feel I have to spend it.
3. I buy things even when I cannot afford them.
4. I spend money to make myself feel better.
5. I overspend on gifts to impress or gain the approval of others.
6. I buy things on sale—just because they're on sale.
7. I indulge in spending rituals such as buying in pairs.
8. I feel secretive about my spending habits.[7]

But spending problems can become more serious when a person tends to be a shopaholic or a compulsive shopper. Women who fall into this category answer, "often" and "very often" to many of the following statements.

1. Shopping is my most common form of entertainment.
2. I feel anxious when I am not shopping.
3. Shopping takes the place of talking and feeling and dealing with the unpleasant realities of my life.
4. I argue with others about my shopping and spending habits.
5. I repeatedly buy things I neither need nor want.
6. I get a rush or a high from the shopping process or even thinking about it.
7. I minimize my purchases or hide them from my family.
8. I buy clothing that does not fit my lifestyle—evening gowns, aerobic wear, or dance shoes—when I rarely, if ever, use them.[8]

Recommended Reading:

Baily, Covert. *Fit or Fat.* Boston, MA: Houghton Mifflin Co., 1977.

Blue, Ron. *Master Your Money: A Step-by-Step Plan for Financial Freedom.* Nashville, TN: Thomas Nelson, 1991.

Hansel, Tim. *You Gotta Keep Dancin'.* Elgin, IL: David C. Cook, 1986.

Hart, Archibald. *Fifteen Principles for Achieving Happiness.* Dallas, TX: WORD Inc., 1988.

Mayo, Mary Ann. *Skin Deep*. Arbor, MI: Vine Books, 1992.
Miller, Holly. *How to Stop Living for the Applause*. Ann Arbor, MI: Servant Publications, 1990. (Help for women who need to be perfect.)
Mundis, Jerrold. *How to Get Out of Debt, Stay Out of Debt, and Live Prosperously*. New York: Bantam, 1989.
Schlayer, Mary Elizabeth. *How to Be a Financially Secure Woman*. New York: Ballantine, 1987.
Seamands, David. *Freedom from the Performance Trap*. Wheaton, IL: Victor Books, 1988.
Stoop, Dave. *Hope for the Perfectionist*. Nashville, TN: Thomas Nelson Publishers, 1989.

Notes
1. Janet Congo, *Free to Be God's Woman* (Ventura, CA: Regal Books, 1988), pp. 51-53.
2. Ibid., pp. 47-70, adapted.
3. Ibid., pp. 70,71.
4. H. Norman Wright, *How to Get Along with Almost Anyone* (Dallas, TX: WORD Inc., 1989), p. 19.
5. Mary Ann Mayo, *Skin Deep* (Arbor, MI: Vine Books, 1992), p. 12.
6. Naomi Wolf, *The Beauty Myth* (New York: Morrow and Co., 1991), pp. 179,180, adapted.
7. Karen O'Connor, *When Spending Takes the Place of Feeling* (Nashville, TN: Thomas Nelson, 1992), p. 69.
8. Ibid., p. 84.

Chapter 4

BEING SINGLE

Single and Happy

Q. WHAT DO I SAY WHEN PEOPLE ASK ME
WHY I AM NOT MARRIED YET?
I AM HAPPY SINGLE.

A. You do not have to answer a question that intrudes into your privacy; do not take the responsibility for a personal question. You can respond to the inquisitive person in several ways such as:

"Why aren't *you* married yet?"

"Is it a problem that I'm not married?" or "It sounds like that's a concern for you. I'm quite happy and satisfied. Are you?"

These are not to be said in a sarcastic manner but simply to request that the other person consider the purpose of the question.

For those who feel they might marry someday, I recommend the book, *Should I Get Married?* by Blaine Smith for a complete presentation of all the necessary factors for being married.

Sexual Feelings in the Single Woman

Q. HOW DO I DEAL WITH MY SEXUAL FEELINGS AS
A SINGLE CHRISTIAN WOMAN?

A. Perhaps the healthiest step is admitting you have sexual drives. You may find yourself noticing an attractive man and experiencing a sexual interest in him. But as a Christian, you should follow specific guidelines for sexual behavior; sexual intercourse while you are single should not be a consideration for you. Consider these thoughts from Bob Burns and Tom Whiteman:

> The single Christian must, therefore, practice self-control of his sexual desires. Of course, that's easier said than done. There are many temptations to sin along this part of the Christian's journey, but it's possible for the sincere Christian to control himself if he honestly wants to.
>
> Let me mention something here that gets at a tremendous problem in contemporary society. I don't believe the satisfaction of the sexual appetite is a basic life need. That may surprise you if you've seen many movies or read many sex books recently. The attitude of much of society seems to be that our sexual appetite *must be satisfied.* We're told that normal, healthy life requires it. We have to eat, drink, and have intercourse to live. But that's simple falsehood. It is possible to live a fully normal, healthy, and happy life without sexual intercourse. You'll die if you don't eat and drink, but you won't die if you abstain from sex. It's the failure (perhaps I should say refusal) to recognize this fact that makes it impossible for many people to honestly consider self-control in regard to their sexual life. Self-control is not only possible, it's also required of the Christian single. It's God's rule of life for us, and we must seek it if we mean to walk with Him.

Let me suggest some things that will help in the struggle for self-control.

First, self-control is simply impossible for the person who refuses to make a commitment to it. Self-control begins with a hard and clear decision to be a certain kind of person. The single person who toys around with his commitment is simply guaranteeing his failure, but the person who honestly determines that he will refrain from sexual intercourse is going to have success.

I want to emphasize the *certainty of success* for those who make a personal commitment to refrain from intercourse. A real commitment made by a person who knows himself well will bring success. I'm talking of a life-and-death determination.[1]

If you want to exercise self-control, you must make a commitment to it. But this involves being honest about your strengths and weaknesses and taking steps to protect yourself in the weak areas. It involves avoiding tempting situations and places, and watching carefully what you look at and dwell upon in your mind. It involves not being alone with someone who is tempting to you. And by all means, become accountable to a group of your friends and allow them to support you.

Premarital Sex

Q. WHAT IS SO WRONG ABOUT PREMARITAL SEX?

A. What is wrong with premarital sex? One word—AIDS! Sex before or outside of marriage is a risky activity today. Not only because of AIDS but many other diseases are running rampant as well. Sex before marriage is not the best choice today. Those who adhere to a value system of no sex outside of marriage and violate it have more difficulty with guilt and resentment in marriage than those with no value system.

Does the Bible really forbid premarital intercourse? Yes, it is very clear. Here are some passages for you to consider.

Biblical Mandates About Premarital Sex

In some passages *(KJV)* fornication refers to all sexual immorality in general: John 8:4; Acts 15:20-29; 21:25; Romans 1:24; 1 Corinthians 5:1; 6:13,18; 2 Corinthians 12:21; Ephesians 5:3. In Matthew 5:32 and 19:9 the word "fornication" is used as a synonym for the word "adultery." In four passages, both the words "adultery" and "fornication" are used, indicating a definite distinction between the two words: Matthew 15:19; Mark 7:21; 1 Corinthians 6:9; Galatians 5:19. In two passages, fornication refers to voluntary sexual intercourse between unmarried people or between an unmarried person and a married person: 1 Corinthians 7:2; 1 Thessalonians 4:3-5. Out of 39 passages, 37 include the concept of premarital sexual intercourse being opposed to the plan and will of God. The only exceptions are the two passages using fornication as a synonym for adultery.

Paul speaks strongly against sex outside of marriage in many of his letters. In 1 Corinthians 6:9-20 *(NASB)*, Paul warns that those who continue to practice fornication or adultery "shall not inherit the kingdom of God" (vv. 9,10). He adds, "the body is not for immorality, but for the Lord" (v. 13). Indeed, our bodies are "members of Christ" (v. 15) and "a temple of the Holy Spirit" who is in us (v. 19). Accordingly, we are to glorify God in our bodies (see v. 20) by fleeing sexual immorality (see v. 18).

Benefits of Waiting

Many benefits are derived from waiting for sexual relations until marriage.

For one, no guilt. God tells us to wait until marriage for sexual relations. Not waiting will create guilt that will hamper your relationship with Him, with your sex partner, and with everyone else. By waiting you can know, because God says so, that Jesus Christ smiles on your marriage bed.

Waiting ensures that you will never have to be afraid, not even to the extent of one fleeting thought, of having to build a marriage on an unexpected pregnancy.

Waiting also ensures that you will never fall into the devastating trap of comparing your spouse's sexual performance with that of a previous sexual partner.

Waiting will help you subject your physical drives to the Lordship of Christ and thereby develop self-control, an important aspect of the fruit of the Holy Spirit. Also, if you get married and are later separated temporarily (for example, for a business trip), this discipline early in your relationship will give both of you confidence and trust in each other during that time of separation.

Waiting ensures that something will be saved for your marriage relationship, for that first night and for the many nights thereafter. The anticipation of the fulfillment of your relationship in sexual union is exciting. Do not spoil it by jumping the gun.

Given our conviction to refrain from sexual intercourse until marriage, the question remains: How far shall we go, short of sexual intercourse, before marriage? The answer to this question depends upon how far along you are in your relationship together (for example, first date or engaged) and upon your abilities to withstand the very strong temptation to have sexual intercourse.

A general principle that applies to everyone is the following: That which has its natural end in sexual intercourse should be saved for your wedding night. This means, at the very least, that heavy petting (direct stimulation of each other's sexual organs and mutual masturbation) should be out. Do not build up your sexual drives and desires to the point of no return, lest your physical relationship become a source of frustration rather than a joy for you.

Finding a Committed Christian Man

Q. WHERE CAN I FIND A CHRISTIAN MAN WHO IS
COMMITTED TO THE SAME SPIRITUAL VALUES AND ACTIVITIES
AS ME? (THE MOST COMMON QUESTION FROM SINGLES.)

A. I agree that it is difficult to find a spiritually committed Christian man. Many women have found a partner at churches that have large, single-adult groups or through Christian computer services. No matter where you meet a man, establish right away your faith in Jesus Christ and commitment to a biblical value system and pattern of behavior. Ask him to share his testimony, the details of his daily interaction with God, in what way he has grown as a Christian over the last year and so on. Yes, you might scare him off but better now than discovering after several months his commitment is shallow.

Keep looking for a man who is a growing Christian instead of dating someone and hoping to either convert him or help him start growing spiritually. And do not hesitate to go early for premarital counseling if it looks promising. If the man you are dating resists going for premarital counseling, move on! That is not harsh. It is realistic. If he is closed to help before marriage, he will be even more closed and resistant after marriage.

Falling in Love with a Loser

Q. WHY AM I ATTRACTED TO MEN WHO
DO NOT TREAT ME WELL?

A. Many women fall into the repetition trap. They keep developing relationships with the same kind of abusive man over and over again. I have seen many reasons for this.

Some women are comfortable with men who do not treat them

well because they know what to expect even though the men have characteristics they do not care for. Some women, unfortunately, feel as though they do not deserve any better. Yet others are driven by unresolved issues with the men in their lives while they were being raised. Others keep selecting the same kind of abusive man with the hope that they might change him so he will treat them better than the others did. But it usually does not work.

Recommended Reading:

Smith, Blaine M. *Should I Get Married?* Colorado Springs: InterVarsity Press, 1990.

Note
1. Bob Burns and Tom Whiteman, *The Fresh Start Divorce Recovery Workshop* (Nashville: TN: Thomas Nelson, 1992), p. 144.

Chapter 5

Stress

The potential for stress is all around us. But how is it really affecting you? And what is creating this feeling of tension and pressure you experience? What is stressful to you may not be stressful to someone else. For some, stress is the worry about future events that cannot be avoided or concern about events after they have occurred. And yet for others, it is simply the wear and tear of daily life. Perhaps you are feeling like a piece of stone that has been hammered on for so long that you have started to crumble.

Any experience that arouses your adrenaline system and keeps your body in that state over a period of time is creating stress.

Causes of Stress

Q. HOW CAN I BETTER DEAL WITH STRESS AND
WHAT ARE THE CAUSES OF STRESS?

 Let's consider some of the causes of stress:

1. *An unresolved relationship.* If you have uncertainties about a relationship such as a friendship or marriage, if you are

wondering if your partner is unhappy or is thinking of leaving the marriage, stress is present.

2. *Environment.* Your environment could contribute to stress. A monotonous and repetitious environment can be just as much a problem as a fast-paced, pressure-filled, competitive atmosphere.

3. *Perfectionism.* Having excessively high standards is a great way to set ourselves up for failure and self-rejection. And a perfectionist is hard to live with. Perfectionism usually means insecurity. Those who are secure are flexible and willing to take risks and make positive changes. When a person has unrealistic expectations and does not live up to them, she begins to despise herself, which leads to depression.

4. *Impatience.* If you are very impatient with others, you are impatient with yourself as well. Not getting things done according to a schedule keeps a person's insides in a turmoil. The word "patience" means, "forbearance, not hasty or impulsive, steadfast, able to bear."

5. *Rigidity.* Inflexibility is closely tied to perfectionism and impatience. Rigid people spend their time prospecting for something to be upset over. Admitting one's error and accepting other people's opinions is a mature and stress-reducing response.

6. *Inability to relax.* Many people find it difficult to sit in a chair for 10 minutes and totally relax. Their minds keep running and they push themselves. Their activity is called stress momentum.

7. *Explosiveness and anger.* If a person's life is characterized by bombs spreading angry shrapnel on others, stress is affecting not only the person but other people as well.

8. *Lack of humor and little enthusiasm for life.* Those who are filled with self-conceit, self-reproach, and therefore stress are probably depressed as well. See Philippians.

9. *Too much competition.* Comparing yourself with others, in terms of what they do and what they have, places unneeded

pressure on you. We do not have to let what others do and have affect our own lives. Some competition in certain areas can be fun and enjoyable, but when it is constant it is no fun.

10. *Lack of self-worth.* A low self-concept is the basis for many difficulties in life. Depression and stress can occur.

Women's Unique Stresses

Women have their own unique set of stressors.

Georgia Witkin has written extensively about stress in both men and women. She says that concerns expressed by women are usually different from those raised by men. In her studies, women spoke of many more stresses that were (1) *long-term* and (2) *beyond their control.* These are the two factors that make stress dangerous to psychological and physical health!

Women talked about the stresses of *unequal pay* and *unequal say.* They talked about the stresses of *double duties,* such as housework and work-work. They talked about *sabotage on the home front*—sometimes intentional, but more often not.

From her years of working with women in counseling, Georgia Witkin identified the following stresses among women:

- The stresses associated with their physiology—breast development, menstruation, pregnancy and menopause.
- The stresses associated with their life changes—becoming a wife, becoming a mother, being either during the divorce boom and economic bust, being female after 40 in a youth-beauty culture, becoming a not-so-merry widow, or reorganizing after children have grown.
- The psychological stress often felt by the supposedly swinging single who was raised in an old-fashioned way; the homemaker who is pressured to get out of the home and develop herself; the career woman who is pressured to get back into her home lest she lose her family; and the lifelong non-assertiveness expert.

- The hidden stresses that distract, distress and deplete—
  tokenism, chauvinism, subtle sexism practiced by both men
  and other women, entertaining, chauffeuring and talking to
  two-year-olds.

- And the stresses of life crises which fall largely on female
  shoulders—caring for an ill or dying parent, parenting a hand-
  icapped child and making sure that life goes on.[1]

Eliminating Stress

How can you eliminate stress? Here are three ways.

Alter your environment. First, you can attempt to alter the environment in order to prevent events that are likely to produce stress. You
could change jobs, move from your neighborhood, or not visit your relatives as often. Unfortunately, people do not realize how many additional changes would have to be made that could create even more
stress.

Alter the symptoms. The second way of dealing with stress is for you
to work on the symptoms. We can attempt to alter our emotional and
physiological response to stress by using medication, tranquilizers, relaxation techniques, meditation imagery (from a Christian perspective).

Alter your attitude. The third way of handling stress is the best way.
This involves altering those beliefs, assumptions, and negative ways of
thinking, that make us more vulnerable to stress. Our perceptions and
evaluations of the world actually can cause stress. Changing our attitudes may be difficult but it may also be the most expedient way to
reduce stress, tension and anxiety.

Handling Stress

What can any woman do to handle the stress in her life?

One step is to evaluate what you do and why you do it. Dr. Lloyd
Ogilvie offers some insights on our motivation and the pressures we
create:

We say, "Look, God, how busy I am!" We equate exhaustion with an effective, full life. Having certain purposes, we redouble our efforts in an identity crisis of meaning. We stack up performance statistics in the hope that we are counting for something in our generation. But for what or for whom?

Many of us become frustrated and beg for time to just be, but do our decisions about our involvement affirm that plea? A Christian is free to stop running away from life in overinvolvement.[2]

In one of Dr. Ogilvie's sermons, he also raised two interesting questions that relate to what we are doing and how we are doing it: (1) What are you doing with your life that you couldn't do without the *power of God?* (2) Are you living life out of your own *adequacy* or out of the abundance of the riches of Christ? Both questions are worth thinking about.

Evaluate all that you do by making a list of all the various activities in which you are involved. Then place each item in the proper column on this chart.

Very Crucial	Very Important	Important	Good

Everything that falls in "Very Crucial" stays in your life. Whatever falls in "Very Important" would probably stay but if necessary could be dropped. Anything that falls in "Important" can either stay or go. And anything in the "Good" column goes.

Identify Your Needs

Identify what you need and what will help you the most.

Build strong, close relationships with other women, even if lack of time is one of your stressors. This will help you in the long run.

In *The Female Stress Syndrome,* Georgia Witkin suggests: (1) do exercises that you enjoy; (2) take steps to feel as though you are in control; (3) learn relaxation techniques (I would suggest Tim Hansel's book *When I Relax I Feel Guilty);* (4) take control of your schedule; (5) prioritize what you do; (6) make decisions and choices; (7) separate your past from your present; (8) accept who you are; (9) learn to say no; (10) give yourself permission to change your mind; (11) become your own permission giver so that you can rest and relax; (12) set limits; (13) expect the best; (14) anticipate the stress of the holidays; and (15) learn to laugh.[3]

After reading such a list you may feel, "There's no way. It takes too much time to do things for me." You may be interested to know that according to the 1991 Bristol-Meyers Keri Report, "The State of American Women Today," the women who allotted enough time for exercise, grooming and nutritional needs felt more in control of their lives and it only took an extra 21 minutes a day.[4]

I have found other ways to handle stress that have helped me. First, I purposely slow down and take a slower pace when I feel rushed and overwhelmed. It gives a feeling of taking back control and puts everything in proper perspective.

Second, when I am in a frustrating situation such as not getting everything done by a certain time, being unavoidably late and getting stuck in traffic, I give myself permission to not get it done, to be late, or to get stuck. If you are stuck in traffic you could say, "All right, this isn't what I wanted. But I can handle it. It's all right. I give myself permission to be late or stuck. It's not the end of the world. I'll make use of the time by praying." It works!

Third, concentrate on the Word of God. Have these verses available on small cards that you keep with you: Psalm 4:8; 27:1; 37:1-9; Isaiah 41:10,13; Philippians 4:6-9; Hebrews 13:6; James 1:2,3; and 1 Peter 5:7.

The Stress of Work and Family

Q. How do I deal with the stress
of work and family?

A. Consider these suggestions from an authority on stress management, Dr. Georgia Witkin:

> It helps to have more of the basic clothes to cut down on washing and trips to the cleaner. As much as possible, hire help you can afford. You can't do it all yourself. Each day schedule an escape even if it means reading a novel in the bath for fifteen minutes while your husband watches the kids. Find some private time just for you. Children can be taught not to disturb you. Find some type of play you enjoy. A number of people I know use their lunch time for this. Learn to rely upon routine and lists. A regular schedule helps to save time and energy.[5]

If you are married, one of the most important steps to take is to enlist the help of your spouse. Too often it is the wife who carries the load of both the household work and her career while the husband has just the career. Each person needs to contribute to sharing the load equally, but you will have to be flexible about who does what. It helps if both of you become adept at all tasks so you can exchange them easily. This is no time for old rigid male/female roles to dictate who does what.

If you are a single mother, suggest that the men of the church or singles group volunteer to watch the children one Saturday a month so you have at least one day that you can count on to be yours.

Burnout

Q. I feel so overwhelmed. I just want
to shut down. How do I cope?

A. This question immediately brings to mind the word "burnout." It is a condition that can strike any of us. Basically it means we have worn ourselves out by excessively striving to reach some unrealistic expectations imposed on us by ourselves or by the values of society.

A person experiencing burnout is "someone in a state of fatigue or frustration brought about by devotion to a cause, way of life, or relationship that failed to produce the expected reward."

If you want a simple explanation of how a person responds in a burnout, just analyze the word itself. The word "burn" brings about the vision of heat, fire, conflagration or anger. Some become angry at their families, their friends or their employers. This is an anger that is just seething beneath the surface, ready to boil up and spill over at the slightest provocation.

The second part of the word is "out." Nothing is left. It is as though you have checked out of life itself. You give up, claiming that nothing can be done and that the entire mess is hopeless. You hurt others by doing nothing. Your energy, integrity, care, love and desire are gone. Burnout is when you are running on empty.

One of the major causes of burnout is false expectation. Unrealistic expectations about life, people or an occupation can lead to burnout. Some women focus upon the goal they wish to accomplish, having no regard for the struggle involved in the attainment process.

Another facet of unrealistic expectations is the belief that "it can't happen to me." Other people collapse, but not me. Other people fail, but not me. Other people burn out, but not me.

What Can Be Done to Overcome Burnout?

1. Evaluate your goals. What are they and what is their purpose?
2. Evaluate your expectations. List them and discover which ones are realistic and which ones are not.
3. Identify times of stress in your life.
4. Be willing to run the risk of becoming close to others. Let others help carry the responsibility.
5. Learn at least one relaxation technique and practice it regu-

larly. This helps to rest critical components of your body's emergency system.

6. Balance your life by exercising regularly. Good physical conditioning strengthens the body's immune system and increases endorphins, which are the brain's natural tranquilizers.

7. Get proper rest. Allow adequate time for sleep. Contrary to what we have been taught in a previous generation, most of us need more sleep than we actually get. Adrenal arousal reduces our need for sleep—but this is a trap because we will ultimately pay the penalty for it.

8. Learn to be flexible. Only the gospel is unchanging. Your ideas and priorities may need to change. Flexibility reduces the likelihood of frustration.

9. Slow down. Remember, God is never in a hurry. "Hurryness" is a human characteristic caused by inadequate planning and poor time management. Hurry speeds up the "wear and tear"of our bodies and minds and increases the production of destructive adrenaline.

10. Pay attention to the "little hassles." They are more likely to kill you than the big ones. The everyday, minor irritations are the deadliest.

11. Focus your work and use of time on essentials. Reduce redundancies, eliminate unnecessary activities, avoid demands that will stretch you too thinly and learn how to say no kindly, without giving offense and without experiencing a sense of guilt.

12. Stay in touch with reality. Do not let your ambitions outrun the limits of your capabilities.

13. Avoid states of helplessness; take control and implement a coping strategy regardless how minor.

14. If you cannot resolve a major conflict area in your life, leave it. Move on if necessary. Notions of being super-human often keep us in severe conflict situations.

ℰ*orry*

ℚ. HOW CAN I CONTROL WORRY?

ℋ. Over the years, I have worked with many people in counseling and in classes who describe themselves as professional worriers. They are very proficient at rehearsing the future in their minds and asking the question, "What if..." again and again.

During a Sunday School class I was teaching on the subject of worry, I asked participants to report on an experiment I had suggested the previous week for eliminating the worry from their lives. One woman said she began the experiment Monday morning, and by Friday she felt the worry pattern that had plagued her for years was finally broken.

What accomplished this radical improvement? It was a simple method of applying God's Word to her life in a new way. I have shared this method with hundreds of people in my counseling office and with thousands in classes and seminars. Perhaps it will help you.

Methods to Eliminate Worry

Take a blank index card and on one side write the word STOP in large, bold letters. On the other side, write the complete text of Philippians 4:6-9. (Use *The Living Bible* or the *Amplified Bible*.) Keep the card with you at all times. Whenever you are alone and begin to worry, take the card out, hold the STOP side in front of you, and say "Stop!" aloud twice with emphasis. Then turn the card over and read the Scripture passage aloud twice with emphasis.

Taking the card out interrupts your thought pattern of worry. Saying the word "Stop!" further breaks this automatic habit pattern. Then reading the Word of God aloud becomes the positive substitute for worry. If you are in a group of people and begin to worry, follow the same procedure, only do it silently.

The woman who shared in the class said that on the first day of her experiment, she took out the card 20 times during the day. But on Friday she took it out only 3 times. Her words were, "For the first time in my life, I have the hope that my worrisome thinking can be chased out of my life."

Another step is to inventory your worries. Whenever worry plagues you, try some or all of the following techniques to help you evaluate your worries and plan your strategy:

1. Face your worries and admit them when they occur. Do not run from them, for they will return to haunt you. Do not worry about worrying! That just reinforces and perpetuates the problem.

2. Itemize your worries and anxieties on a sheet of paper. Be specific and complete as you describe them.

3. Write down the reasons or causes for your worry. Investigate the sources. Is there any possibility you can eliminate the source or the cause of your worry? Have you tried? What have you tried specifically?

4. Write down the amount of time you spend each day worrying.

5. What has worry accomplished in your life? Describe this in detail.

6. Make a list of the following: (a) the ways your worrying has prevented a feared situation from occurring; (b) the ways your worrying increased the problem.

Recommended Reading:

Hansel, Tim. *When I Relax I Feel Guilty.* Elgin, IL: David C. Cook, 1979.

West, Sheila. *Beyond Chaos—Stress Relief for the Working Woman.* Colorado Springs, CO: NavPress, 1992.

Witkin, Georgia. *The Female Stress Syndrome.* New York: Newmarket Press, 1991.

Wright, H. Norman. *Afraid No More!* Wheaton, IL: Tyndale House Publishers, 1992.

Notes

1. Georgia Witkin, *The Female Stress Syndrome* (New York: Newmarket Press, 1991), pp. 16,17.
2. Lloyd Ogilvie, *God's Best for Today* (Eugene, OR: Harvest House, 1981), February 3 devotion.
3. Witkin, *The Female Stress Syndrome*, pp. 290-307, adapted.
4. Ibid., p. 125, adapted.
5. Ibid., pp. 142,143, adapted.

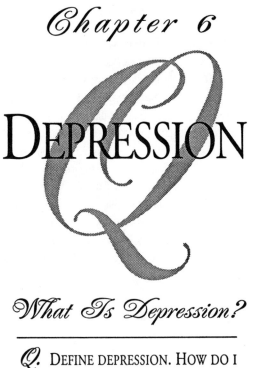

Chapter 6

DEPRESSION

What Is Depression?

Q. DEFINE DEPRESSION. HOW DO I
KNOW IF I AM DEPRESSED?

A. Depression—a common term in a woman's vocabulary. I hear it constantly. It can describe many things. When I counsel a woman who says she is depressed, I usually ask her what she means by the term. The word "depression" can have a hundred different meanings, and each woman may have a slight variation in the way she experiences it. But, what is it like? In working with a counselee I often ask this series of questions:

Do you find it difficult to get out of bed in the morning? If you have responsibilities for other family members, do you let them shift for themselves? Are you becoming indecisive and forgetful? Has your ability to concentrate vanished? Do you feel like laughing anymore? Has food lost its taste and sex its appeal?

Do you seem to be withdrawing into a shell, not wanting to be bothered by family or friends? Have you lost your desire to talk on the phone or attend the social gatherings you used to enjoy? Are you starting to sever all contact with other people?

Do you have difficulty falling asleep at night? Do you wake up in the middle of the night and thrash about until dawn, bothered by negative and gloomy thoughts? Would you like to sleep 16 hours a day or take frequent naps? And even if you do, do you still feel exhausted?

Are your thoughts filled with a sense of hopelessness? Do you feel there is no way out of your circumstances? Do you feel no one cares about you, and you do not particularly care for yourself? Are there any positive feelings about yourself? Do you feel there is a dark thundercloud hanging above your head following you wherever you go?

Have you noticed some changes physically? Do you have a number of new, vague pains or aches? Do you suspect that you have some serious disease?

This is depression.

Forms of Depression

Emotional depression. This is probably the most common symptom in our country today. One out of eight of us is expected to receive help for depression at some time in our lives. No one is immune. Being a Christian does not make you immune either. And this can add an even greater depth to your depression because of a disbelief that as a believer you should not be depressed!

Your depression has a purpose, strange as it seems. Depression is a sign that something is not right in your life. It is a message system telling you, "Listen to me!" It is trying to point you to the cause. And in many cases depression is a healthy response to what is taking place in your life.

And please, hold on to this next statement: *Being depressed is not a sin!* That is right, it is not a sin to be depressed. Throughout God's Word, we see examples of people who were depressed and the depression was there for a purpose. Listen to the account of Jesus as He went into the garden:

And taking with Him Peter and the two sons of Zebedee, He began to show grief and distress of mind and was deeply depressed. Then He said to them, My soul is very sad and deeply grieved, so that I am almost dying of sorrow. Stay here and keep awake and watch with Me (Matt. 26:37,38, *AMP*).

Jesus' sense of loss was expressed through His feelings.

Spiritual depression. Some causes of depression can be traced to sinful behavior and thoughts. If your behavior is in conflict with your Christian value system, the result could be guilt and depression. This we call spiritual depression. It is vital to recognize and identify the sinful cause and deal with it so the depression has an opportunity to lift. This is where the healing resources of Jesus Christ will be your solution. It is important to remember that even after confessing the sin, repenting and accepting Christ's forgiveness, some depression may linger. This is normal because the biological changes that occur during depression take time to heal.

Ignoring a depression instead of facing it and seeking assistance, or refusing to follow guidelines to overcome the depression, has been considered sinful by some. In James 4:17 we read, "Therefore to him that knoweth to do good, and doeth it not, to him it is sin" *(KJV)*. Perhaps the "good" here for some depressed Christians is the knowledge that they can do something to get out of their depression. And this can have an effect on recovering from depression. Neglecting the body by lack of proper sleep, food and exercise can be a violation of maintaining the body, which is a temple of the Holy Spirit.

Sometimes people use their depression selfishly to elicit self-pity and sympathy from others, and even to control others. This prolongs the malady and turns depression into a weapon.

Do not overfocus on sin when you are depressed. Depression may be the consequence of sin, but the depression itself is not sin. An excessive tendency to engage in self-condemnation exists when you are depressed; along with a preoccupation on how terrible everything is and will continue to be. The good news is, if sin is involved, forgiveness and acceptance are available. This is a healthy focus.

You are experiencing a normal, although painful, response to what is happening psychologically and physically when you are depressed. Depression is an inner scream telling us that we have neglected some area of our lives. We need to listen to the depression, for it is telling us something we need to know. Respond to it and deal with the cause.

Depression has both spiritual and emotional elements to it as its darkness gradually draws a veil over your life. Your joy and peace will be replaced by unhappiness and discontentment. Instead of being filled with the Spirit, there is barrenness. Faith and hope give way to doubt and despair. You do not feel loved and forgiven. If anything, you feel unworthy, guilty and abandoned. We all feel as though we have been left alone to tromp through the darkness in isolation. And we doubt and doubt and doubt. We have no assurance of God's loving care, and we feel like orphans.

If you have experienced these symptoms, you are not alone. Remember, you cannot depend upon good, bubbly feelings to confirm your faith when you are depressed. When you are unable to feel God's presence, hold firmly to the facts of the Word of God that tell us He is there and we are not alone. If we believe that God is not present because we do not feel Him, then we will not reach out by an act of faith to rely upon Him. But the outstretched arms of Jesus Christ are always near. Sometimes we may need to ask a friend to loan us his or her faith so that we can reach out and accept God's help.

High Risk Groups for Depression

I usually do not go into this much detail with a counselee, but this is important for you to know. Various subgroups of the population are clearly at higher risk to experience depression than others. Let's consider some of these risk factors:

> 1. *Gender.* An overwhelming body of research shows a higher rate of depression in women than in men.
> 2. *Age.* Recent community surveys report a higher prevalence

of depressive symptoms in young adults (18-44) than older adults. This is a change from the early twentieth century when reports indicated older adults were more depressed. But the elderly are also becoming more prone to depression as their life span is lengthening.

3. *Marital status.* Separated and divorced people show a higher incidence of depression than do those who have never married or those who are currently married. Rates are lower among married than among single people. But an unfulfilled marriage is a major cause of depression.

4. *Religion.* A relationship between religion and depressive symptoms has not been found except in a few small religious groups that have inbred through closed marriages. Here, the more serious forms of depression are four times as common, presumably because of the strong genetic factor.

5. *Social class.* Whether defined by occupational, financial or educational level, strong evidence shows that rates of depressive symptoms are significantly higher in persons of lower socioeconomic status.

6. *Genetic factors.* Over the past 10 years, tremendous forward strides in studies have shown that genetic factors can cause depression. Compelling evidence exists that hereditary factors predispose one to the bipolar disorders (previously called manic-depressive disorders). Hereditary factors are less clear in other forms of depression.

7. *Biological factors.* Almost monthly, research into the functioning of the brain and its connection with the body reveals some new complexity. There is growing acceptance that clinical depression can be triggered by the brain in a number of different places in the body. The interactions are complex and still unclear. Physical illness almost certainly increases one's risk for depression, but so does having a certain "high risk" physiology.[1]

Depression

Reasons for Women's Depression

Q. I AM DEPRESSED AND CONTINUALLY CRYING.
HOW DO I OVERCOME MY DEPRESSION?
HOW DO I DEAL WITH A
MEANINGLESS LIFE?

A. In the United States, women are two to six times more likely to be diagnosed as depressed than men. Sometimes people have decided that these lopsided figures are the result of poor interpretation of statistics, female hormones or because women seek help more readily than men. But most studies do conclude that many more women than men are depressed.

Seventy percent of all antidepressants are prescribed for women. More women are in therapy for depression than ever before. Alcoholism, which used to be primarily a male problem, is on the increase among women. And it does not matter whether a woman is employed outside the home or is an isolated housewife. Both are prone to depression and experience it for the same reasons.

Many reasons are given for the high incidence of depression in the female population.

First, our western culture pressures women to take a dependent, passive role. Many women have never been encouraged to become self-sufficient, and a link connects "learned helplessness" with depression. This still exists. Furthermore, in the past, some women were taught to lower their personal aspirations and depend upon dominant males for their well-being. This did not do much for healthy self-esteem, and often contributed to depression.

Second, some women's marriages contribute to depression. Some men are insensitive to their wives' moods. Instead of being helpful and supportive, husbands often respond with criticism, put-downs and an unwillingness to listen.

Third, many women are depressed because they bring certain unresolved issues with them into adulthood. Maggie Scarf, in her excellent book *Unfinished Business: Pressure Points in the Lives of Women*, says that no woman reaches maturity without having taken on a freight carload of unresolved issues. These include the following:

1. *Uncompleted growing tasks.* It is important to work through the growing stages of life such as adolescence, emotional separation from parents, the 20s and 30s and so on. A woman who is shortchanged in these needed transitions can get bogged down and depressed.

2. *Unresolved trauma.* Some women enter adulthood with psychological bills left unpaid. Many cases of depression occur because of being victimized as a child through abuse or incest. Anger, depression and guilt are common companions to these past traumas.

3. *Unfinished business.* Some women have evaded important business from the past. Unforgiven grudges or resentments can produce depression. And often when depression occurs, a woman looks for surface causes, ignoring the hidden roots. Hormone imbalance and hypoglycemia have often been unjustly blamed for deeper sources of depression.[2]

Our society traditionally allows women to admit weaknesses or problems and to seek help, but insists that men maintain stability and put up a brave front.

Most women were not encouraged to learn to express their anger as they were growing up and this lends itself to a great deal of repression, which soon turns into depression.

Another factor that can contribute to women experiencing more depression than men is that their brain structures cause them to be more sensitive. Women use their brains holistically, which has definite advantages. They are more people-oriented, form more intense love bonds, are the nurturers, and learn more "shoulds" as a child.

Another major cause of depression is that women become more attached to others than men do. Any loss, especially relational, can precipitate depression.

Brenda Poinsett describes this so well in her book *Understanding a Woman's Depression:*

> A woman puts so much of herself into her relationships. She cements herself to the ones she loves. And very often, without even realizing it, her very identity gets wrapped up in her love bonds. Who she is has meaning in terms of whom she loves.
>
> Depression for women, when it occurs, happens in one kind of context more than any other. This context is the loss of the love bond or relationship.
>
> It is around *losses of love* that the clouds of despair tend to converge, hover, and darken. Important figures leaving or dying; the inability to establish another meaningful bond with a peer-partner; being forced, by a natural transition in life, to relinquish an important love-tie; a marriage that is ruptured, threatening to rupture, or simply growing progressively distant; the splintering of a love affair or recognition that it is souring and will come to nothing...[3]
>
> A woman's love bonds are her joy, but they are also her sorrow.[4]

Early Detection

Perhaps you remember the story of the frog and the boiling water. If you drop a frog in a pan of cool water on the stove it begins to swim about. It is enjoying itself. If you turn on the flame under the pan and gradually warm up the water, the frog is not aware of the change in temperature. It adjusts to the water as the temperature changes. In time the water becomes very hot, then boils, and finally the frog is cooked. But the heat comes so gradually and subtly that the frog does not realize what is happening until it is too late.

Depression is like that: It is often difficult to detect in its early stages. You may experience some of the symptoms but not understand what they are until they intensify. And when you have moved deeper into depression it is much more difficult to break out of its hold. Notice the three stages of depression described below.

Three Stages of Depression

1. Light depression. Your mood may be a bit low or down. You have a slight loss of interest in what you normally enjoy. A few feelings of discouragement may also be present. Your thinking is still normal. You might have a few physical symptoms, but your sleeping and eating habits remain normal. You may have a slight spiritual withdrawal at times.

If you can recognize these symptoms as indications of depression (and if this is a reaction depression), you are still in a position to reverse the depression. Ask yourself these questions: What is my depression trying to tell me? What may be causing this reaction? What would be the best way to stabilize myself at this time? Would sharing this with another person help, and if so, with whom will I share this? What Scriptures would help me at this time, or what other resource would be helpful? Having a preplanned reading program in mind would be beneficial. This can include a devotional book and specific passages of Scripture.

2. Moderate depression. All of the above symptoms are intensified. A prevailing feeling of hopelessness now emerges. Thinking is a bit slow as negative thoughts about yourself increase. Tears may flow for no apparent reason. Sleeping and eating problems may emerge—either too much or too little. You have a greater struggle spiritually as the tendency to retreat from God increases. During this stage you will probably need someone else to help you handle the depression. But your tendency may be not to share your difficulty with anyone else. However, keeping your problems to yourself just compounds the dilemma.

3. Severe depression. All of the previous symptoms occur at a very intense dimension. Personal neglect is obvious as appearance and cleanliness are ignored. It is a chore to complete daily tasks. Spiritual symptoms are obvious—either withdrawal or preoccupation. Crying is frequent, along with intense feelings of dejection, rejection, discouragement, self-blame, self-pity and guilt. Patterns of eating and sleeping are disrupted. Sometimes a woman becomes so despondent that she begins thinking about suicide. But this does not happen to everyone who is depressed.

A person who recognizes light depression does not want it, but often she does not know how to get rid of it. To keep from going into moderate or deep depression it is vital that we "let go" of light depression. Letting go before you plunge into the depths is the key to thwarting long-lasting and heavy depression.

Let's say you are swimming and you discover you are a little more tired than you thought you were. Or perhaps the water is deeper and the current swifter than you expected. By taking action immediately you can quickly head for shore and avert a possible disaster. And you hope you learn something from the experience. You can take similar action when you are in the light stage of depression.

But if the current is too strong, or if you are totally exhausted and on the verge of drowning, you will need the help of a lifeguard. If you are already in the moderate or severe stage of depression, if your depression has immobilized you and you feel helpless, you need the help of someone who is loving, firm, empathetic and a good listener to help pull you out of it.

You might be thinking, *Well, this is all background about depression. What do I do about it? How do I get out of my depression?*

How to Detect Depression

If you find you are becoming depressed, first check for any physical reasons for your depression. You may want to see your medical doctor. If there is no physical cause, then your next step is to ask yourself two key questions. You may want to ask your mate or a good friend to help you think them through:

1. What am I doing that might be bringing on my depression? Check your behavior to determine if it is consistent with Scripture. Ask yourself if you are doing anything to reinforce the depression.

2. What am I thinking about, or in what way am I thinking that might be making me depressed?

   Look for your depression "trigger." Some triggers are obvious and you are readily aware of what prompted the depression. Other causes are more difficult to discover. You may want to keep the following questions on a card, and when you are depressed refer to them to help you recall the thought or event that triggered the depression: What did I do? Where did I go? With whom did I speak? What did I see? What did I read? What was I thinking about?[5]

Please, do not attempt to deal with your depression by yourself. If it has been with you for some time, talk to a trusted friend and seek out a professional Christian counselor. But do something. The lethargy that is a by-product of being depressed causes us to behave in such a way that we reinforce our depression. Reading the recommended books for this section may help you; but if you are experiencing any of the symptoms listed below, please seek out someone trained in helping others with their depression. Let me suggest what Brenda Poinsett recommends; she experienced a deep depression herself and writes about it in her book, *Understanding a Woman's Depression.*

We need help when we don't know what caused the depression. The black cloud of despair came out of nowhere. The despair is dark and deep; and in all honesty, we cannot fathom a cause.

We need help if we are having suicidal thoughts.

We need help if we are having delusional thoughts.

We need help if we can't sleep, or we are losing a serious amount of weight, or we are experiencing severe physical discomfort in which our health may be affected.

We need help if we have had repeated depressive episodes in our life.

We need help when the depression is hurting our marriage, our family, or our job.

We definitely need help if the depression has lasted longer than one year.

A woman fitting any of these conditions needs to consider seeking outside help in getting over her depression. Depression is a treatable illness. While there is not one simple cure that works for everyone, there are a number of treatments available.

If one method doesn't bring you out of depression, another likely will. Any woman suffering from depression needs to know how to get help and what kind of help is available.[6]

It is not a sign of weakness to seek professional help. This may be the step to enable you to turn your depression from a life-crippling experience to an experience of reconstruction.

Spiritual Factors to Consider

Q. AS I AM A CHRISTIAN, WHY CAN'T I KEEP FROM GETTING DEPRESSED AND ANXIOUS?

A. Let's consider what happens to us spiritually when depression occurs. Are there any predictable symptoms or tendencies? Two extremes usually occur.

The most common is to *withdraw from God.* You will tend not to pray or read the Scriptures as you once did. Why? Possibly because you feel God has either rejected you or abandoned you. Because guilt is a part of depression, you may tend to feel that God is punishing you by rejecting you, and this provokes spiritual withdrawal. But God does understand what you are going through. He is neither rejecting you nor is He punishing you. Cutting yourself off from God only serves to reinforce your depression.

Just the opposite can also occur. Depression may lead you to *become overinvolved in spiritual things.* This could be a compensation for guilt feelings. Hours are spent each day praying and reading Scripture, but it does not lift the depression. This intense activity can actually limit the lifting of depression, for you neglect other areas of your life that need attention.

Guidance from Scripture

Can you imagine your life being better after your depression than before? Perhaps not, but many have experienced just that. Remember the passage in the last chapter of Job? "And the Lord blessed the latter days of Job more than his beginning" (Job 42:12, *NASB)*. Through your depression, you can develop a new perspective about life, a greater awareness of who you are as well as your abilities, a new way of seeing and relating to others and a deeper relationship with God. This latter step occurs as you feed upon His Word.

Keep me safe, O God, for in you I take refuge (Ps. 16:1).

I have set the Lord always before me. Because he is at my right hand, I will not be shaken (Ps. 16:8).

You, O Lord, keep my lamp burning; my God turns my darkness into light (Ps. 18:28).

The Lord is my light and my salvation—whom shall I fear? The Lord is the stronghold of my life—of whom shall I be afraid? (Ps. 27:1).

Hear my voice when I call, O Lord; be merciful to me and answer me (Ps. 27:7).

God is our refuge and strength, an ever present help in trouble (Ps. 46:1).

Have mercy on me, O God, according to your unfailing love; according to your great compassion blot out my transgressions (Ps. 51:1).

Recommended Reading:

Hart, Archibald D. *Dark Clouds, Silver Lining.* Colorado Springs, CO: Focus on the Family Publishing, 1993.

Hirschfeld, Robert, M.D. *When the Blues Won't Go Away; New Approaches to Dysthymic Disorder and Other Forms of Chronic Low-Grade Depression.* New York: Macmillan Publishing Co., 1991.

McGrath, Ellen. *When Feeling Bad Is Good: An Innovative Self-Help Program for Women to Convert Healthy Depression into New Sources of Growth and Power.* New York: Henry Holt & Co., 1992.

Notes

1. Archibald Hart, *Depression in the Ministry and Other Helping Professions* (Dallas, TX: WORD Inc., 1984), pp. 26-28, adapted.
2. Maggie Scarf, *Unfinished Business: Pressure Points in the Lives of Women* (New York: Doubleday and Co., 1980), pp. 10-80, adapted.
3. Used by permission from Brenda Poinsett, author of *Understanding a Woman's Depression*, R. 13, Box 445, Bedford, IN 47421.
4. Ibid., p. 57.
5. Hart, *Depression in the Ministry*, p. 68, adapted.
6. Poinsett, *Understanding a Woman's Depression*, pp. 131,132.

Chapter 7

HEALTH ISSUES

Premenstrual Syndrome (PMS)

Q. WHERE CAN I LEARN ABOUT PMS AND HOW
DO I EXPLAIN IT TO MY HUSBAND?

A. Premenstrual tension is real! The many wives and husbands who have told me their stories and the books I have read about PMS have convinced me! Unfortunately, not all medical doctors are convinced PMS is real, so it is important to find a doctor who believes in its reality and understands what help to provide. Approximately 90 percent of women experience some PMS symptoms during the 7 to 14 days prior to menstruation. And it ranges in intensity and severity. The symptoms can include the following:

- headaches
- anxiety and nervousness
- fatigue/lethargy
- depression and/or crying jags

- moodiness (alternating highs and lows)
- backache and/or pelvic pain
- fluid retention and bloating
- food cravings (typically candy, cake and chocolate)
- hot flashes
- distended stomach with or without stomach upset
- irritability
- breast engorgement and tenderness
- temperature changes
- migraine headaches
- lowered sex drive
- increase in accidents and errors
- acne, blotching
- flaring of allergic reactions
- sweating
- swelling of the legs
- changes in bowel rhythms
- outbursts of aggression
- thirst
- loss of concentration

The triggers for these symptoms are found within the body. It is not abnormal to experience PMS. It is an indication that the hormones in your body are working the way they are supposed to work. And treatments are available. The treatments can include regular exercise, diet, nonhormonal medications as well as hormonal therapy.

As I am not a woman nor a specialist in this area my answer will be brief. If you struggle with PMS, read, find a knowledgeable doctor and educate your family members. I would recommend that every woman and her husband read both of the recommended books. If necessary, take your husband with you to talk with your physician. Let him know that help is available and it will be to his advantage to cooperate with you in any of your endeavors to find the help both of you are looking for. I have talked with many men about the reality of PMS in their wives, and found they were willing to learn more about it and to be more sympathetic to the problem.

Q. HOW CAN I LIVE WITH THE MEMORIES OF TRAUMA IN MY LIFE OVER MY ABORTION? HOW CAN I RESOLVE THE GUILT AND SHAME I FEEL? HOW CAN I FORGIVE MYSELF FOR THIS? I KNOW I HAVE TO, BUT I CAN'T. CAN GOD FORGIVE ME FOR MY ABORTION?

A. Millions of women are suffering with the memories and residue of an abortion. It is not easy to admit and talk about because many people are judgmental. Too many women bear their guilt and pain in silence.

Abortion is one of life's greatest losses and yet one of the most unique losses to be experienced. You do not have any external evidence that your baby existed. You had no baby to hold or to say good-bye to. Your baby lived in your heart and mind. And in most cases there was no ritual such as a funeral. Even though abortion is legal it is socially unacceptable. So who is there to give you permission to grieve? More guilt is experienced regarding abortion than most any other action.

What did you experience after the abortion? Rejection? Disapproval? Anger? Humiliation? Judgment? Relief? Isolation? Who helped you recover? Who could you talk to? Here are some suggestions I hope will help you at this time in your life:

Seek Help

1. Find a support group even though the abortion may have occurred years ago.

2. Grieve and give yourself plenty of time to grieve. Find someone to help you grieve.

3. It helps to name your baby if you have not done so. Giving a name and visualizing what your baby looked like will make your baby real for you and make it easier to grieve.

4. Use the gift of your mind and envision your baby in the arms of Jesus.

As Dr. Jack Hayford points out in his book, *I'll Hold You in Heaven,* your child is alive in heaven and you, as a believer in Christ, will be reunited with him one day (see 2 Sam. 12:19-23). As well, there will be no resentment or anger in your reunion—only joy.

There is no pain or sorrow in heaven. God sees you as though this act had never occurred. God has already forgiven you. Ask Him to help you understand and feel forgiveness. Begin responding to yourself as though you were a forgiven person. Trust in the truth of the Scripture:

> If we [freely] admit that we have sinned and confess our sins, He is faithful and just [true to His own nature and promises] and will forgive our sins (dismiss our lawlessness) and continuously cleanse us from all unrighteousness—everything not in conformity to His will in purpose, thought and action (1 John 1:9, *AMP*).
>
> Come now, and let us reason together, says the Lord; though your sins be as scarlet, they shall be as white as snow; though they be red like crimson, they shall be as wool (Isa. 1:18, *AMP*).
>
> For I will be merciful and gracious toward their sins and I will remember their deeds of unrighteousness no more (Heb. 8:12, *AMP*).

5. Perhaps the next step will be difficult but it is vital. Forgive those whom you blame for having been involved in the abortion.

6. Realize that because of all the debates over this issue, you

may struggle again and again with some of your feelings. When you do, start the steps over again.[1]

7. Give your memories to God and ask Him to heal them. Listening to the tape series "Biblical Psychology" by Dr. David Seamands can help you with this step.

8. Avoid being promiscuous to prove you are no good. Do not purposely become pregnant just to atone for the abortion. Your baby cannot be replaced.

9. Realize that some of the people who hear about your abortion will be critical. But when you tell about it, do it without acting like a martyr or a condemned person. Conclude your sharing with the statement, "But thank God, I am a forgiven person and it is by His grace that I can move ahead with my life."

Barrenness

Q. HOW CAN I COPE WITH MY BARRENNESS? I DON'T FEEL WHOLE AS A WOMAN BECAUSE I CANNOT BEAR CHILDREN.

A. Most women have a dream for their lives and they cherish this dream from childhood. They nurture it and expect it to come true someday. For many women, it is one of the transitional points that establishes identity—it is having a child.

Not being able to bear a child is a loss that is not really tangible nor visible and can easily be overlooked. It is a longing for something that will never be. Perhaps the feeling is best expressed by Rachel in Genesis 30:1: "Give me children, or I'll die." This loss is an issue that can exist for 15 to 20 years in a woman's life. If you cannot have children, then you know the feelings. If you can have them, be very sensitive and supportive to those who cannot.

How to Cope

What can you do? You need to acknowledge and experience the loss. You need to mourn for what will never be. Face every little loss. Think about it and imagine and write out each loss. You will never feel your baby stir within you, hold your child, caress her, feed her strained carrots, rock her to sleep, see her take her first step, hear her laugh, comfort her when she falls down and so on. It is a massive list. Identify and mourn for each part.

I am not a woman. I cannot fully understand or empathize as another childless woman can. But I can understand more than you may realize and so can my wife, Joyce. We raised a profoundly retarded son until he died at age 22. We do know about not experiencing what other parents experience and take for granted. To have a son and never hear him say "Daddy" or "Mommy" is a loss.

Perhaps as you work through your loss you will experience blame—of yourself and others. Face your anger, release it and forgive. Write a daily letter or journal of forgiveness, pray for the one you blame or have a verbal or written dialogue with that person.

Do not try to work through your grief alone. Fortunately, support groups are available.

Many childless women make a point to include children in their lives. These are not meant to be a substitute. Nothing else will compensate for being childless. But you can choose different roles you want to play in your involvement with children and identify what you want to experience with them.[2]

Perhaps the biggest issue you have to face is developing your identity, discovering who you are apart from being a mother. Too many women build their identity upon being a mother and when their children leave, they face a crisis. You need to design and build your world apart from being a mother. It is a slow process of acceptance. But it can happen. Counter your negative messages about yourself with the truth of your value as God sees you.

Cancer

Q. I AM STRUGGLING WITH A SERIOUS MEDICAL PROBLEM. I
HAVE CANCER. HOW DO I COPE WITH THIS?

A. When any of us face a serious illness, we evaluate our values.
Our priorities and use of time may experience a shift of emphasis.
You are faced with your immortality and you feel as though you are
living on borrowed time. We all are. That is a fact of life.

Guidelines for Coping

No matter what your illness is, here are some guidelines (if you have
a friend who is ill you may want to share these with her).

The first step is to face your illness and call it by what it is—cancer—if it is the big *C*.

Do not let denial keep you from handling it in a healthy way. It
is important to live life one day at a time. Thank God for each day
and count each day one of God's blessings. Use the functions you
have to their fullest whether they are physical or mental. Find others
to pray with you and to be accountable to so you do not become
stuck in depression or self-pity. Talk, talk and talk about your feelings. It helps to talk to others who are suffering from the same illness.

I have a friend who has had Multiple Sclerosis for the past 15
years and has researched the disease thoroughly. I have sent a number of counselees who are struggling with the same disease to talk
with him. He has been a tremendous source of help and encouragement to them. Give your friends guidelines on how you want them to
respond to you.

When you are facing a terminal illness, be sure to complete any
unfinished tasks you feel need to be done such as telling your loved
ones how much you love them. Search out facilities that would be

helpful to you, such as a hospice. Above all, let the Scriptures comfort you. Read the following passages:

Psalm 39:4,5; 139:1-18,23,24; 2 Corinthians 4:16,17; 5:2,8.[3]

Anxiety Attacks

Q. HOW CAN I COPE WITH THE ANXIETY AND
PANIC ATTACKS I AM EXPERIENCING? AM
I BAD BECAUSE I SUFFER FROM AN
ANXIETY DISORDER?

A. A person is not a bad person because she has an anxiety problem or any other problem for that matter. Anxiety is experienced frequently by people in today's society with its stressors and pressures. But some experience it more than others and for some it can become a suffocating experience. You are part of 20 to 30 million people in our country who have an anxiety disorder. This is the number one mental-health problem for women and the second largest for men.

Anxiety can come in many forms. It can be the sudden and unexplained uneasiness that lasts for a few hours or it can be a constant state of being. It can be fear that causes avoidance of specific situations or intense worry. These reactions still fall into the normal range but they turn into "anxiety disorders" when they become intense, go on for months, or interfere with normal functioning in your life. These can include:

- *Agoraphobia:* fear of being in open spaces, having panic attacks, or being in a place where escape would be difficult;
- *Social phobias:* fear of being embarrassed;
- *Simple phobia:* fear of a specific object or situation;

- *Generalized anxiety disorder:* persistent worry that continues at least six months;
- *Obsessive-compulsive disorder:* recurring yet senseless ideas, thoughts, images, or impulses (obsessions) and the behaviors (compulsions) that are intended to alleviate the anxiety produced by the obsessions.[4]

Anxiety attacks happen because of an emotional overload. If you suffer from anxiety, there is a good possibility you do not recognize or deal with your own feelings. You may have learned to deny, conceal or disguise your feelings; but denying them gives them incredible power and control over you. Why does this happen to some people and not others? The causes range from a parent modeling an anxiety disorder, your unique temperament, childhood experiences, and misdeveloped, mistaken beliefs that create fears of failure, rejection and punishment.

Steps for Improvement

What can you do? A bottom-line answer is to learn healthy ways to express your emotions. For anxiety problems and disorders, I highly encourage individual counseling as well as a recovery group. You can take two steps to make this easier for you.

1. Whenever an attack occurs, call a friend who is aware of the problem and can help you. Educate this person so she knows what you are experiencing and what you need.
2. Plan ahead so you know what to do when an attack hits. Often anxiety makes thinking difficult. Do you know what you will do the next time an attack hits? Develop a plan to follow when the attacks hit. This could include practicing relaxation techniques, calling a friend, playing a prerecorded tape, reading preselected (with page numbers) Scripture passages, listening to praise tapes, listing five of your most recent blessings and so on. Add to this list items you have found helpful in the past.

Compulsive-Obsessive Behavior

Q. HOW CAN I OVERCOME OBSESSIVE-COMPULSIVE
BEHAVIOR? THIS INCLUDES OVEREATING,
DRINKING, SHOPPING SPREES AND
ADDICTIVE RELATIONSHIPS.

A. All of us are capable of obsessional thinking. Many people have a troublesome thought that persistently runs through their minds. But if you have an obsessional disorder, your obsessions are more severe, persistent and resistant. These take professional help to overcome. I do not know what level your obsessive or compulsive behavior is at, so perhaps the best way to answer your questions is with some basic information that might help you decide on the next step to take.

Obsessive Characteristics

Let's start with obsessions. Do your obsessional tendencies have any of the following characteristics?

- They involve repetitive, uncontrollable thoughts.
- The obsessional thoughts are meaningless or unwelcome.
- The obsession affords no pleasure.
- The obsession always produces a loss of energy and a sense of ambivalence.
- Severe obsessions destroy healthy mental functioning.
- They involve denial of the underlying anxiety, but not of the thoughts themselves.[5]

Compulsive Characteristics

Compulsions, on the other hand, have other characteristics and can be a minor problem or create great discomfort. Do you relate to any of these compulsive symptoms?

- They are repetitive, unwelcomed, and alien.
- They are meaningless urges, essentially unconnected with or out of proportion to the relief they provide.
- Often they are trivial or ritualistic.
- The actions are performed against one's will.
- The behavior can be silly or terrifying, or somewhere between these extremes.
- Like obsessions, *they give no pleasure.* Their essential function is to provide *relief* from underlying anxiety.[6]

Addictive Characteristics

There is a difference between obsessions, compulsions and addictions. If you have an addiction, you have a controlling need or desire for that substance, object, action or behavior because you receive a pleasant reaction, which is either stimulating or relaxing. But you deny that it is controlling you. Unlike addictions, compulsions and obsessions result in pain and the person does not deny that she is unable to control the problem. Sometimes obsessive and compulsive disorders can lead to addictions.

Several kinds of addictions exist; some are learned and some come from deficiencies. An addiction serves the purpose of removing you from your true feelings. It is an escape. Do you have any behaviors that fit this classification?

I have seen addictions to food, sex, shopping, stress, work, helping, religious service, religious ecstasy, love, romance, adrenaline, alcohol and drugs. All the possibilities are there. Do not try to handle these difficulties by yourself. Go for help to a professionally trained and licensed therapist; most helpers in churches are not trained to deal with these problems.

Pornography

Q. IS WATCHING OR LOOKING AT PORNOGRAPHIC
MATERIAL FOR THE PURPOSE OF STIMULATION ALL RIGHT?

A. Pornography is one of the worst diseases we have in the world. It degrades people and places an overemphasis on sex rather than intimacy. It puts sex as an end in itself, cheapens the experience and leaves out the aspect of love. Those who appear in pornographic films and photos are often the exceptions physically, and the photographers use various touch-up techniques to achieve deceitful appearances. The participants are not the norm and yet we sometimes use them as the basis from which to compare others.

Pornographic material is often violent and both men and women who use this material often want to bring what they have seen into their marriage or another relationship. Research conducted upon men who watched hard-core pornography regularly has identified four phases in the men's response to this stimuli.

> First, it leads to an addiction. The first phases of excitement lead to repeated and deliberate involvement with the pornographic material for the purpose of sexual excitement. Then there is an escalation phase in which the man wants rougher and more sexually exciting input in order to attain the previous level of sexual excitement. The next phase is desensitization in which the pornography is boring. The man is not repulsed by what he sees and has no compassion for the people involved. The final phase is the inclination to act out. What the man has seen actually becomes part of his repertoire of sexual behavior.[7]

Pornography is especially degrading to women and puts them in a state of being victimized. There is no place for it in anyone's life. I have seen the negative results of pornography in many relationships. Programs are available to help sexual addicts.

Consider the pornography issue in light of this Scripture passage from Philippians:

> For the rest, brethren, whatever is true, whatever is worthy of reverence and is honorable and seemly, whatever is just, whatever is pure, whatever is lovely and lovable, whatever is kind and winsome and gracious, if there is any virtue and excellence, if there is anything worthy of praise, think on and weigh and take account of these things—fix your minds on them (Phil. 4:8, *AMP*).

Masturbation

Q. IS MASTURBATION A SIN? IF SO, HOW DO I
HANDLE SEXUAL URGES AND FEELINGS?

A. Is masturbation a sin? This is one of the more frequently asked questions we hear from youth and adults alike. The majority of people have masturbated to orgasm at some time in their lives. It is a common and normal stimulus and yet it is just as normal for people not to participate in masturbation.

Scripture is totally silent on the subject of masturbation. If people attempt to show you that the Word of God does say something about it, they are using Scripture for their own benefit. The act of masturbation is not so much the problem. It is not self-abuse. But if someone engages in it excessively several times a day, this obsession is indicating some other emotional difficulty. Some people use masturbation to deal with their feelings of loneliness or their inability to develop meaningful friendships and relationships. Instead of dealing with the problem, they rely upon their fantasies.

Whether the act of masturbation is lustful or not depends upon what is going on in the person's mind. Some do not think of another person when engaged in self-stimulation. Others say they think about their spouses. Still others engage in lust and if they use photos or pornographic material it can lead to an addiction. A rich sexual fantasy life can make it difficult for the marital partner as it is hard to compete with the fantasy in the other person's mind. Few can compare to the unrealism conjured up in a person's thought life.

Consider what Joyce and Cliff Penner say about this:

> If our adult self-stimulation takes something away from our partner, then the behavior is not loving. On the other hand, if one partner desires a great deal of sexual activity and the other is less frequently interested, the couple might decide that masturbation is the most loving act the highly interested person can do, so as not to put the spouse under pressure. There may be periods when abstinence from intercourse is necessary. At such times it may be most loving and adaptive to enjoy a sexual release brought about either by self-stimulation or by mutual stimulation. Some of these occasions might be during extensive periods of separate travel or illness. When there is extreme outside pressure for one individual either relationally or vocationally, that person may prefer that the other take care of his or her own sexual needs. Or there may be times when one partner needs to be free from the pressures of sex for emotional reasons. So while it is possible that self-stimulation could be an unloving act, there is also the possibility that using it to relieve pressure would be the more loving act, not only for the self-stimulator but also for the partner.[8]

For the purposes of release, there is no reason why both singles and marrieds should not engage in masturbation.

Recommended Reading

Anton, Linda Hunt. *Never to Be a Mother.* New York: Harper and Row, 1992.

Baughan, Jill. *A Hope Deferred—A Couple's Guide to Coping With Infertility.* Portland, OR: Multnomah Press, 1989.

Garton, Jean Staker. *Who Broke the Baby?* Minneapolis, MN: Bethany House Publishers, 1979.

Hart, Archibald. *Healing Life's Hidden Addictions.* Ann Arbor, MI: Servant Publications, 1990.

Hayford, Jack, with Hanes, Mari. *Beyond Heartache.* Wheaton, IL: Tyndale House, 1984.

Hayford, Jack. *I'll Hold You in Heaven.* Ventura, CA: Regal Books, 1986.

Koerbel, Pam. *Abortion's Second Victim.* Wheaton, IL: Victor Books, 1986.

Kuenning, Delores. *Helping People Through Grief.* Minneapolis, MN: Bethany House, 1987.

Lauersen, Niels H., M.D., and Stukane, Eileen. *PMS: Premenstrual Syndrome and You.* New York: Simon and Schuster, Inc., 1983.

Love, Vicky. *Childless Is Not Less.* Minneapolis, MN: Bethany House Publishers, 1984.

Randau, Karen. *Anxiety Attacks.* Houston, TX: Rapha Publishing, 1991.

Seamands, David. "Biblical Psychology" tapes. Available from Christian Marriage Enrichment, 17821 17th St., Suite 290, Tustin, CA 92680.

Sneed, Sharon, and McIlhaney, Joe S. Jr., M.D. *PMS—What It Is and What You Can Do About It.* Grand Rapids, MI: Baker Book House, 1988.

Wright, H. Norman. *Afraid No More!* Wheaton, IL: Tyndale House Publishers, 1992.

Wright, H. Norman. *Recovering from the Losses of Life.* Tarrytown, NY: Fleming H. Revell, 1991.

Notes

1. Delores Kuenning, *Helping People Through Grief* (Minneapolis, MN: Bethany House Publishers, 1987), pp. 129-133.
2. Linda Hunt Anton, *Never to Be a Mother* (New York: Harper and Row, 1992), pp. 10-160, adapted.
3. Kuenning, *Helping People Through Grief,* pp. 204-206, adapted.
4. Karen Randau, *Anxiety Attacks* (Houston, TX: Rapha Publishing, 1991), p. 4.

5. Archibald Hart, *Healing Life's Hidden Addictions* (Ann Arbor, MI: Servant Publications, 1990), p. 76.

6. Ibid., p. 78.

7. Victor Cline, cited by Jerry Kirk in *A Winnable War* (Colorado Springs, CO: Focus on the Family Publishing, 1987), p. 9.

8. Cliff and Joyce Penner, *The Gift of Sex* (Dallas TX: WORD Inc., 1981), p. 234.

Chapter 8

SPIRITUAL ISSUES AND HEALING THE PAST

God's Love

Q. HOW CAN I BE SURE THAT GOD LOVES ME?

A. The certainty that God loves you is found within the Scriptures. In Jeremiah, we read:

> And I will give them one heart and one way, that they may [reverently] fear Me for ever, for the good of themselves and of their children after them.
>
> And I will make an everlasting covenant with them, that I will not turn away from following them, to do them good; and I will put My [reverential] fear in their hearts, that they shall not depart from Me.
>
> Yes, I will rejoice over them to do them good, and I will plant them in this land assuredly and in truth with My whole heart and with My whole being (Jer. 32:39-41, *AMP*).

Think about these passages as John Piper illuminates the truth of these verses.

Not only does God promise not to turn away from doing

good to us, he says, "I will rejoice in doing them good" (Jeremiah 32:41). "The Lord will again take delight in prospering you" (Deuteronomy 30:9). He does not bless us begrudgingly. There is a kind of eagerness about the beneficence of God. He does not wait for us to come to him. He seeks us out, because it is his pleasure to do us good. "The eyes of the Lord run to and fro throughout the whole earth, to show his might in behalf of those whose heart is whole toward him" (2 Chronicles 16:9). God is not waiting for us, he is pursuing us. That, in fact, is the literal translation of Psalm 23:6, "Surely goodness and mercy shall pursue me all the days of my life." I have never forgotten how a great teacher once explained it to me. He said God is like a highway patrolman pursuing you down the interstate with lights flashing and siren blaring to get you to stop—not to give you a ticket, but to give you a message so good it couldn't wait till you get home.

God loves to show mercy. Let me say it again. God loves to show mercy. He is not hesitant or indecisive or tentative in his desires to do good to his people.[1]

You are loved so much that God decided to adopt you as His own. You have been chosen and you belong to Him. *Think about that.* Ephesians 1:4 and 5 says, "In love he predestined us to be adopted as his sons through Jesus Christ."

Look at the rights and privileges you have because of this adoption.

- You have been guaranteed eternal life, as evidenced by the presence of the Holy Spirit in your life (see Eph. 1:14).

- You have hope in Christ, your glorious inheritance (see Eph. 1:18).

- You have experienced the incomparable power that raised Jesus Christ from the dead and seated Him at God's right hand (see Eph. 1:19,20).

- You are the recipient of God's incomparable grace that saved you apart from anything you have done or can ever do (see Eph. 2:8,9).

- You now have access to the Father through His Spirit (see Eph. 2:18).
- You can know the love of Christ, which will enable you to receive God's fullness (see Eph. 3:19).

Perhaps the best way to bring home the reality of this is through the example of the honeymoon experience, as illustrated by Piper.

> Sometimes we joke and say about a marriage, "The honeymoon is over." But that's because we are finite. We can't sustain a honeymoon level of intensity and affection. We can't foresee the irritations that come with long-term familiarity. We can't stay as fit and handsome as we were then. We can't come up with enough new things to keep the relationship that fresh. But God says his joy over his people is like a bridegroom over a bride. He is talking about honeymoon intensity and honeymoon pleasures and honeymoon energy and excitement and enthusiasm and enjoyment. He is trying to get into our hearts what he means when he says he rejoices over us *with all his heart.*
>
> And add to this, that with God the honeymoon never ends. He is infinite in power and wisdom and creativity and love.[2]

I hope you are able to grasp a bit better how much you are loved.

God's Forgiveness

Q. AFTER WHAT I HAVE DONE, HOW CAN
GOD POSSIBLY FORGIVE ME?

A. You could have done nothing that God has not already forgiven. His forgiveness is so extensive, it is difficult to comprehend. And that is the problem; our minds cannot possibly grasp how God could just wipe out, blot out and totally erase the worst possible and imaginable sin you could have committed. In 1 John 1:9 we read:

> If we [freely] admit that we have sinned and confess our sins, He is faithful and just [true to His own nature and promises] and will forgive our sins (dismiss our lawlessness) and continuously cleanse us from all unrighteousness—everything not in conformity to His will in purpose, thought and action *(AMP).*

Perhaps what I said recently to one of my counselees may help. When you ask for forgiveness, it is given. And God wants you from that moment on to think like a forgiven person and to behave like a forgiven person. Consequently, in time you will begin to feel like a forgiven person. Sometimes it helps to imagine what it would feel like if you were forgiven. And then realize, "It's true. This *is* me. I am forgiven." Consider this. If you believe that God has forgiven you, He expects you to accept His gift fully and reflect it from this moment on. It can happen to you.

Knowing God's Will

Q. HOW CAN I TRULY HEAR GOD'S VOICE SO I KNOW I AM FOLLOWING HIS WILL FOR MY LIFE?

A. Perhaps you would be surprised to know that the first step in knowing God's will is *the desire to know His will.* My pastor, Lloyd Ogilvie of the First Presbyterian Church of Hollywood, has said that you and I would not even be desiring God's will for our lives if He were not speaking to us seeking to make it known. Wanting to know His will is a clear sign that you indeed have been chosen by Him.

I have read various formulas and plans for discerning what God wants us to do to know His will. I am not sure there are specific formulas to follow. I do know that praying specifically for something and being open for a change of plans is part of the process. Reading Scripture and gaining wisdom from others is also helpful.

To make wise decisions, consider these 12 questions to assist you in seeking God's guidance:

1. Is what I am considering consistent with the Ten Commandments?

2. Will it deepen my relationship with Christ?

3. Will there be an extension of Christ's life and message, and will it further the work of the kingdom?

4. If I do it, will it glorify Jesus Christ and enable me to grow as His disciple?

5. Is there a scriptural basis for this desire?

6. Will this need the Lord's presence and power to accomplish it?

7. Has prayer and thought produced an inner feeling of "rightness" about it?

8. Is it something for which I can praise Him in advance of doing or receiving it?

9. Is it an expression of genuine love, and will it benefit the lives of the people involved?

10. Will it be consistent with my basic purpose to love the Lord and be a communicator of His love to others?

11. Will this decision enable me to grow in the talents and gifts I have been given?

12. Will my expenditures in this decision still allow tithing and generous giving of my money for the Lord's work and the needs of others?[3]

Have you submitted your decisions to questions such as these? It is worth trying.

#

Q. IF I AM A CHRISTIAN I SHOULDN'T BE SUFFERING OR HAVING PROBLEMS, SHOULD I?

A. Over the years, an overabundance of improper theology has been taught by many well-meaning Christians. And much of it pertains to the pain, suffering and misfortunes of life that we all encounter. Many people expect that, by loving and following God, we will be immune to misfortunes. If we believe that, then it is easy to also believe, "If you are suffering it must be that you are sinning." Neither is true. God causes the rain to fall on the just as well as the unjust. All misfortune is caused by sin but it is the result of sin in the human race.

You see, God never promised that if you accept His Son, follow Him, and do wonderful things for Him, He would insulate you from the problems of life. Yes, He may choose to intervene but I do not have the right to demand His intervention. It will be through the misfortunes of life that our greatest growth will occur.

I know. I have been there. I have walked the same path others have. But I would not trade the experience, because I learned from it. My only son, Matthew, was a profoundly mentally retarded boy who never developed to be more than an 18-month-old mentally. When he was 22, I watched him slowly die in the hospital over a 2-week period. Matthew's simple life made my wife, Joyce, and me grow. We could have made the decision to become bitter and blame God. But we made a choice not to. That is what it means in James 1:2,3:

> Consider it wholly joyful, my brethren, whenever you are enveloped in or encounter trials of any sort, or fall into various temptations.
>
> Be assured and understand that the trial and proving of your faith bring out endurance and steadfastness and patience *(AMP)*.

Count it all joy can mean *make up* your mind to regard adversity as something to welcome or be glad about.

Other people are quick to give us formulas to follow and reasons for our suffering. They do this out of their own anxiety about the event for they too are threatened by what is happening.

I do not have an answer for all the suffering. I do not understand it at times. None of us does. Isaiah tells us:

> For My thoughts are not your thoughts, neither are your ways My ways, says the Lord.
>
> For as the heavens are higher than the earth, so are My ways higher than your ways, and My thoughts than your thoughts (Isa. 55:8,9, *AMP*).

When you continue to fight against a problem or difficulty with God, the energy that could be used to discover some benefit from the problem is drained away. When you face your problem and say, "All right, this is not what I would have chosen but it's here. How can I learn from this and how can God be glorified through this?" then you are in a position to grow and learn and experience the depth of His care. God does not make all the problems go away. He never said that. What He did say was:

> Fear not, for I have redeemed you—ransomed you by paying a price instead of leaving you captives; I have called you by your name, you are Mine.
>
> When you pass through the waters I will be with you, and through the rivers they shall not overwhelm you; when you walk through the fire you shall not be burned or scorched, nor shall the flame kindle upon you" (Isa. 43:1,2, *AMP*).

God gives us the grace, strength and comfort to go through a difficult experience. And the problems that occur are not because God is weak, or does not care. They do not happen without His permission. I like what my pastor said:

God's purposes are not thwarted by our problems. He is in charge and no problem is too big for Him. In fact, a careful study of history indicates that He works out His plan through the problems He allows in our lives. God is not the helpless victim of the problems we bring on ourselves, those caused by other people, or those that are the mischief of the force of evil in the world.

God gave us the awesome gift of freedom so that we could choose to love, glorify, and serve Him. The refusal to do that is the cause of many of the problems we bring on ourselves and is often the cause of problems we face with others. Humankind's rebellion is often collusive in social evil, injustice, and suffering.

We live in a world fallen from God's original purpose. And yet He never gives up on us. He intervenes in our lives, reveals His loving and forgiving heart, and uses the problems we face. In fact, God uses them to get our attention and to force us to realize we can't make it on our own. And He draws us into a deeper relationship with Him as we learn to trust Him for strength to cope with and overcome our problems.

The bracing truth is that no problem can happen without God's permission. And what He allows is always for a greater blessing than we could ever realize if we had no problems.[4]

Six Principles to Guide You

Here are six principles to assist you when you are struggling with the issues and problems of life.

1. We can be assured of God's phenomenal love and forgiveness. Much of our suffering is not due to our personal sin. But even when it is, God assures us that He still loves us and is ready to forgive us. He promises, "If we confess our sins, He is faithful and righteous to forgive us our sins and to cleanse us from all unrighteousness" (1 John 1:9, *NASB*).

2. God has allowed all the suffering we face. This is difficult for some to comprehend but He is sovereign and retains ultimate control of the universe. The problem has passed through the sieve of His permissive will.

3. God will never give you more than you can bear. God always sets limits on the amount of suffering or misfortune that occurs in your life.

> No temptation [or suffering] has overtaken you but such as is common to man; and God is faithful, who will not allow you to be tempted [or suffer] beyond what you are able; but with the temptation [or suffering] will provide the way of escape also, that you may be able to endure it (1 Cor. 10:13, *NASB*).

4. Often it is God's desire to deliver you from your current suffering. "And Jesus was going about...healing every kind of disease and every kind of sickness. And seeing the multitudes, He felt compassion for them, because they were distressed and downcast like sheep without a shepherd" (Matt. 9:35,36, *NASB*).

5. God always cares and will be with you through the suffering. Although God may not deliver you immediately from suffering, He is always very concerned about you when you are confronted with difficulty. He will always go through it with you; although you feel He is distant it does not mean He is.

Scripture clearly states that God is aware of the minutest details of our lives—He even has numbered the hairs on our heads. He certainly cares about whatever pain you may be having. "For God has said, 'I will never, never fail you nor forsake you.' That is why we can say without any doubt or fear, 'The Lord is my Helper and I am not afraid of anything that mere man can do to me'" (Heb. 13:5,6, *TLB*). Though God may not *feel* close when your body is racked with suffering, *God is with you.*

6. God makes all things work together for ultimate good. If we are open and yield to Him, He can take the worst situation in our lives and ultimately use it for good. "And we know that God causes all things to work together for good to those who love God" (Rom. 8:28, *NASB*).[5]

Time for Growth

Think of it this way. What God allows us to experience is for growth. It may not seem right or fair, but what is your other option? Bitterness and resentment is usually the outcome. God arranged the seasons of nature to produce growth. He arranges the experiences of the seasons of our lives for growth as well. Some days bring sunshine and other days bring hurricanes. Both are necessary; but remember, He knows the amount of pressure we can bear and He knows our limits.

You may have asked, "God, where are you?" He is there.

You may have asked, "God, when? When will you answer me?" So did the psalmist. "How long wilt thou hide thy face from me? How long shall I take counsel in my soul, having sorrow in my heart daily? How long shall mine enemy be exalted over me?" (Ps. 13:1,2, *KJV*).

It is all right for you to cry out, complain and become angry at God. But make the choice not to stay there for that keeps your pain deeply ingrained in your life and blocks the opportunity for healing.

God has a reason for everything He does and a timetable for when He does it: "'For I know the plans I have for you,' declares the Lord, 'plans to prosper you and not to harm you, plans to give you hope and a future'" (Jer. 29:11). Give yourself permission not to know what, not to know how, and not to know when. All of this unknowing will help you learn to become more dependent upon God and put your trust in Him for your source of strength.

In the meantime, pray. Let others know your struggles and ask them to pray with you and for you. Read the Scriptures. Read books of help and inspiration such as those listed in the recommended reading section. In addition, two other writers have been a tremendous blessing to me and thousands of others with the devotional focus of their writing. Max Lucado has written books such as *The Applause of Heaven, In the Eye of the Storm, Six Hours One Friday, The Angels Were Silent*. Ken Gire has written *Intimate Moments With the Savior* and *Incredible Moments With the Savior.* Spend time in these books and let the insight and inspiration encourage you.

Newness in Christ— Healing the Past

Q. WHEN I BECAME A CHRISTIAN, WHY DIDN'T EVERYTHING BECOME NEW, INCLUDING MY PAST?

A. When you invited Jesus Christ into your life, you became a new creature. All that transpired up to that point remains a historical fact—with the exception that all of your sins have been forgiven. They were wiped away. But the Christian life is a life of growth. We do not snap our fingers to find that all the pain and horrendous memories of the past have immediately vanished.

The Bible teaches that the Christian life is an ongoing walk. In Matthew 5:48 we read, "Be perfect as, your heavenly Father is perfect." This is talking about *reaching* toward maturity. Scripture says, "Be conformed to the likeness of his Son," (Rom. 8:29) which is a promise of *growing* into the fullness of Christ. We are also changing for the better, "Being made new in the attitude of our minds" (see Eph. 4:23).

These Scripture verses indicate that this is all a process that takes time. And the more you rely upon the grace of God for attitude change, belief change and behavior change, the more you will see yourself growing. You will undergo many changes again and again in the transformation from a caterpillar to a butterfly. Your past will remain the same but now you have new resources to deal with the negative effects of the past. In time, your remembrance of the past will shift from an emotional remembering to a historical remembering. In the emotional, you feel the pain accompanying the memory but with the historical you will remember the event but the pain and its controlling force will be gone. When the memory comes to mind you can say, "Yes, that did happen, but it doesn't affect me now. I have more positive and important things in my life that affect me."

Effects of the Past

Q. HOW DO I DEAL WITH PAINFUL ISSUES
IN MY PAST (CHILDHOOD) THAT ARE
AFFECTING THE WAY I LIVE TODAY?

A. We cannot change the facts of the past but we do have something to say about the effects of the past. To desire change is an important first step. Often in counseling I will ask the counselee to tell me two specific things. (1) Why do you want to change, (2) and what do you want to change? It is essential to identify what it is from your past that still bothers you, affects you, influences you or hinders you. Often I ask counselees to complete the following exercise to give clarity to what they want. List your reasons.

I want to change because...

1.
2.
3.
4.
5.
6.

When counselees say, "I am being affected by my past," I like to know in what way. Specifically, how and in what way do you want to be different? When you say your family was unhealthy or dysfunctional, can you describe that for me? Many can but others are vague. Knowing what the problem was is one step but then deciding how you want to be different is another. If you want your current family life to be different and healthy, can you describe what kinds of change you want? For some, it is helpful to suggest a possible model of a healthy family.

Model families usually reflect the following:

- The climate of the home is positive. The atmosphere is basically nonjudgmental.
- Each member of the family is valued and accepted for who he or she is. There is regard for individual characteristics.
- Each person is allowed to operate within his or her proper role. A child is allowed to be a child and an adult is an adult.
- Members of the family care for one another and they verbalize their caring and affirmation.
- The communication process is healthy, open and direct. There are no double messages.
- Children are raised in such a way that they can mature and become individuals in their own right. They separate from Mom and Dad in a healthy manner.
- The family enjoys being together. They do not get together out of a sense of obligation.
- Family members can laugh together, and they enjoy life together.
- Family members can share their hopes, dreams, fears and concerns with one another and still be accepted. A healthy level of intimacy exists within the home.[6]

If this is what you want, what do you need to do to make it a reality? Set specific small and attainable goals you can measure for each area of your life. Sometimes my next question takes a person off guard and it might throw you a bit too. "What has kept you from changing in the past? Do you know what you are doing to keep yourself from moving ahead?"

Many people have learned to use what we call victim phrases:

"I can't." How many times a day do you say these words? Have you ever kept track? Do you realize these words are prompted by

some kind of unbelief, fear or lack of hope? Think about it. Those three factors often hinder us from moving on with our lives.

When you say "I can't," you are saying you have no control over your life. It is no harder to say, "It's worth a try," and you will like the results of this positive phrase much better.

"That's a problem." Sometimes instead of saying, "That's a problem," we say, "He's a problem" or, "She's a problem." People who see life's complications as problems or burdens are immersed in fear and hopelessness. Life is full of barriers and detours. But with every obstacle comes an opportunity to learn and grow—if you hold the right attitude. Using other phrases such as, "That's a challenge" or, "That's an opportunity for learning something new," leaves the door open for moving ahead.

"I'll never..." This victim phrase is the anchor of personal stagnation. It is the signal of unconditional surrender to what exists or has happened in your life. Such negative words do not give yourself or God an opportunity. Instead say, "I've never considered that before" or, "I haven't tried it, but I'm willing to try," and open the door to personal growth.

"That's awful." Sometimes this phrase is appropriate in view of the shocking, dire situations we often hear about in the news. But those events are extraordinary. In everyday experiences, "That's awful" is an inappropriate overreaction that holds us back. Make it a point to eliminate its use for life's everyday problems. Instead, respond by saying, "Let's see what we can do about this situation" or, "I wonder how I can help at this time" or, "I wonder how I can do this differently."

"Why is life this way?" This is a normal response to the deep pains and sudden shocks of life. Some people experience one hurt and disappointment after another. Others experience a major setback and choose to linger in its crippling aftermath without recovering. They inappropriately use this question over and over again for months and years.

"Why is life this way?" and its companion statement, "Life isn't fair," are overused for the normal, minor upsets of everyday life. Life is unpredictable. Life is unfair. Life is not always the way we want it to be. But our response to life is our choice, and the healthiest response is reflected in James 1:2,3:

> Consider it wholly joyful, my brethren, whenever you are enveloped in or encounter trials of any sort, or fall into various temptations. Be assured and understand that the trial and proving of your faith bring out endurance and steadfastness and patience *(AMP)*.

These verses encourage us to make up our minds to regard adversity as something to welcome or be glad about. Joy in life is a choice. Growth in life is a choice. Change in life can be a choice, and choice comes before joy, growth and change.

Change is possible for you if you have a relationship with Jesus Christ. Why? Because faith in Christ is a life of continuing inward change that leads to outward change. Allowing Him to change us on the inside is the starting point. Paul wrote, "I am again in the pains of childbirth until *Christ is formed in you*" (Gal. 4:19, italics added). He is telling us that we must let Jesus Christ live in and through us. When you grasp the fact that Christ is working inside you, your hope will soar for the changes you desire to make.

In Ephesians 4:23,24 we are told, "Be made new in the attitude of your minds;...put on the new self, created to be like God in true righteousness and holiness." The new self must be put on from the inside. We are able to put on the new self because God has placed Jesus Christ within us. We are to let Him work within us. This means we must give Him access to those "impossible" concerns in our lives that need to be changed. What door do you need to open in your life today to allow Christ to work?

When you accepted Christ, you became a new creation in Jesus Christ. You are now identified with Him. In 2 Corinthians 5:17, Paul says, "Therefore, if anyone is in Christ, he is a new creation; the old has gone, the new has come!" Then in Romans 6:6 Paul says, "Our old self was crucified with him...that we should no longer be slaves to sin." By believing in Jesus Christ, we have died with Him and have been raised a new creation with Him. All things are indeed new.

Letting Go of a Loved One

Q. HOW DO YOU LET GO OF SOMEONE YOU LOVE?

A. Letting go of someone you love takes time and work. You need to recognize that the one you loved is no longer a part of your life, and you need to grieve over the person as though he or she died. I would suggest reading grief recovery books, going through a grief recovery group or a divorce recovery program. You will probably need some assistance in learning to counter the amount of thinking you engage in about this person. You may feel as though you are a victim and out of control. The best step is to take control and this can be done in several ways. You will need to act on the facts, however, rather than your feelings. Watch out for the memories, the fantasies and your self-talk about the person. The more you dwell on these the more difficult it will be to recover.

You can take control in the following ways:

1. List all of the losses you are now experiencing because of the loss of this person. Write out how this loss is affecting you.

2. Anticipate that you are fully recovered from this loss. Describe how you will feel and what your life will be like.

3. Set aside the same time each day for a programmed cry about this loss. This is the time to look at pictures or reflect upon the good memories to help you cry.

4. Write a good-bye letter to the person and the relationship and read it out loud at least once a week.

5. Write a eulogy and read it out loud as you imagine your relationship being lowered into a grave.

6. Begin to sift through the items you want to keep from the relationship and those you wish to discard.

7. Identify the significant dates that could cause you pain and plan something special for yourself on that day.
8. If you are avoiding any songs, places or special events because of the pain, decide when you will once again visit or engage in any of these so you can take charge of them.
9. Let others know how you would like them to respond or talk to you about this person. Do what is best for you.
10. Pray each day for your hurt and your welfare and read passages of Scripture that give you comfort.
11. Develop a chart so you can plot your recovery. It will help you realize that you are recovering.

Recommended Reading:

Carlson, Dwight, and Wood, Susan Carlson. *When Life Isn't Fair.* Eugene, OR: Harvest House, 1989.

Mann, Gerald. *When the Bad Times Are Over for Good.* Brentwood, TN: Wolgemuth and Hyatt Publishers, 1982.

McGee, Robert S. and Springle, Pat. *Getting Unstuck.* Dallas, TX: WORD Inc., 1992.

Ogilvie, Lloyd John. *Discovering God's Will in Your Life.* Eugene, OR: Harvest House, 1982.

Schmidt, Kenneth A. *Finding Your Way Home: Freeing the Child Within You and Discovering Wholeness in the Functional Family of God.* Ventura, CA: Regal Books, 1990.

Smedes, Lewis. *How Can It Be All Right When Everything Is All Wrong?* San Francisco: HarperSan Francisco, 1982.

Stoop, Dave. *Making Peace With Your Father.* Wheaton, IL: Tyndale House Publishers, 1992.

Wright, H. Norman. *Making Peace With Your Past.* Tarrytown, NY: Fleming H. Revell Co., 1985.

Wright, H. Norman. *Recovering From the Losses of Life.* Tarrytown, NY: Fleming H. Revell, 1991.

Notes

1. John Piper, *The Pleasures of God* (Portland, OR: Multnomah Productions, 1991), p. 19.

2. Ibid. pp. 194,195.

3. Lloyd John Ogilvie, *Discovering God's Will in Your Life* (Eugene, OR: Harvest House, 1982), pp. 173,174, adapted.

4. Lloyd John Ogilvie, *If God Cares, Why Do I Still Have Problems?* (Dallas, TX: WORD Inc., 1985), p. 20.

5. Dwight Carlson, and Susan Carlson Wood, *When Life Isn't Fair* (Eugene, OR: Harvest House, 1989), pp. 90-92, adapted.

6. H. Norman Wright, *Always Daddy's Girl* (Ventura, CA: Regal Books, 1989), p. 143.

Section Two

MARRIAGE
ISSUES

Chapter 9

SEX, INTIMACY AND ROMANCE

Male/Female Sexuality

Q. HOW CAN I MAKE MY HUSBAND RECOGNIZE
THE DIFFERENCE BETWEEN HIS AND MY SEXUALITY?

A. An age-old confusion exists about male/female differences and
one of the vast differences is in male/female sexuality.

We are all sexual, but most men are extremely sexual and they
think about sex more than women do. Even Christian men think
about it more. Both men and women look at a person of the opposite sex with appreciation for the way that person looks. But often a
woman's sense of appreciation is more romantic and a man's is more
sexual.

Sexual thoughts flit in and out of a man's mind all day long. Men
think about, dream about and daydream about sex far more than you
probably ever realized. Even though men slow down in their
thoughts about sex when they are in their 40s and 50s, they still think
about it several times a day. Men tend to dream about sex at least
three times as often as women, and their dreams rarely involve their
own wives. Women tend to dream about men they know. Recently in

one of my seminars a wife commented about men and sex. "Their 'on' button is never 'off'!" she said.

Men's Daydreams

The daydreams of men are rich, varied and detailed. Fantasies can create all kinds of sexual experiences and sex that is never disappointing. This creates problems because very few women can compete with a man's fantasies and often men are disappointed with their real sexual experiences. This is usually not the fault of the woman, for very few could ever attain the level of performance and ecstasy a man dreams about.

Feelings and Behavior

Often I am asked the question, "Why aren't men more loving?" But men do feel love! It is the expression of love that creates the problem. Men know they are in love but they do not always show that love. Women tend to see feelings and behavior as the same thing. They act upon their feelings and the feelings are seen in their actions.

When a man does not act in a loving manner, how is it interpreted? It translates as if "he doesn't have feelings of love."

The assumption is: no loving behavior equals no love.

But men do not see behavior and feelings in the same way as women. The two are not linked together and are often seen as unrelated. A man's behavior can be a form of camouflage hiding his true feelings. You cannot always tell what a man's feelings are based upon his behavior. A worried, anxious man may appear very calm; an angry man could appear happy and content; a man in love could appear indifferent and uncaring. Women have their own way of evaluating and determining love. Men have a different perspective and the two oftentimes clash.

Defining Love

Men and women define love differently. All too often men confuse love with sex. For the most part they have a limited perspective on love. It is too narrow. It needs to be broadened and it can be! Men have a lot to learn from a woman's perspective. The problem is they do not want to admit this fact! It is a threat.

Women have a fuller range for love than do men. Love to a woman involves time spent together and having significant interchange. It involves personal concern and empathy for one another. Fortunately, I have seen men who are willing to learn new ways of expressing love to their wives. Your husband could be one of them! I like the way Dennis Rainey explains the difference:

> Nothing will melt the icicles in many marriage beds faster than the husband realizing that women are built with a different sexual time clock and with different perspectives and expectations concerning sex. The "Differences in Sexuality" chart is a *general* guide to how men and women can be so different in this area of sex. (Obviously, this chart cannot be 100 percent true. It compares the general tendencies and differences between men and women and how they view sex.) These differences cause certain expectations on the part of men and women which often lead to misunderstanding, frustration, and disappointment.
>
> Men put a much higher priority on sex than women do and women have a different orientation that demands a different approach. As the chart shows, the man's orientation is physical, a woman's is relational. A man wants physical oneness, the woman desires emotional oneness. The man is stimulated by sight, smell, and the body. The woman is stimulated by touch, attitudes, actions, words, and the whole person.
>
> A man needs respect and admiration, to be physically needed, and not to be put down. The woman needs understanding, love, to be emotionally needed, and time to warm up to the sexual act.

DIFFERENCES IN SEXUALITY

	MEN	WOMEN
ORIENTATION	Physical	Relational
	Compartmentalized	Holistic
	Physical oneness	Emotional oneness
	Variety	Security
	Sex is high priority	Other priorities may be higher
STIMULATION	Sight	Touch
		Attitudes
	Smell	Actions
		Words
	Body-centered	Person-centered
NEEDS	Respect	Understanding
	Admiration	Love
	Physically needed	Emotionally needed
	Not to be put down	Time
SEXUAL RESPONSE	Acyclical	Cyclical
	Quick excitement	Slow excitement
	Initiates (usually)	Responder (usually)
	Difficult to distract	Easily distracted
ORGASM	Propagation of species	Propagation of oneness
	Shorter, more intense	Longer, more in depth
	Physically-oriented	Emotionally-oriented
	Orgasm usually needed for satisfaction	Satisfaction possible without orgasm

The man's sexual response is acyclical, which means any time, anywhere. The woman's response is cyclical, which means she goes through times when she is more interested in sex than others. A man responds sexually by getting excited quickly, while the woman is much slower.

During sex, a man is single-minded, while a woman is easily distracted. The woman wants to know, "Are the kids all asleep?" "Have you checked to see if they're all covered?" "Is the door shut?" "Is it locked?" "Are the windows closed?" "Are the blinds down?" "I think I hear the bathroom faucet dripping."[1]

Men's Sexual Apprehensions

You may think that men have few or no apprehensions about sex. That is not true! Men are concerned about their performance, partly because they equate so much of their maleness or manhood with their sexual ability. They want to be sure they can have an erection, maintain it, satisfy the woman and be certain to have an orgasm.

The performance trap that men create overflows into the sexual arena as well as most other aspects of life. They are uncomfortable with times and situations that are unstructured and spontaneous. This same orientation is brought to sex. If a man takes time to create a romantic atmosphere having ample conversation, it is a necessary step in his mind in order to bring about sex. Because of their goal orientation, it is often difficult for men to focus on what is happening in the present. And when the sexual act is concluded, rather than finding it enjoyable, men tend to move on to another goal. Have you noticed this in your own relationship?

Men's Sex Fears

Men have fears about sex. The sexual fear is bound up in one word: impotence. This is the inability to either achieve or maintain an erection. Erections are a normal part of male life. Men have four or five erections a night and often wake up with an erection. This early morning erection is a healthy sign as it indicates that a man is still capable of functioning. The male hormone, testosterone, becomes depleted during the day and is replenished during sleep. It peaks around 5 A.M. and is as much as 40 percent higher than the night before. Men are more capable of sex in the morning but this time is often difficult for a woman because the lovemaking has not been preceded by a time of loving communication. Thus, his early-morning erection has nothing to do with thinking about sex. Sometimes it merely means he has a full bladder! Many wives believe that every such erection means he wants sex and that is not true. Talk about it.

Men's Reasons for Sex

Men want sex for several reasons, such as physical release; giving or receiving comfort or affection; love; proving one's popularity, masculinity or sexual ability; and expressing tenderness or hostility. Many men use sex to prove their manhood.

Consciously or subconsciously men are looking for some spoken or unspoken admiration from others when they talk about their exploits.

Whether men realize it or not, they do want more in a relationship than sex. They do want closeness and intimacy. But they do not know how to ask for it or admit to it.

Men do not have the sexual endurance of women. Nor do they have the long-term capability for enjoyment that women have. Most men are capable of expressing love and affection through the sexual experience. But what they need to learn is to give love and affection in nonsexual ways.

One of the most common complaints I (and countless other marriage therapists) have heard from wives is, "I wish he could understand that each time I kiss him or hug him or caress him when I walk by him in the house is NOT an invitation to the bedroom. I even hesitate giving these little responses because we seem to end up in an argument. Why can't he understand? I don't even respond now when he comes up and kisses or holds me. I just know that he has sex on his mind. If we could have a lot of nonsexual contact I would respond much more and he would really be surprised and delighted!"

A man often interprets his wife's sexual response as a signal of how she feels about him in general. In reality, how often a wife responds or what she agrees to do sexually with him may have little or no bearing on her feelings toward him. This is why I request that men I work with read *Sex Begins in the Kitchen* by Kevin Leman and *If Only He Knew* by Gary Smalley. Tell your husband that what you want for your birthday or anniversary is for him to read the books with you!

Sex is used differently by men and women in a love relationship. Many women view sharing as being close and men view being close as something sexual. Women view sex as one way of being close and too many men view it as the *only* way to be close. For women, tenderness, touching, talking and sex go together. For some men, sex is sufficient, especially if they do not know how to relate in other expressions of intimacy.

Most men substitute sex for sharing. Sex is an expression of emotion and also substitutes for emotion. As one woman expressed her feelings about sex with her husband, "To me being close means sharing and talking. He thinks being close is having sex. Maybe that's the difference in the way we love. When he's upset or mad or insecure, he wants sex. I guess it reassures him. But I wish he would talk about the feelings. When I get home from work and I'm wound up with a lot of baggage, I want to talk about it. When he comes home that way, he doesn't want to talk, he wants sex. When I'm sad, what I need is a shoulder to cry on and someone to hear me out. When he's sad, he wants to be seduced out of his feelings." Is this your experience?[2]

One husband said, "Sex means many things to me. Sometimes I want sex with my wife because I feel romantic and want to be loving and close. Other times I just want the release or diversion. I don't need to talk about it all the time. I wish she could understand that."

Sex and Communication

Many men believe that sex can substitute for all other kinds of communication in a relationship. Sex is the vehicle couples take to share their personal and private selves. It is as though a husband says to his wife, "You ought to know I love you because I make love to you." For women, sex is only one means of intimacy out of many and not always the best one. For many men, sex is the only expression of intimacy.

Men tend to compress the meaning of intimacy into the sex act and when they do not have that outlet, they can become frustrated and upset. Why? Because they are cut off from the only source of closeness they know. Men are interested in closeness and intimacy but they have different ways of defining and expressing it. Here again is an area where perhaps you and your husband need to talk, listen, understand one another's view of sex and in some way learn to speak each other's language.

Men hesitate to talk with their wives about sex because of their fear of making fools of themselves. They are supposed to be the strong, tough ones, so they are afraid to make themselves vulnerable. Men are supposed to be the ones whose feelings should not get hurt. But they can be vulnerable.

Men's Sexual Performance

Sexual relief is important to a man but what really makes him uncomfortable is nongoal-directed holding and caressing. Thus he approaches sex in a mechanical manner. Sex becomes work rather than play. The end result—rather than the process—becomes important. Sex becomes an act rather than a means to being close. This ignores the fact that a man's sexual response is also an expression of who he is. It is directly tied to his feelings and desires and is also a reflection of the quality of the material relationship.

Younger men especially tend to prove themselves through their sexual performance, but as a man grows older and matures he wants greater intimacy. The intense sexual drive and view of physical affection he had as an adolescent begins to change. As he matures, he is able to tell the difference between his need for emotional reassurance and nurturing and his need for sex. Communication becomes more important for some men. If your husband approaches you with a hug and a kiss and you wonder what he wants, ask! Find out if he wants a pat, kiss, caress, five minutes of fondling or sexual intercourse. You may be surprised! Encourage him to let you know. Do not be afraid to let him know what you want as well.

Men's Fear of Impotence

Earlier I mentioned that a major fear of men is impotence. Men worry about their erections. They need foreplay just as women do. They cannot always perform on command. Atmosphere is important to them as well. Occasionally a man cannot achieve an erection at all, even though he feels aroused and loving. This can be a normal response. If it continues over time, however, it is an indication of some difficulty. As men grow older, their erections may not be as firm and they may take longer to occur. All men will experience a time of impotency during their lifetime and often it is situational. Ninety percent of the cause lies in the man's head rather than in his physical condition. If impotency persists, additional information or help may be needed.[3]

Performance anxiety is one of the reasons why a man loses interest in sex. Men have different levels of interest in sex. Sometimes a woman's drive is much stronger and she is the one constantly pushing her husband.

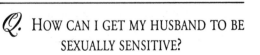

Sexual Sensitivity

Q. HOW CAN I GET MY HUSBAND TO BE
SEXUALLY SENSITIVE?

A. Here are some approaches that have worked for some women.

Let him know you are interested in having the best sexual relationship possible and you have learned some information that you would like to share with him to enhance his enjoyment.

1. Ask your husband to read a book with you, such as *The Gift of Sex* by Cliff and Joyce Penner, or to listen to Dr. Ed Wheat's tape series, "Sex Techniques" and "Love Life."
2. Attend a sexuality seminar by Joyce and Cliff Penner.
3. Suggest that you see a counselor together. If he prefers not to go, let him know you are still going so you can learn more about sexual intimacy in marriage.

If your husband is bypassing your affection needs, present him with Kevin Leman's book, *Sex Begins in the Kitchen*, and give him a list of your affection responses that you want from him.

Sexual Intimacy

Q. DOES INTIMACY ALWAYS HAVE TO MEAN, OR INCLUDE, SEXUAL ACTIVITY?

A. Do you know what the word "intimacy" means? It comes from a Latin word meaning, "inmost". Intimacy suggests a strong personal relationship, a special *emotional* closeness that includes understanding and being understood by someone who is special. Intimacy has also been defined as "an affectionate bond, the strands of which are composed of mutual caring, responsibility, trust, open communication of feelings and sensations, as well as the non-defended interchange of information about significant emotional events."[4] Intimacy means taking the risk to be close to someone and allowing that someone to step inside your personal boundaries.

If intimacy is not existent in a relationship, love or romance will not be present either. And as you see from the definition, feelings play an essential part of this process. If one or both are blocked emotionally you won't experience much intimacy.

You can have intimacy without sex. You can also have sex without intimacy! Intimacy has a multifaceted nature as it has six different dimensions. Consider the following as expressed by Dr. Donald Harvey:

1. *Emotional intimacy.* When you are emotionally intimate, you "feel" close to one another. You feel emotionally supported and cared for by your mate. There is a sharing of hurts and joys and a sense that each of you is genuinely interested in the well-being of the other. Attentiveness and understanding seem to be characteristics of this dimension of intimacy.

2. *Social intimacy.* When you are socially intimate, you have many friends in common as opposed to separate social calendars. This is not to say that you do not have some separate friendships. But "separate friendships" are not the totality of your socializing. Having time together with mutual friends is an important part of your shared activities.

3. *Sexual intimacy.* True sexual intimacy involves more than the mere performance of the sex act. In truly intimate marriages, sexual expression is an essential part of the relationship. It is a communication vehicle and not just a duty. If your relationship is sexually intimate, you are satisfied with your sex life. You are comfortable with one another and do not see your activity as routine. Genuine interest, satisfaction, ability to discuss sexual issues—these are characteristics of a sexually intimate relationship.

4. *Intellectual intimacy.* Intellectual intimacy involves sharing ideas. In short, when you are intellectually intimate you talk to each other. More than just superficial conversations about the weather, you seek input from your mate regarding issues of importance. You value your mate's opinion and want to share your own. There is an attitude of mutual

respect. Feeling "put down," feeling conversations are futile, feeling as though your mate is constantly trying to change your ideas—these are absent in intellectually intimate relationships. Instead, conversations are stimulating and enriching.

5. *Recreational intimacy.* When you are recreationally intimate, you enjoy and share in many of the same "just for fun" activities. You have many similar interests. Whether they be outdoor activities or indoor, you like "playing" together. Even in the midst of hectic schedules, you find time to do fun things. And in so doing, you feel closer to one another.

6. *Spiritual intimacy.* For you to be spiritually intimate, three criteria must be met:

a. you must share common or similar beliefs about God;

b. these beliefs must be important or significant to your lives; and

c. you must honestly share where each one of you is in your own spiritual quest.

Having only one or two of these prerequisites to spiritual intimacy will not do. All must be present. If couples do not share their journey with one another, even those who have been raised in the same denomination and who personally value their religious commitment may be no more intimate spiritually than couples who are unequally yoked. Dutiful attendance at religious activities is no guarantee that spiritual intimacy exists within a marriage. This form of closeness requires much more.[5]

Now go back and evaluate each dimension. On a scale of 0-10, indicate your level for each of the six dimensions of intimacy. Then evaluate each one as you feel your husband would. Now, indicate what you can do to enhance the level in each dimension. It might be interesting to ask your husband to do the same evaluation, first as he sees each dimension in your marriage and then how he thinks you would respond. It could make an interesting discussion.

Sexual Behavior

Q. WHO SETS THE STANDARD FOR NORMAL SEXUAL
BEHAVIOR? IS ORAL SEX ALL RIGHT IN MARRIAGE?

A. In a marriage relationship, each person participates in setting the sexual standard in light of what Scripture teaches and what each person enjoys. Neither one is to have power over the other in prescribing what is their standard. The New Testament teaches that men and women are equal in terms of value, ability and position before God. Men do not have sexual rights that women do not have. Each has as many rights as the other.

The passages in the New Testament that teach about the husband-wife sexual relationship either begin or end with a command for mutuality. Each are to have their needs met and this means both are to discover what is pleasing to the other.

One of the barriers to the sexual relationship is ignorance, both of Scripture and the sexual process. What have you read that clearly and objectively states what Scripture says about sex? What have both of you read about the sexual response? Have you read *The Gift of Sex* by Joyce and Cliff Penner? This is a must read for couples of every age, even those who have been married for 30 years or more. Why? Because I have found more misinformation with couples who are married longer than those who are younger.

Probably the most frequently asked question about sex is about oral sex. Oral sex refers to oral stimulation of sexual organs by either partner using the tongue or mouth on the partner's organs. Cliff and Joyce Penner point out in their book, *The Joy of Sex,* that The Song of Solomon refers to the couple's stimulating one another in this manner (Song of Songs 4:16-5:1). It would seem to indicate from Scripture that nothing is wrong with this practice. But this is just an inference as Scripture is not fully clear about it being right or wrong.

Any wrongness that could occur is when one partner attempts to force oral sex upon the other. Nothing should be done that violates the other person. Oral sex could be a problem if it loses its purpose of increased stimulation for the purpose of completing the sexual act of intercourse and becomes a substitute for intercourse. In some cases, even when a woman does not enjoy oral sex for herself, she will give in to her husband's requests. Then, he loses interest in fulfilling her needs through sexual intercourse.

Oral sex is just as natural as stimulation of the breasts, mouth or ears. Some express concern about it being an unclean act. If the body is washed and clean, contamination will not be spread from either the genitals or the mouth. The most important principle to follow is to discover what your partner enjoys, and do not request or force anything that would violate them. The book *The Gift of Sex* includes the best detailed discussion of this subject.

Recommended Reading and Listening:

Penner, Cliff, and Penner, Joyce. *The Gift of Sex.* Dallas, TX: WORD Inc., 1981.

Wheat, Ed. *"Sex Problems and Sex Techniques in Marriage"* (audiotapes).

Wright, H. Norman. *Holding on to Romance.* Ventura, CA: Regal Books, 1992.

Notes

1. Dennis Rainey, *Staying Close* (Dallas, TX: WORD Inc., 1989), pp. 254-256.
2. Michael McGill, *The McGill Report on Male Intimacy* (New York: HarperCollins, 1985), pp. 188,189, adapted.
3. H. Norman Wright, *Understanding the Man in Your Life* (Dallas, TX: WORD, Inc., 1987), pp. 191-197, adapted.
4. Source unknown.
5. Donald Harvey, *The Drifting Marriage* (Tarrytown, NY: Fleming H. Revell, 1988), pp. 38,39, adapted.

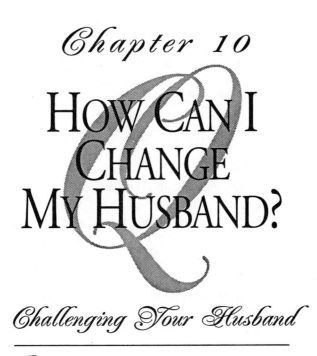

Chapter 10

HOW CAN I CHANGE MY HUSBAND?

Challenging Your Husband

Q. HOW CAN I CHANGE AND CHALLENGE MY
HUSBAND SO THAT I CAN LIVE WITH HIM? SOME
OF HIS BEHAVIOR IS FRUSTRATING TO ME.

A. Counselors and pastors constantly hear women's concerns about
changing a husband. One person in the marriage is interested in
growth and change and the other appears to be stuck. The motiva-
tions for change vary and so do the methods wives use to try to
change their husbands.

You can motivate your husband and effect change, but it is not
easy. Without careful forethought, some of your responses can backfire. As well, your own motivation and reasons for wanting change
must be considered carefully. Does trying to change a spouse fall
under the mandate of Scripture? Shouldn't we just totally let the other
person be and learn to accept everything? No, for if we did we would
be saying that each of us is perfect and that we don't have room to
grow.

In this chapter we will consider (1) what the Scriptures say; (2) an overall plan for change; (3) and some specific issues regarding changing a partner. I hope something in this chapter will be applicable to your marriage as well as other kinds of relationships.

Biblical Examples

How does the biblical mandate to exhort and encourage one another apply to the marriage relationship? The Word of God gives us examples of how we should respond to one another (italics have been added).

> And when [Apollos] wished to cross to Achaia [most of Greece], the brethren wrote to the disciples there, *urging* and *encouraging* them to accept and welcome him heartily (Acts 18:27, *AMP*).

> I *entreat* and *advise* Euodia and I entreat and advise Syntyche to agree and to work in harmony in the Lord (Phil. 4:2, *AMP*).

> Let the word [spoken by] the Christ, the Messiah, have its home (in your hearts and minds) and dwell in you in [all its] richness, as you *teach* and *admonish* and *train* one another in all insight and intelligence and wisdom [in spiritual things, and sing] psalms and hymns and spiritual songs, making melody to God with [His] grace in your hearts (Col. 3:16, *AMP*).

> But we beseech and earnestly exhort you, brethren, that you excel [in this matter] more and more (1 Thess. 4:10, *AMP*). Therefore encourage (admonish, exhort) one another and edify—strengthen and build up—one another, just as you are doing (1 Thess. 5:11, *AMP*).

Who determines what we are to exhort another person to do? Who determines what we are to teach or encourage another person to do?

The word "exhort" in these passages means to urge one to pursue some course of conduct. It is always looking to the future. Exhorting one another is a three-fold ministry in which a believer (1) urges another person to action in terms of applying scriptural truth; (2) encourages the other person with scriptural truth; and (3) comforts the person through the application of Scripture. In Acts 18:27, "encourage" means to urge forward or persuade. In 1 Thessalonians 5:11, it means to stimulate another person to the ordinary duties of life.

Therefore, what are we to exhort another person to do? To answer this you need to look at your motives for change. When you begin to understand what your motives really are, you may discover that it is not really necessary for your spouse to change. Perhaps your needs can be fulfilled in other ways, which allow your partner not to have to change. If you can discover why you want your spouse to change, you may discover what you want changed in your own life. The key is to understand your own motives.

A Strategy for Change

When you ask your husband to change some of his behavior that you dislike, he will interpret the proposed change in one of four ways: (1) as a destructive change; (2) as a threatening change; (3) as having no effect upon him; or (4) as a change that would help him become a better person. Thus it is important in requesting a change to present the suggestion in such a way that he sees it as an opportunity for growth. How can this be done?

Give your husband information. Each person has a different need for and capacity for handling information. The more information you provide about a desired change the less the resistance. Why? Because there is more opportunity for him to see the request as a step toward growth.

"John, I appreciate your interest in the children and their education. I'd like you to help me in two areas with them—David needs your assistance with some of his projects and I need your help in talking to his teacher. I understand that this may take some time, but your opinions and knowledge can help David more than mine. If we both talk to the teacher we'll be able to share our ideas and present a united front to both the teacher and David."

Your husband needs to know *what* you *expect* of him, *why* you *expect* it, and *what* may be the *results.*

Involve your husband. This will lessen resistance in exploring various alternatives for change. Your husband will be less defensive if he has a chance to express his ideas and make suggestions.

"Jim, you know that we've been able to talk a bit more lately about how the home is kept and also our scheduling difficulties. I'm wondering if we could explore some possible alternatives that might work. This doesn't mean we're going to accept whatever idea is shared, but so we can come up with more ideas to work with. What do you think?"

Start out slowly. Is the requested change an overwhelming and gigantic step, or have you broken the request down into small increments that can actually be accomplished? If the requested change is for increased communication, start out by sharing for 7 minutes 1 night a week. Your ultimate goal may be 30 minutes a night, 4 nights a week, but that is too much to expect at first. Having the garage cleaned and kept clean is a typical request. But developing a specific small-step plan to accomplish this over a 4-month time period may be workable.

Create intimacy. Resistance is a normal response when one partner mistrusts and fears the other. If motives or intentions are questioned, how can a suggested change be seen as anything but damaging? If trust and intimacy are present, your husband may see the request as one way to achieve even greater intimacy in the marriage. A husband who has responded favorably to his wife's previous suggestions for change will be open if:

1. His wife acknowledges his change in a positive way. She doesn't say, "Well, it won't last," or "It's about time," or "I can't believe it."

2. She doesn't mention his change or lack of change in front of others to embarrass him.

3. She is open to change herself.

4. He knows she loves him whether he changes or not.

5. He sees her request for change as something that will enhance his life.

Resistance to Change

Why does your husband resist change? Why is it difficult to comply with the requests of others? Too often the reasons we give are covers for the real source of resistance.

If a husband does not respond positively to a request to change, his resistance can take many forms.

Some simply stop listening. This is an expression of their unwillingness to change. They cut off the conversation, leave the room or busy themselves with some task. A man may stay late at the office or say he has to leave early for an appointment to prevent further discussion.

Some do not follow through on the request. Some people agree with the request, but do not follow through. Why? They have no intention of doing so. This is a stall tactic to get the person making the request to back off! But after many requests with no follow-through, you become suspicious and angry.

Or perhaps the person counters with, "Why don't *you* change?" This completely turns the request around and the result will probably be an argument.

Reluctance to Change

Why are all of us so reluctant to change?

Habit. A simple reason for not changing is habit. Day in and day out we maintain a fairly predictable routine. Inside of us we have a selection of comfortable responses that make us feel secure. We do not have to think about or work at new ways of responding. But the habits that make us feel secure may be an irritant to others. Habit is probably the most frequently used form of resistance. Why? Because it works so well.

Have you ever used these excuses or heard them used? "I've always done it this way." "After 28 years, it's too late to change now." "Why change? I'm comfortable. This way works." "How do I know the new way is better? I don't have to think about this one. I just do it."

Perhaps you live with a husband who is messy. He does not pick up after himself, put items away, or hang up his clothes when he comes home from work. He neglects to change into old clothes before he does a messy chore, pick up the paper and magazines he dropped on the floor or clear his own dishes away from the table.

You may have tried to correct him by begging, pleading, threatening, letting the mess accumulate for days or even weeks, but nothing has worked. He probably was accustomed to having people pick up after him while he was growing up. If this is the case, he may have developed the belief that he is special and deserves to be waited on. If he was waited on and picked up after for many years and now you are saying, "Pick up after yourself," the message he is receiving is, "You no longer deserve to be catered to." Thus his self-esteem is under attack. The way he thinks about himself has been challenged. This is the real reason why he resists. If he changes, he will have to change some perceptions he holds about himself.

Habits can be changed. A habit of 25 years can change as quickly as one of 10 years or 1 year once the source of resistance is discovered. And the change is easier than most people realize.

Ignorance. Others plead ignorance as their resistance. They say, "I didn't know that's what you wanted" or "I don't know how to do that. Who do you think you married? Superman?" Ignorance can be an effective tool because it puts the person making the request on the defensive. You begin to question whether you told your husband what he wanted or whether he is expecting too much.

Control. Another resistance frequently used is control. If someone asks me to change I may not comply because of my fear of losing control. I want to stay in control of me and even you. We do not like others determining how we are to behave. The request may not be a control issue but we interpret it in that manner.

Uncertainty or anxiety. This is an honest resistance response.

"How will this change affect me?" "Will I be capable?" "Will people still respond to me in the same way?" "What if I still can't please you?" We anticipate some threats and fears coming into play. We feel our self-esteem being challenged and threatened, and this again is the key: Any perceived threat to our self-esteem is going to be resisted. Will I still receive affirmation? Will I be as secure?

Do you really think all your requests for change should meet with instant applause and compliance? If your partner resists your request for change, do you become angry, despondent, perplexed, stubborn? Can you see value in resistance? Probably not. But consider the possibilities.

If your requests are resisted, perhaps this will cause you to consider why you want the change, how intensely you want it, and how committed you are to pursuing the change. What does your commitment level to this change tell you about your own needs at this time?

Perhaps the resistance will assist you in being more specific concerning what it is you wish changed. Have you considered your mate's resistance as a unique form of communication? He could be telling you something new about himself—what he values, what elements are involved in his self-esteem. If his resistance is too strong, you may be convinced to try another approach.

Motivating Your Husband to Change

Q. HOW CAN I COPE WITH AN UNMOTIVATED HUSBAND?

A. We have been told for years that we cannot change others, only they can change themselves. That is true. But we can help to create the conditions under which another person would desire to change. Here are some of the main means you can use to bring about change.

Ineffective Methods

First of all, here are several ineffective but frequently used means of bringing about change.

Show me tactic. "If you loved me you would..." Have you ever asked your husband to change for this reason? The response he probably gives back is: "If you loved me, you wouldn't ask!" This is manipulation.

Trade off. "Look, I'll change _____ if you'll change _____."
This is like saying, "I've got a deal for you!" It doesn't work.

Still others use the demand, "You better do this or else I will..." This is risky and can backfire.

Power and coercion. For centuries people have used power and coercion to bring about change. Threats, demands and rewards are frequently used, including giving or withholding verbal or physical affection. As well, sometimes abuse takes place. Power can work, but what are the consequences? None of us likes to be dominated by another person.

Discomfort. Others make people worry, feel uncomfortable, or ill at ease about what they do. If we can create guilt or anxiety, we think we can bring about change. But the change is usually not real or lasting. Instead of bringing about the change you seek, your husband may actually withdraw from you. We don't like to be around people who make us feel uncomfortable. It is difficult to develop intimacy between people when either power or discomfort is used as a means of bringing about change. And I think more intimacy is probably what you want.

Effective Methods

Here are some effective methods that can be used to promote change.

Provide new information. This is based upon believing that your husband will examine new data and make a rational decision to change. Hopefully he will discover that what he is currently doing will not achieve his goals as readily as the new approach. The information approach may be effective, but it is slow. He must clearly see the consequences of the new suggestion and the way it will enhance his feelings of self-worth.

The growth approach. If your husband can see little or no risk involved to himself and his self-image, he may be open to change. "If I don't have anything to lose, I may try it." The key is to eliminate risk! This means he needs to be assured that his self-image will remain intact or be enhanced. This is the ideal. There will always be some degree of risk, however.

Trust. Of all strategies for change the most vital is trust. Trust is paramount if you wish to bring about change. If you have a solid basis of trust already established, your requests may find a response. If there is no pattern of trust, it may take awhile to build it. And if trust has been destroyed, you may never rebuild it. Trust and credibility (yours!) are at stake.

To build trust, and to request change based on this trust, requests for change in the beginning should be simple and trivial. Think of how safe the other person feels now. How safe and secure will he need to feel before he responds to your request?

If your husband is going to change he must see that you are trustworthy and that you seek the best for him. And all you can do is *request* change. It is up to him to *decide* to change and to do it. Before you begin, are the changes you request in harmony with the pattern of living as stated in Scripture? Or do the changes reflect your own insecurities?

Consider Your Actions

Change can occur if *you* will do the following:

1. Examine and clarify your reasons and desires for change. Examine your need.

2. Evaluate the requests in light of Scripture. Is this a change that Scripture calls upon us to make?

3. Understand how your husband sees himself and what his self-esteem is built upon.

4. Present change in a way that enhances his self-esteem.

5. Consider your own willingness to change. Are you willing to stand by your husband and encourage, edify and build him up? Are you open to change and is that openness obvious to others? A yes answer to these questions is vital.

6. Reinforce, reinforce and reinforce! If your husband makes a requested change and you ignore it or take it for granted, he will feel violated, let down and will revert back to his previous behavior. We all need feedback and reward for making a change. Then our self-esteem remains intact. Changes are fragile and must be strengthened. When I *experience* affirmation as a person for my new behavior I feel like making it a part and parcel of my life-style. If I feel uncertain with this new behavior, then I will return to the certainty of the old. And the new experience and reinforcement needs to be strong. Otherwise, I remember my old experience, which is a natural part of my life and is not easily overcome. The reinforcement must come at a time when it can be linked to the new behavior. This means right after it occurs.

7. Be persistent and patient. Do not expect too much too soon and do not become a defeatist.

How to Motivate a Husband Spiritually

Q. WHY DOES MY HUSBAND HAVE NO DESIRE TO BE THE HEAD OF THE HOME IN SPIRITUAL ISSUES? HOW CAN I GET MY HUSBAND TO BE THE SPIRITUAL HEAD OF MY FAMILY?

A. A major concern for many Christian wives is the disparity between their own spirituality and the spiritual life of their husbands. Unfortunately, many engaged women never evaluate a fiancé thoroughly enough in this realm prior to marriage. Or perhaps the husband-to-be gave the impression of being alive spiritually when actually he was not.

Let's consider several questions about this issue.

Prior to marriage, perhaps you had expectations for your husband's spirituality. Or perhaps these expectations have developed since then. Were these expectations ever discussed with him? If so, what was his response?

Are you comparing your husband's expression of his faith with the way you express yours? If so, are you taking into consideration personality differences, length of time as a believer, or whether he had any kind of role model spiritually when he was growing up, whether he exhibits strong leadership in other areas of his life? Sometimes we place unrealistic expectations on our spouse. Is what you want for him to his benefit and can he learn to be comfortable with it?

Susan Yates, a minister's wife, says,

> God speaks to each of us in different ways. The expression of our faith may be different, our spiritual gifts may be different. God is not going to make us copies of one another.
>
> Spiritual growth is not a race. We're not competing. Spiritual growth is more like a walk through a garden. We're not sprinting to the finish line; we're walking from one incredible array of beauty to the next. Granted, there are weeds and rocks along the way, but we're exploring, not racing. We're both going to notice different things, and go through different seasons in our growth. And as we walk through that garden, we need to love one another, pray for one another, and learn from one another.[1]

I will always remember a statement I read years ago regarding what we expect of a spouse.

We try to change people to conform to our ideas of how they

should be. So does God. But there the similarity ends. Our ideas of what the other person should do or how he should act may be an improvement or an imprisonment. We may be setting the other person free of behavior patterns that are restricting his development, or we may be simply chaining him up in another behavioral bondage.[2]

Many men were not raised with a role model of what a husband was to do as a spiritual leader. As well, they were never instructed in the basic attributes of spiritual leadership. They were simply admonished to be "the spiritual leader in the home."

Coupled with inadequate preparation and a desire to be in control and succeed, is it any wonder many men are hesitant to be the spiritual leaders in their homes? For years when I spoke at Forest Home Conference Grounds Family Camp, the most popular and well-attended seminar was an optional session held at four in the afternoon. It was for men only on the subject, "How to pray with your wife." The desire is often there but very little guidance and instruction is available. What can you do?

1. Pray for your husband.

Carole Mayhall, writing in *Today's Christian Woman,* suggested the following:

> *How to Pray "Just for Him":*
>
> Make it a point to commit five minutes a day to pray just for your husband. Pray a different scripture for him each month, as well as other specific requests that God puts on your heart. And keep a prayer list specifically for him. The list might look something like this:
>
> For my husband: (put the date you begin praying)
>
> A. Colossians 1:9-11
>
> • That he would be filled with the knowledge of God's will.
>
> • That he would have spiritual wisdom and understanding.
>
> • That he would live a life worthy of God.

- That he would please God in every way.
- That he would be strengthened with God's power for patience and endurance.
- That he would have a thankful spirit.

B. That he would develop a friendship with a committed Christian who would challenge him.

C. That God would give him a hunger and thirst for himself and his Word.

Write down the answers when they come and date them.

After a friend of mine had been praying specifically for her husband for several months, she called me, excitement lilting in her voice.

"Guess what!" she exclaimed. "Bill just told me a new co-worker asked him if he'd be willing to attend a new early morning Bible study, and Bill said YES! And something else. I tried not to show my astonishment when Bill brought home a brochure on a Marriage Enrichment weekend and said he'd signed us up to go."

My friend and I rejoiced together in this new beginning.[3]

2. Apply the information in this chapter to this subject area.

A husband refusing to accept the Lord is not a cause for divorce. I have seen wives wait a year, 10 years and 30 years for a husband to respond to God's message. They were patient, prayed and responded according to 1 Peter. God does not put a timetable on a person. Susan Yates suggests the following:

Although it's hard to accept at times, you need to remember that you are NOT responsible for your husband's salvation. Not long ago a woman came up to me after I had finished talking at a retreat. She told me a little about her life, and before long she was in tears. She felt tremendous guilt that her husband hadn't come to Christ. I assured her she was not guilty because of what her husband did or did not believe. Her husband's faith was between him and God. I encouraged the woman to be concerned that SHE grew in Christ. The Holy Spirit is the one who convicts of sin—not wives...

Your husband is not your adversary; he is your partner— for life. Therefore, a good question to ask yourself is, "Am I allowing this difficulty to draw me closer to the Lord or am I becoming bitter?" Tell God your hurts and disappointments and ask him to draw you closer to himself. Read his Word, and listen to him, for he has something special to teach you.[4]

3. Encourage your church to develop programs and ministries to equip husbands to be spiritual leaders. Encourage your husband to consider the spiritual dimension of life by giving him testimony books by authors in his vocational or recreational interest field. Often someone else saying essentially what you have said will gain his listening ear more than you can.

4. Work with him to become the spiritual leader. Discuss what this concept means to him and discover what he would be comfortable in doing. Supply him with tools and resources to make it easier.

Read the book by this author, *Quiet Times for Couples* (a daily devotional) two to three minutes a day.

Building Resentment

Q. I FEEL RESENTMENT BECAUSE MY HUSBAND DOES NOT TAKE ON LEADERSHIP IN OUR HOME. I HAVE TO DO EVERYTHING!

A. One of the difficulties that occurs in marriage when there is an overfocus on changing the other person is the buildup of resentment. Each time you run the risk of being vulnerable and experience disappointment and hurt, a process of hurt collection begins, which in time turns into resentment. This issue soon begins to consume the structure of the marriage. Perhaps it can be best described in this way.

We have an abundance of insects in California. One type is rarely seen but it definitely makes its presence known. It is the destructive termite. Hidden from view, the termite slowly and steadily continues to feast its way through the skeletal structure of a house month after month. Some homeowners may be aware of termites as telltale indications of infestation are discovered from time to time. But too many ignore the warning signs and fail to take appropriate steps to evict the invaders.

The subtle erosion continues and eventually the damage becomes apparent and the problem can no longer be ignored. But by the time the termites' work has reached the visible surface, the internal damage is extensive and major repairs and expensive reconstruction are often necessary.

In marriage, the destructive counterpart to the unseen termite is resentment. An insidious disease, this feeling of ill will is a barrier to the growth of romance and intimacy as well as being a corrosive acid that eats away at the existing relationship. Resentment is usually bred from a real or imagined hurt that we hold against the perpetrator.[5]

Resentment almost becomes an addiction or an obsession. Resentment hinders solving problems because your focus is shifted to the hurt and resentment rather than the problem-solving skills. Your emotions reflect fear and defensiveness. Your reasoning ability is hooked into justifying your own reactions. Solving the problem is not primary now, revenge is the source of satisfaction. And when resentment exists, you replay the video of the disappointment and hurt time and time again. You begin to feel self-justified.

It can feel good to hold on to resentment because it eases the pain of marriage dissatisfaction. And the use of resentment increases and soon becomes a habit. I have met resentment addicts. It begins to feed on itself because the more you resent, the more you need to justify the place of all this resentment, and a vicious cycle develops. And unfortunately it tends to reinforce the behavior or problem you detest in your partner that contributed to the resentment in the first place.

Does resentment have any place in your life at this time? If so, what is it feeding on? What keeps it alive and well?[6]

The alternative is the one that can heal any relationship. It is expensive but not to you. It cost God a great deal, but for you it is free. It is called forgiveness. You might try it.

Characteristics of an Unmotivated Husband

Q. WHAT ARE THE CHARACTERISTICS OF AN UNMOTIVATED HUSBAND? I WANT MY MARRIAGE TO GROW, BUT MY HUSBAND DOESN'T SEEM TO BE INTERESTED. WHAT CAN I DO?

A. Let's consider some characteristics you may encounter in an unmotivated husband. Do you experience any of these responses from your husband?

He is *undependable* though quite charming and witty when courting you. In time, however, especially when you need him the most, he tends to become invisible when he grows bored or when responsibilities are placed upon him. How frequently does this occur? Give an example_____

He is *rebellious*. When you make a request, he interprets it as a demand. His ways of rebelling are many and varied. Two passive responses are procrastination and forgetfulness. How frequently does this occur? _____ Give an example_____

He is helpless with several problems with which he cannot cope. You are drawn into assisting him with problems that seem to overwhelm him but that he should be able to handle. How frequently does this occur? _____ Give an example _____

He is *narcissistic* or in love with himself. Who does he think about? Himself! HE comes first and he cannot empathize. He can't understand why you get upset. How frequently does this occur? _____ Give an example _____

He tries to elicit *pity* from you. Pouting and sulking are common. He attempts to appeal to your mothering instincts. He is a great complainer but makes little effort to change his unhappy circumstances. How frequently does this occur? _____ Give an example

_____

Guilt exists, especially in his relationship with his parents. Usually he is resentful toward Mom but longs for a close relationship with his dad. How frequently does this occur?_____ Give an example

_____

In many ways, he is *dependent*. He will not reciprocate love, concern or care unless you get on his case—and even then his response won't last. How frequently does this occur?_____ Give an example _____

Words such as "manipulator," "con artist" and "dishonest," appear on your lips when you think of him.

Often you are drawn to the "little boy" in him, but when you reach out in an attempt to get close, he withdraws. He is very *secretive*. How frequently does this occur? _____ Give an example

_____

There is a sense of *emotional paralysis* because his emotions are stunted. He tends to express a different emotion from the one he is experiencing. Anger is expressed as rage. He may tell you he loves you but somehow forgets to express it. How frequently does this occur? _____ Give an example_____

_____

Another kind of husband is *socially impotent*. Though he is involved with others and inwardly suffers from acute loneliness, he cannot make friends. Unable to face the fact that the inadequacies in his relationships lie within himself, he may attempt to buy friends.[7]

How frequently does this occur? _____ Give an example
_____

What are you feeling right now? Does this last kind of man sound like your husband? This kind of man has been described as having the Peter Pan Syndrome and it is easy to end up mothering them.

*Help Your Husband
Be Responsible*

_____

Q. WHAT CAN I DO TO ENCOURAGE MY HUSBAND
TO BE MORE RESPONSIBLE? I FEEL LIKE
I AM STRUGGLING ALONE.

_____

A. In one week's time, reflect on how you respond to your husband. List what you do that may be reinforcing him to respond in the way you *don't* want.

Here are several suggestions to stimulate your thinking. The purpose of these suggestions is to help you with your own personal growth and to encourage your husband to become a caring, mature person. If he tends to overreact, and in one way or another attempts to get you to excuse his behavior or failings or appease his guilt—be sure you *don't* let him out of his responsibility. Say something such as, "I'm sure you did the best you were able to do" or "Others were at fault and you were the victim of circumstances." Do not support any of his rationalizations.

Do Not Rescue Him

What can you do? You could ask him how it feels to make a mistake. You can ask him what he could have done differently. What did he learn from this mistake and what will he do differently the next time? Say, "We all become angry and that is quite normal." Then offer some alternatives. Watch out for the anger that will be directed your way when you do not feel sorry for him. It will come. Be sure you do not take responsibility for his problem or his anger.

He needs to experience the consequences of his irresponsible behavior. Do not rescue him!

Help Him Remember the Important Dates

If your husband has the habit of forgetting important dates and appointments—including your anniversary or birthday—be sure you do not drop subtle hints, complain to others about him or try to shame him.

You can place the dates in bright bold letters on the calendar and just before the important date tell him it is about to occur.

Let him know how important remembering dates is to you and why it is important. Ask him how he will develop his plan to remember the dates the next time. If he says, "I just forget. I need you to remind me," don't buy this line. I am sure he remembers some dates that are important to him. Say, "No, I am not going to remind you, but I will work with you to develop the plan you are going to follow in order to remember."

Quit Doing for Him

Quit doing things for him he could and ought to be doing for himself. Your words and the tone of voice of your responses will be very important. Do not pick up after him. Do not rush to bring him whatever he wants when he wants it. If you are busy you have every right to say, "I'm sorry. I'm tied up. Could you please get it or find it yourself?" Do not hesitate to ask him to help you either.

Avoid Manipulation

One of the traps you want to avoid is manipulation. It may bring about some change but it is deceitful in its process and the change does not last. There are ways to break through into the world of your husband and gain his attention in a positive way. Remember, you may be confronting many of his past issues in this process.

Presenting Requests

Q. MY HUSBAND REFUSES TO TAKE INITIATIVE IN
THE HOME. WHAT SHOULD I DO? HOW DO I
PRESENT THE CHANGES I WANT?

A. Let's consider some ways to present requests and not demands to your husband. Above all, do not demand.

Demands are an ineffective way to force people to meet our needs. It won't work to insist your husband do something he does not enjoy, though you may gain pleasure from it. If he complies, he won't like it and, as a result, he will never be in the habit of helping you.

Demands are also thoughtless. Our gain comes at someone else's expense. We do not care how the other person feels as long as we get our way. For that reason, when any of us make demands of our spouse, we rob our marriage of love and closeness. Demands breed resistance.

A better alternative to demands are thoughtful requests. There are three steps: (1) Explain what you would like and ask how your husband would feel fulfilling your request; (2) if he indicates that the request will be unpleasant to fulfill, withdraw it; (3) discuss alternative ways he could help you and feel good about it.

Thoughtful requests reward your husband's efforts on your behalf and help to turn the needed behavior into a habit. You turn what might have been considered a selfish demand into a thoughtful request by simply asking how your husband would feel about it. And this can make a significant difference.

If you do not ask how your husband feels, he may think you are taking him for granted. In many situations, he will agree to help you because you asked for his opinion. Knowing that you care makes the job more acceptable and he does not feel put down.

The second step is a bit more difficult: If your husband indicates that the request will be unpleasant to fulfill, withdraw it.

This step is difficult to take if you believe your husband owes you this, has a responsibility to meet your needs, or must do what he is told.

No one has the right to make demands of another person. It is self-defeating and will create more distance.

Being considerate means behaving in a way that takes your husband's feelings into account. If you suspect that your husband will find meeting your request unpleasant, you may win the battle but lose the war. But if you do not push, how will your basic emotional needs be met?

If your marriage is healthy, your husband probably wants to help you or meet your needs even if he resists your request. It is the way you want your spouse to help that often causes the problem as well as the *way* you present it in terms of tone of voice and body language.

If you do not present your requests thoughtfully, you will not get what you want—but you will get what you do not want. Your long-term goal is to eventually generate help without having to ask your husband. You want your husband to develop the *habit* of helping you. The best way to help your spouse do that is to be thoughtful and flexible and when he does respond, be appreciative. At times he may be reluctant to begin with, but when he discovers there are benefits he will be less reluctant the next time.[8]

Recommended Reading:

Harley, Willard. *Love Busters.* Tarrytown, NY: Fleming H. Revell, 1992.
Walker, James. *Husbands Who Won't Lead and Wives Who Won't Follow.* Minneapolis, MN: Bethany House Publishers, 1989.
Wright, H. Norman. *Quiet Times for Couples.* Eugene, OR: Harvest House Publishers, 1990.

Wright, H. Norman. *Understanding the Man in Your Life.* Dallas, TX: WORD Inc., 1987.

Notes
1. Gloria Gaither, Gigi Graham Tchividjian, and Susan Alexander Yates, *Marriage: Questions Women Ask* (Portland, OR: Multnomah Productions, 1992), p. 130.
2. Author and source unknown.
3. Carole Mayhall, *Today's Christian Woman,* May/June 1991.
4. Gaither, Tchividjian, Yates, *Marriage: Questions Women Ask,* p. 138.
5. H. Norman Wright, *Holding on to Romance* (Ventura, CA: Regal Books, 1992), pp. 103,104.
6. Mark J. Luciano and Christopher Merris, *If Only You Would Change* (Nashville, TN: Thomas Nelson, 1992), pp. 10,11, adapted.
7. Dan Kiley, *The Peter Pan Syndrome* (New York: Aron Books, 1983), pp. 9-11, adapted.
8. Willard Harley, *Love Busters* (Tarrytown, NY: Fleming H. Revell, 1992), p. 81, adapted.

Chapter 11

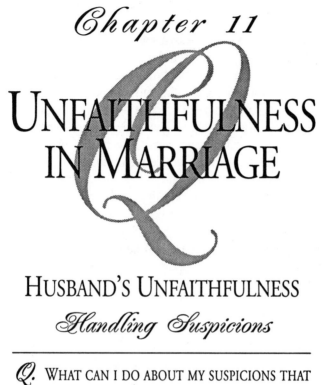

Unfaithfulness in Marriage

Husband's Unfaithfulness

Handling Suspicions

Q. WHAT CAN I DO ABOUT MY SUSPICIONS THAT
MY HUSBAND IS NOT FAITHFUL?

A. Handling suspicions of an unfaithful spouse is never easy. First
of all, I need to ask you several questions. Are the suspicions just your
own or are others feeding you information? If others are coming to
you, what are the specifics of what they are saying? Is it just a "feeling"
they have or do they have facts? I have seen damage done to a relationship in which a third party suspected something was happening
but there was no hard evidence. If it is just your own suspicion, what
is it based on? Have you made an actual list of what you see happening? Is your energy being taken up by suspicion and in trying to discover if he is faithful, or are you continuing to love and give to him?

Have you discussed your concerns with your husband? Perhaps
you are afraid to confront him for fear you might be wrong. Well,
what other alternatives do you have?

One counselee said she was suspicious of her husband and one day brought up her suspicions to him. She approached him by saying, "Honey, I have a serious concern. You may be offended, shocked or even angry with me for bringing this up but I can handle whatever reaction you have. I have noticed the following (she proceeded to identify the behaviors that were giving her concern, such as lack of sexual interest, more time spent away from home, suspicious phone calls and so on). I just want a simple yes or no answer. Are you having an affair with another person?"

Whatever response is given at that time needs to be accepted. I have seen cases in which the husband has confessed right then and there, or has lied and later confessed. Still others said no they were not and they were telling the truth. If he is not having an affair, this could provide an excellent opportunity to correct the problems that are contributing to the suspicion.

Winning Back an Unfaithful Spouse

Q. HOW CAN A WIFE WIN BACK HER UNFAITHFUL SPOUSE? AFTER SO MANY YEARS OF MARRIAGE AND SO MANY CHILDREN, HE IS NOW SEEING ANOTHER WOMAN. HOW DID I MISS SEEING THIS COMING? WHAT IS WRONG WITH ME?

A. The question of winning back a spouse indicates that you have "lost" your husband. This would imply that you were the cause of him having an affair. It is important that we do all we can to love our partners. But I have seen many situations in which a beautiful wife demonstrated her love for her husband sexually, emotionally and every other way, and yet he still chose to run around on her.

No matter what defects exist in a marriage, no one forces a husband to seek solace elsewhere in place of working to correct the problems. In many of the marital affairs I have witnessed in the past 25 years, a large proportion of those marriages have had intimacy deficits. Unfortunately, many women deeply desire intimacy but their husbands either do not want to work at it or are unable to.

Myths About Infidelity

Many Christians live with a list of myths about infidelity that can catch them off guard. How many of these do you believe?

1. "Lust is the basis for the majority of affairs." All the other reasons far outweigh this one.

2. "You can inoculate yourself against an affair by a strong Christian faith." It *will* reduce it but we are all still vulnerable.

3. "If you have a good marriage you don't need to be concerned since affairs rarely happen in good marriages." Unfortunately, affairs are likely to occur within 75 percent of the marriages of young and middle-aged couples!

4. "If the unfaithful person is an evangelical, a strong biblical confrontation will usually be all that is needed to stop the affair." Rarely does this work.

5. "An affair is an indication that the unfaithful person's spouse is not an adequate partner." An affair can point up difficulties but it does not always indicate something is wrong with the unfaithful partner's spouse.

6. "A man almost always chooses a woman who is physically more attractive than his spouse." In many cases the woman is less attractive. The emotional attraction is a stronger incentive.

7. "Most affairs end in divorce." Divorce from an affair occurs in about 50 percent of the general population, but with Christians a majority are able to work out their problems.

8. "If you are certain that your marriage is solid and 'affair proof' then it could never happen to you." If you believe this, you are in trouble.

9. "A Christian woman who is a close friend of another Christian woman would never have an affair with that woman's husband." Yes, this does happen.

10. "Affairs can improve a stagnant marriage." Affairs are painful and destructive.

11. "If a man has an affair, that proves he does not love his wife." Only in a few cases is that true.

12. "When you discover an affair, it is best to act as though it is not happening and avoid an upset." This is definitely not true.[1]

What *Not* to Do

Here are several steps *not* to take to try to win back your husband:

1. If you are suspicious that he is involved in an affair, but are not sure, you may try to bury the idea. The unhealthy tendency is to invest time and energy in your children or other activities that do not generate anxiety over your concerns. This won't work.

2. You could verbally attack and denounce him but this would provide him with greater justification for what he is doing.

3. You could tell as many others as possible about the affair, including his friends, fellow workers and especially family. But this only creates additional alienation between the two of you. And asking other people to talk to him usually does not work either. You may need to talk with one or two friends regularly but be certain this will be kept in confidence.

4. You could increase the frequency and variety of your sexual activity with the hope of winning him back. In many cases, however, it is not so much the sexual intimacy that is the problem but the emotional intimacy. If your husband is having an affair, you should stop all sexual

involvement at this time because of the abundance of sexually transmitted diseases including AIDS. Before any sexual involvement is resumed, he needs to be tested for sexually transmitted diseases (STDs). You cannot give the other person the benefit of the doubt in the world in which we are now living.

5. You could go on a self-improvement campaign by changing your hairstyle and wardrobe, or by losing weight in an attempt to catch his eye, but it usually does not work. Do not try to compete with the other woman or become the "perfect wife." It is a good way to feel worse about yourself and wear yourself out.

6. Some women have gone to see the other woman to see what she is like (if they do not know) to attack her and scare her off or to plead with her. This does not draw back your husband.

7. Do not go to him and apologize for not being a good enough spouse.

Give Him a Choice

What needs to occur is to change your marriage relationship. Once you have discovered an affair is in process, you must do two things. One is to experience, release and work through the multitude of feelings you are experiencing. Then you must force a choice. He needs to decide now to either leave the other woman and work toward restoring your marriage or lose the marriage relationship completely. It cannot be done slowly or gingerly or subtly, it must be confronted directly either in person or through a letter. You may need to have your minister or a counselor help you with the steps involved. Reading *Love Must Be Tough* by Dr. James Dobson may help. You are not forcing your husband to do anything or to demean him. You are simply letting him know he must make a choice. In his excellent book *Torn Asunder* (which I would recommend every person in this situation read), Dr. Dave

Carder gives an example of a letter you could give to your husband:

Dear Richard:

This letter is the hardest I've ever written. You are the love of my life, and I thought I was the love of yours. But I'm beginning to wonder if I was wrong.

Now with the revelation of your involvement with Julie, I just don't know what's true anymore.

Were our eighteen years together just a lie?

Am I having a nightmare just now in trying to believe that you've been with her on the sly for almost a year? In my heart it seems like a bad dream, but in my head I know it's true.

I've had my faults as a wife, I know. And I'm willing to work on them. But at this most difficult juncture in our marriage relationship, I want to let you know clearly that I'm releasing you to your choices.

I love you very much, and I made a commitment before God and a promise to you to love you, and you only, forever. However, true love really sets people free.

I hope you will choose to stay with me as my husband, but I would not want you to do so out of compassion over how your departure would affect me. Should you ultimately choose to leave, it would be extremely difficult for me, but I am an adult and know that God will help me recover. I would eventually go on with my life.

If you choose to come back, I want you to know that I am fully willing to accept my responsibility for putting this marriage back together in a more mutually satisfying way. I know that I need to make personal changes for any future relationship to be successful. I also know that if you choose with me to save our marriage, our mutual recovery will very probably be slow, difficult, and painful.

We both will surely feel like quitting along the way, and working through our issues will stretch both of us to the breaking point. But you have my commitment to this process, and I hope and pray that you will join me in it.

But you, too, are an adult and are free to walk away if that's what you truly desire. I only ask that, should you choose to leave, you carry out your decision appropriately and without deceit.

I think this letter states clearly my true feelings, and I thank you for listening. I ask you to search your heart and make a decision within the near future as to whether you want to restore our marriage or not.

Richard, regardless of your final decision, I wish you the very best.

Love,
Ashley[2]

Dr. Dobson recommends that if the unfaithful partner desires to be free of the marriage, he should be given the freedom to leave. When this is done, three things are likely to happen:

1. The trapped partner no longer feels it necessary to fight off his spouse, and their relationship improves. It is not that the love is rekindled, necessarily, but the strain between the two partners is often eased.

2. As the cool spouse (i.e., the one who wants to leave) begins to feel free again, the question he has been asking himself changes. After having wondered for weeks or months, "How can I get out of this mess?" He now asks, "Do I really want to go?" Just knowing that he can have his way often makes him less anxious to achieve it. Sometimes it turns him around 180 degrees and brings him back home!

3. The third change occurs...in the mind of the vulnerable one (the one who was begging). Incredibly, she feels better—somehow more in control of the situation. There is no greater agony than journeying thorough a vale of tears, waiting in vain for the phone to ring or for a miracle to occur.

Instead, the woman (who gives her partner permission to leave) has begun to respect herself and receive small evidences of respect in return.[3]

Reasons for Affairs

Q. WHY DOES MY HUSBAND SEEK SEXUAL STIMULATION ELSEWHERE (PORNOGRAPHY, AFFAIRS, ETC.) WHEN HE HAS ME?

A. I do not know if you are aware of the many reasons men and women have affairs. The majority of people do not set out consciously to have an affair. In all the literature concerning this issue, 10 categories seem to emerge. Perhaps these will help you to better understand what has happened.

1. The unfaithful person has a personality disorder.
2. The person has a sexual addiction.
3. Some developmental crisis in the person's life has not been handled.
4. Your partner was involved in temptation-filled situations.
5. There were either unconscious, unrealistic, or uncommunicated expectations of the unfaithful partner.
6. There was a failure to meet realistic, communicated expectations of the unfaithful spouse.
7. There was a failure to meet the esteem needs of the unfaithful person.
8. There were unconscious, unrealistic, or uncommunicated expectations of the faithful partner, which were expressed in unhealthy ways.
9. Psychopathology, including codependency, of the faithful spouse was the cause.

10. Other reasons resulted from the family relationship either past or present.[4]

As you can see, the first five reasons are primarily the responsibility of the unfaithful spouse. In the next four, the faithful partner did not cause the affair but contributed to a situation in which the other person became more vulnerable to an affair. Each person is responsible for his or her responses and reactions. The book *Broken Promises* by Dr. Henry Virkler discusses these reasons in detail and is must reading for any minister or counselor. It is helpful for laymen as well.

Is your husband a sexual addict? It is not an easy issue to face but many do find themselves caught up in an addiction that controls their lives. For some it is x-rated movies and hard-core pornographic videos. For others it is pornographic magazines. For some it also includes other women. If that is the case and if you see a repetition of this pattern, your husband needs outside help. The best you can do at this time is to educate yourself more about sexual addiction and encourage your husband to seek help. Many recovery groups are designed to help those who want assistance.

Reestablishing Trust

Q. HOW CAN I LEARN TO TRUST AND FORGIVE MY HUSBAND WHEN HE HAS BETRAYED MY TRUST THROUGH AN AFFAIR?

A. When an affair occurs, plan on a time of pain, disruption, rebuilding and hopefully restoration. If your husband admits to the affair but does not want to talk about it or deal with it, you have another choice facing you—you can either let it go or you can use an intervention to shake him out of his complacency. I would advise the latter. It is better to take this step rather than wait around to see what might occur. (Please refer to chapter 10 of *Torn Asunder* by Dave Carder for specific guidelines for an intervention.)

The costs of an affair are great and perhaps the greatest is the loss of trust. When you trust your partner you can depend upon him to be faithful—he is somewhat predictable. You can rely on him. But when an affair occurs, all of this vanishes as though erased from a chalkboard. You discover that your partner's past behavior was not what he led you to believe, so you do not have any basis from which to predict his future behavior. You wonder, *Do I know or did I ever know this man?*

Making your marriage work will require a mutual commitment and a reestablishment of trust. It will require the ability to take things a day at a time to build a positive track record.

The causes of an affair are often complex and in the rebuilding stage must be identified and examined. This is necessary but the timing may vary with each couple.

Both of you will need to grieve about the affair because of the many losses sustained. You, as the faithful partner, need to define what you would like from your spouse to help you rebuild trust. Trust for you may be the emotional feeling that grows when you know your partner is repentant and committed to fidelity. What commitments do you need from your partner? Many times the faithful one will ask for a consistent caring attitude from the other, an openness and willingness to talk about the strengths and weaknesses of the marriage, and a recommitment to spiritual values.

Steps to Rebuilding Your Marriage

When an affair comes to light, both of the partners are plunged into a crisis and action needs to occur immediately. Here are some steps you can take.

1. I recommend the approach of Dr. James Dobson in his book, *Love Must Be Tough*. Here is what Dr. Dobson says the wife must do.

   [She] must make it clear that *never* again—and I mean *never*—will she tolerate sexual unfaithfulness. (Her husband) needs this motivation to go straight. He must know, and *believe* that one more romp with another lover and the sky will surely fall. (His wife) must convince him that she means business. If he wavers, even slightly, she should give him another month or two to sit somewhere wishing he could come home. Better that they continue at the door of matrimonial death now than go through the misery of infidelity again in a few years. Finally, (the wife) should insist on some major spiritual commitments within the family. This couple is going to need the healing powers of God and His grace if they are to rebuild what sin has eroded.[5]

2. A commitment to the marriage must be made by both of you, which means going for marriage counseling for as long as necessary.

3. A pattern of honest communication must be established no matter what. This means not withholding any information.

4. Accountability is essential, especially through volunteering information about scheduling and whereabouts.

5. The unfaithful husband must commit himself to fidelity in thought and action. This can include staying away from situations and places that could create problems for him. As well, I recommend he read the book *Running the Red Lights* by Charles Mylander.

6. The unfaithful spouse must accept the responsibility for his actions and for the pain you are experiencing. He also must accept the fact that your recovery will run in cycles—one day you may be fine and the next day you might be back to anger, questioning or crying. That is normal. Your part in this is to recognize and accept your ups and downs and, on a down day, recall that you do have good days and you are improving. It also means giving your husband the benefit of the doubt.

7. You both must work on building the positives in your marriage.

8. Work toward a time when forgiveness is complete; renew

your marriage vows and publicly make Christ the head of your marriage.[6]

The grace of God as expressed in your forgiveness of your partner is the healing agent. I would encourage you to read the books recommended on this subject. You cannot rush forgiveness. It takes time to grow. If you try to forgive too soon you will bury your pain alive and suffer even more loss. If you want to forgive your husband, know what is involved. Read Ephesians 4:31 and Proverbs 17:9.

WIFE'S UNFAITHFULNESS

Wife's Attraction to Another Man

Q. WHAT CAN I DO ABOUT MY ATTRACTION TO ANOTHER MAN WHO IS NOT MY HUSBAND?

A. High-risk attraction—it can happen to any of us. No one is immune. Do you feel like a ticking time bomb just waiting to go off? You could be close to an affair.

1. Have you been thinking of having an affair with someone you know?

2. Have you fantasized about an affair with someone?

3. Have you ever hoped that something would "happen" to your spouse or he would do something so you would feel justified in having an affair?

4. Did you ever wish your husband would die so you would be free?

5. Have you ever wished you did not have children so you could do what you want without hurting them?

If so, you are at high risk!

Steps to Overcome Fantasy

What can you do to reverse your direction? First, answer the above questions honestly. Then, quit thinking and fantasizing about this person. What you are thinking is unrealistic. Your spouse cannot compete with your fantasies. Make a list of everything you will lose if you have an affair. You will lose your self-respect, your sense of right and wrong, a clear conscience in the sexual area, and unhindered sexual expression with your spouse. You will lose being comfortable with friends because you will wonder, *Who knows?* You will also lose your personal integrity and potentially your life by AIDS.

Now can you think of any other losses?

Perhaps you feel justified in leaning toward someone else because of the state of your marriage. It may be empty; perhaps your needs are not being met. Have you shared your specific needs with your husband so he will know how to close the intimacy gap? Are you giving your energy to help develop and enhance your love toward your spouse, or is it being drained away by your fantasies? Perhaps you are becoming addicted to the excitement of your attraction and feelings? What is the state of your devotional life? Are you asking the Lord for guidance?

If you really want to change the direction in which you are headed, you must take several steps.

First, give up all interaction with this person. Then acknowledge your sin and ask God to strengthen your conscience. Take action at once. No more contact, phone calls or working together at church. If contact is unavoidable, make sure all interaction carries a businesslike tone. A caution—this may be tough and you may falter and rationalize. Don't! If you have a trusted friend, confide in her and make yourself accountable to her. I have seen this work with both men and women. A friend can support you in prayer and encourage you when you feel vulnerable. Write an unmailed good-bye letter to this other man and read it aloud to your friend or to yourself, then burn it and thank God for being your source of strength. Read the helpful book, *The Snare* by Lois Mowday, which says:

We will struggle with desire, temptation, and attraction. We will be in situations where we have friendships with those of the opposite sex. We are to heed the teaching of Scripture, accept our sexuality, remove ourselves from romantic settings with others and continually feed, nurture and maintain a need-fulfilling marriage. Remember, however, even a healthy marriage is not a guaranteed safeguard against an affair. We may be redeemed creatures but we are still fallen with a distortion of the image of God within us. We must commit not just our behavior to God but all our thoughts and feelings. An intimate, honest prayer life as a couple and a commitment to His Word are ways He gives us victory over temptation.

There hath no temptation taken you but such as is common to man: but God is faithful, who will not suffer you to be tempted above that ye are able; but will with the temptation also make a way to escape, that ye may be able to bear it" (1 Cor. 10:13, *KJV*).

"In conclusion, be strong in the Lord—be empowered through your union with Him; draw your strength from Him—that strength which His [boundless] might provides" (Eph 6:10, *AMP*).

"But thanks be to God, Who gives us the victory—making us conquerors—through our Lord Jesus Christ (1 Cor. 15:57, *AMP*).[7]

If You Have Had an Affair...

Q. SHOULD I TELL MY HUSBAND ABOUT MY AFFAIR?
I WOULD RATHER LIVE WITH IT MYSELF THAN
DESTROY MY MARRIAGE.

A. Opinions vary, but I believe you should tell your husband if you have an affair. I realize there will be problems because there is no way to predict how your partner will respond. Confession will bring about a crisis that will last for months and produce tremendous pain. And if your spouse has insecurities and emotional problems he may never get over it. And yes, it could bring about a divorce. I have seen that happen.

The other side of the coin, however, is that confessing an affair is the best opportunity to start a new marriage built on trust. When you do not confess, you perpetuate deception and can become adept at living a lie. Trust and honesty then are not part of your relationship. And are you certain that your partner does not know or suspect? Often men do know and therefore both of you are living with the tension.

The following are what I believe to be the most important reasons for telling your husband. At some time in the future, whether it is a few months or 15 years, the affair is usually discovered. You may let it slip or someone else will tell about it. The discovery or confession of it years later makes recovery more difficult because the other partner feels he has been deceived for all those years. He begins to suspect other problems as well. Adultery is a violation against God and His teachings and against the marital vows and the marriage partner. That is why it needs to be confessed to both God and your husband—and this includes so-called "one-night stands."

Before you confess, it is important to write out exactly what you want to say. You can state that you have been unfaithful, have sinned against God and your partner and are asking forgiveness. Indicate that you are willing to do whatever needs to be done to restore the relationship. Let your husband know you understand how devastating this is to him and that you realize forgiveness will take time. Do not give a lot of detail, for it is more difficult for him to get those items out of his mind. Often it is best to share this in some public place such as a restaurant or a park. Have a counselor or pastor lined up to see immediately.[8]

It will not be easy. But it is best. I have seen scores of marriages restored after an affair. It does not have to be the end of the world.

Recommended Reading:

Carder, Dave. *Torn Asunder.* Chicago, IL: Moody Press, 1992.

Coleman, Paul. *The Forgiving Marriage.* Chicago, IL: Contemporary Books, 1982.

Dobson, James. *Love Must Be Tough.* Dallas, TX: WORD Inc., 1983.

Hart, Archibald. *Healing Life's Hidden Addictions.* Ann Arbor, MI: Servant Publications, 1990.

Mowday, Lois. *The Snare.* Colorado Springs, CO: NavPress, 1988.

Mylander, Charles. *Running the Red Lights.* Ventura, CA: Regal Books, 1986.

Smedes, Lewis. *Forgive and Forget.* New York: HarperCollins, 1984.

Virkler, Henry A. *Broken Promises.* Dallas, TX: WORD Inc., 1992.

Notes

1. Henry A. Virkler, *Broken Promises* (Dallas, TX: WORD Inc., 1992), pp. 4-9, adapted.
2. Dave Carder, *Torn Asunder* (Chicago, IL: Moody Press, 1992), pp. 136,137.
3. James Dobson, *Love Must Be Tough* (Dallas, TX: WORD Inc., 1983), pp. 48,49, adapted.
4. Virkler, *Broken Promises,* pp. 10,11, adapted.
5. Dobson, *Love Must Be Tough,* pp. 78,79.
6. Virkler, *Broken Promises,* pp. 224-226, adapted.
7. Lois Mowday, *The Snare* (Colorado Springs, CO: NavPress, 1988).
8. Virkler, *Broken Promises,* pp. 144-148, adapted.

Chapter 12

COMMUNICATION IN MARRIAGE

Dealing with a Silent Husband

Q. WHEN MY HUSBAND COMES HOME FROM WORK, I WANT TO TALK BUT HE WANTS PEACE AND QUIET AND IS SILENT. WHAT CAN I DO?

A. One of the most common complaints I hear is the issue of the noncommunicative husband. Most wives either engage in a direct frontal attack, which doesn't work, or withdraw into resentment, which does little to encourage a husband to open up.

Perhaps you tend to rescue your husband. A silent spouse is not always ready to give more than a yes or no response. One of your tendencies may be to rescue him by filling the uncomfortable silence with your own words. Do not feel you must ease the pressure by elaborating on or illustrating your question or putting words in his mouth. You might say, "I'm interested in what you have to say, but you may need to think about it for a while. That's fine with me, take your time. When you're ready to talk about it, let me know." Giving permission for silence will take the pressure off both of you.

Another way to invite your spouse to interact is to address his silence directly. You could say, "Honey, I'm looking for a response from you and you appear to be thinking about something. I'm curious what your silence means at this time." Then wait.

Or, "The look on your face tells me that you have something on your mind. I'd like to hear what it is." Or, "You may be concerned about how I will respond if you share what's on your mind. I think I'm ready to listen." Or, "It appears that you're having difficulty speaking right now. Can you tell me why?" Or, "Perhaps your silence reflects a concern about saying something correctly. You can say it any way you'd like."

One wife used the direct approach and said, "Sometimes when I want to talk with you, you seem preoccupied or hesitant. I wonder if it's the topic or if there is something I do that makes it difficult for you to respond. Maybe you could think about it and let me know later." Then she stood up and began to leave the room. But her quiet husband said, "Let's talk now. I'm ready to comment on your last statement."

The direct approach is most successful when you invite your partner to tell you how you have been making interaction difficult for him. But it is important to listen to him and not become defensive, regardless of what he says. What he shares may not be accurate from your perspective, but that is how he sees it. Be careful not to say something that might cause him to retreat deeper into his shell.[1]

Basic Communication Guidelines

Q. WHY ARE MY HUSBAND AND I UNABLE
TO COMMUNICATE CLEARLY?

A. Here are some basic communication guidelines to assist you in the important aspect of marriage: communication.

1. Know when something needs to be said and say it straight. This means you do not assume your husband knows what you think, feel, want or need. Communication should be clear and direct. None of us can attend a school for mind reading. I have heard women say, "We've been married for 20 years. Why should I have to tell him...?" "He should know how much that hurt..." Or, "It was so obvious. Why should anyone have to express it?" But obvious to whom? Clearly not to your husband.

Communicating directly means you do not make assumptions, you do not hint, you are not devious, and you do not go through other people to share your message. All these approaches lead to distortions.

2. Be aware of the importance of timing. Proverbs 15:23 *(AMP)* says, "A word spoken at the right moment, how good it is!" Most emotions should be shared at the moment you experience them, because delaying distorts them. When you respond immediately, it allows your husband to learn what you feel and what you need. For example, what is important to you in a conversation may not seem significant to him. Therefore, delaying your response may allow him to totally forget what you said. Then he wonders what you are talking about when you bring it up later, and you wonder why he is so insensitive in not remembering. Has this ever happened?

Speaking of timing, have you asked your husband when the best time is to talk with him? For some the last thing at night or the minute he arrives home is not the best time. Many men need to recuperate awhile before they are ready to engage the family. Be sure the TV is off whenever you do converse. You cannot compete with it.

3. Know exactly what you are going to say and say it. When you talk with your husband, do you want to share your *feelings, needs, thoughts* or *observations?* Or do you share all four? Sometimes we blend and run these together so much that we lose all clarity.

When you share a thought, you offer him your conclusions, observations, value judgments, beliefs and opinions. How do you state these? In such a way that he understands and wants to continue listening. Do you ever indicate that what you are sharing is a thought, compared to a feeling?

4. Understand male-female differences in communication and adjust accordingly. In all cultures throughout the world, linguistic differences exist between men and women, both in style and substance. In our American culture, men tend to resist expressing themselves directly. You may be one of the many wives who are frustrated because your husband only hints about certain things, rather than speaking about them directly. This is especially true in areas involving expression of feelings and answering personal questions such as, "What's bothering you?"

The topic of feelings is a major source of frustration in couple relationships. Most men do not have a feeling vocabulary, and thus putting into words what they are experiencing is a real chore. They often hide their feelings behind a facade of facts, which only serves to further distance them from their wife's feelings. Men tend to talk more about tasks and facts than feelings, reflecting their tendency to be goal oriented.

This primarily male trait also carries over into communication. Your husband's response to what you may consider an intimate conversation is, "What's the purpose here?" or "What will this accomplish?" Men want an agenda. They tend to give a one-two-three solution to problems—even when no one requests an answer. Whereas a woman tends to empathize, men want to be in control, in conversation as well as other areas of life. To help alleviate this problem, present your material in this way.

Does your husband interrupt you? Men do tend to interrupt more than women.

In the choice of words, women tend to use more descriptive words—more adverbs of intensity. The descriptive adjectives used by men and women vary significantly. You seldom hear men talking about the "beautiful mauve drapes" or the "gorgeous sunset, streaked with lavender." Women use terms such as "taupe," "beige," "violet" and "mauve" to describe an item, whereas a man may describe the same item as "red" or "green."

A man might describe an event or experience as "fine," while his wife might describe it in several sentences, her choice of words and inflections painting a very descriptive picture. This frustrates many wives, who feel they cannot get close to their husbands because they

are on different wavelengths. The scarcity of words, minimal inflections, and little or no emotion used by men tends to lead to sterile
conversation.[2] Encourage your husband to give more descriptions.

Amplifiers and Condensers

Often I describe people as amplifiers or condensers. The amplifiers give
a number of descriptive sentences as they talk, while condensers give
one or two sentences. In approximately 70 percent of marriages, the
man is the condenser and the woman is the amplifier. Neither is a bad
trait, but the amplifier wishes his/her partner would share more, while
the condenser wishes his/her partner would share less. It is only when
each of you adapts to the style of your partner that real communication
occurs. If your husband is a condenser, match his style. It works.

We also know that when men and women talk to one another,
both make adjustments, but women make more adjustments than
men. They are also influenced by men's topics and tend to follow
their lead.[3] You may end up feeling you are doing all the work!

Timing, pacing, pausing and agenda difference in listening may
complicate a couple's attempts to develop ongoing intimacy. If your
husband uses intermittent pauses when talking or speaks at a slower pace, you may jump in with your own thoughts or tend to hurry
him along. Understanding and accepting these differences can be
helpful to your relationship.

Some women are overly long talkers and can never seem to get to
the point. They fail to identify the subject, ramble around the barn
several times, and give unnecessary details. If your spouse is a linear
communicator who identifies the subject immediately, he will be
especially put off if you use this style.

Listening Styles

Listening also reflects a difference in style between men and women.
Men tend to offer verbal responses quite infrequently, and when they
do they are meant to indicate, "I agree with you." But women interpret these statements to mean, "I am listening." Why? Because women

respond more frequently when someone is talking to them, and this means or signifies they are listening to the person talking. Thus a wife may think her husband is not listening to her, when in reality he is simply more of a passive listener.[4]

Every couple must find a mutual language or communication style if they are going to establish any level of intimacy in their relationship. I am not suggesting that you make all the adjustments. Your husband needs to as well. But this is a book for women and that is why these suggestions have been made. And by all means, be sure to read the section in this author's book *Holding on to Romance* on how to speak your spouse's language.

Men's Blind Spots

Sometimes men have difficulty with personal relationships. Some of the difficulty occurs because of blind spots created from certain beliefs.

Many men believe they will be loved for performing or achieving. They expect appreciation and recognition for economically providing for the family. But when they do not receive appreciation, they feel let down or betrayed. Many men believe the more successful they are, the more their wives will appreciate them and enjoy the recognition of their accomplishments. They do not see that some of the same qualities that led to their success may actually alienate others and cause people to resent them. A man may believe his perception of reality is the only one that exists and that his wife also accepts his views. He fails to see that other people may not accept his ideas or act on them.

Many men believe that any personal problem can be solved with impersonal, mechanical solutions. They think "how to" answers are the way to solve personal problems. Logic, willpower and self-control are the answers, and they fail to see that their own relationship problems come from their behavior and how they relate to others. They tend to forget from one situation to another and thus repeat their negative experiences again and again.

Many times a man enters a relationship believing that he is the strong one and his wife is the weak one. And thus, when problems arise, he tends to feel anxious and guilty over these difficulties. Some men have difficulty identifying and recognizing the pain in a relationship or the upset of their partners. When it finally does register, an incredible amount of damage to the relationship has already occurred. The man believes that by expressing his ideas more forcibly when he feels he is not being heard, he will get through to his wife. But this just tends to push her farther away.

If you would like your husband to open up and reveal himself to you, be careful that you do not contribute to his reluctance in doing so. Husbands tend to feel helpless and hopeless if they hear accusations that they are unloving or insensitive. If he is accused of being hostile, cold or sexist, or is barraged by a flood of tears, it is an encouragement for him to withdraw and close up.

Listen to what he is attempting to say as he intends it. It may not be in your language, but some sensitive, caring, clarifying questions on your part may help translate it into a language compatible with your own. A man tends to express love differently than a woman, so you might not believe that what he is doing to show love is really love. Some men do have difficulty expressing themselves in a way that is seen as loving. I have talked with many men who feel both resentful and helpless when they are accused of being unloving. They feel the accusations are unfair and unwarranted. Most men do not do too well with accusations.

Men live with their own set of fears and insecurities. They do not always admit their fears directly but they are often reflected in other ways such as rigidity, explosiveness and insatiable quests. Men's fears are also reflected through some of their intense competitiveness and by how hard they are on themselves when they do not achieve. This is a reflection of their fear of losing and failing.

Many men are afraid of being powerless and this is reflected in both the need to control as well as the tendency to avoid situations in which they do not feel in control. They live with a fear of not being useful, which is reflected in needing a goal or purpose to be motivated. Many men fear being weak, dependent and vulnerable so they avoid acknowledging needs and tend to withdraw when they are troubled. The fear of losing control emotionally and being weak and vulnerable is seen in holding on to logic and facts as the way to solve issues in life.[5]

Turn-off Triggers

Certain responses are guaranteed to push most men away from their wives. Often these responses are referred to as triggers. Have these ever appeared in your responses to your husband?

1. Make him feel guilty about his behavior, responses or problems you feel he causes you.

2. Use tears and other expressions of upset that you accuse him of causing, but he really does not understand how he caused them. When he feels unfairly blamed, it is a definite trigger.

3. Accuse him of being selfish, only thinking of himself, or saying, "You don't know how to love," or "I'm not loved because you have a problem with your mother."

4. Criticize the way he treats others.

5. Become a judge on his actions and his reasons for them. Making statements such as, "You're afraid of being intimate." "You don't even want me to get close to you." "You're behaving this way because of what happened at work."

6. Compare him to other husbands and other men. He feels her disappointment in him as a person but will see this as a personal attack rather than an effort to draw close. It creates the very thing she does not want.

7. Continue to talk about the relationship problems again and again even though he is already aware of what you have said. Positive action is far better than excessive talking.[6]

To draw your husband closer to you, encourage him to talk about his experiences in your marital relationship and listen to what he says. Ask about his major concerns as well as what he does appreciate.

Ask what it is you do that upsets him. This will encourage him for it lets him know you are listening and acknowledging him. Talk about things that interest him that are safe and remember the subjects that are sensitive and threatening to him. Approach those with caution.[7]

Resolving Marital Conflicts

Q. HOW DO I HANDLE OUR MARITAL CONFLICTS?
WE DON'T EVEN SEEM TO BE ON THE
SAME WAVE LENGTH MOST OF THE TIME.
WE CAN HARDLY TALK WITHOUT
FIGHTING. WHAT DO WE DO?

A. Entire books have been written on the subject of resolving marital conflicts and I would encourage you to do some extensive reading. But for now let me offer some suggestions to get you started.

Here are some questions to help you identify some of the issues. Answer each one carefully.

1. What happens over and over in your relationship that causes the conflicts? (What do you fight about most frequently?)

2. How does the whole thing start? (Who does or says what first?)

3. Then what happens? (What do you or your spouse do or say in response?)

4. What happens next? (What do you do or what does your husband do in response?)

5. How does it all end? (What do you or your husband do or say to end the fight?)

6. How do you feel afterward? (Are you mad, sad, scared, worried, numb, etc.?)

Go back and look at your answers. Decide at which step or steps you might handle things differently in the future.

How do your quarrels usually end? When couples come for counseling to talk about their conflicts, their usual first response is, "He or she started it." I am more interested in how their conflicts end! If you would divert your attention to the sequence of events, at the conclusion of your argument or quarrel you will be better able to discover the triggers that are pulled to set them off. All couples send out peace signs. Do you know what they are?

During baseball and football season (which you may or may not enjoy), following the game there is a postgame wrap-up or analysis. In football, the day following the game the players are subjected to a detailed analysis of their performance. That is how they benefit from their mistakes and prepare to do a better job the next time. It works the same way with relationship conflicts. If you want them to end, analyze them. Here are some questions to consider following each conflict.

1. How do you feel about the way you reacted? About the way your husband reacted?

2. Do you still feel the way you felt during the conflict? During the 12 hours following?

3. Are you resentful toward your husband or embarrassed by what you did or said during the conflict?

4. Do you feel you are realistically remembering what occurred? How would your spouse describe what happened?

5. Identify the following:

   a. Where the fights usually occur.

   b. When they usually occur.

   c. What is the trigger that sets them off? Often it is a repetitive behavior or statement.

Sometimes bad timing can set things off. Discussing issues right after you arrive home from work, late at night or before you have eaten may be part of the problem. Ask yourself, *"When* is it that I am most likely to have the kind of discussion that I want from my husband?" Have you ever asked what is the best time for him?

    6. Describe for your husband what you remember happening, using two versions:

        a. Describe it from an emotional perspective (your feelings).

        b. Describe it from a factual perspective.

    7. Have you fully faced your hurt or anger and feelings of distance?

    8. What can you learn from your husband's presentation? Be sure to share your response from a positive perspective.

    9. Describe how you see your husband dealing with conflicts.

   10. Ask your husband, "What else would you like me to share about the conflict?"

   11. Describe what responses and behaviors you would handle differently the next time. Describe what you would be willing to give at this time to resolve the conflict.

   12. What will you do the next time to make it easier on yourself and your husband?[8]

Tape-Record Conflicts

If you are brave, the next suggestion is for you. But it is not for the fainthearted. For years I have asked couples to use tape recorders at home. I suggest that they tape their discussions and conflicts. Naturally, I have heard many excuses why this won't work. These include, "If we know it's on, we'll behave differently." Perhaps, but in a few minutes most people forget it is on and resort to their previous behavior.

Others say, "We might be in another room and the recorder isn't there." One wife solved this problem by wearing the recorder around her waist. And this was before the miniature Walkman recorders! The fact is, if a couple wants to change their style of resolving conflicts, they will find a way!

Agree to tape-record your next three disagreements. That is all.

Ask your husband. You do not have to tape any more than three. But *both* of you must agree that you will record your interaction. When the conflict is over, wait awhile and then listen to the tape. It may be best for each of you to listen alone while you respond to the questions below. After listening and analyzing what happened, write out the changes you will make. *Do not* list the changes you feel your husband should make.

Five Ways to Handle an Argument

Q. HELP US TO UNDERSTAND EACH OTHER BETTER AND LEARN TO COPE BETTER. ARGUMENTS ARE GETTING OUT OF CONTROL. WE NEVER GET OUR PROBLEMS SOLVED. WE QUARREL ALL THE TIME.

A. Did you know that you have a choice in the way you handle conflicts? Here are five approaches.

1. Withdrawal. If you have a tendency to see conflict as a hopeless inevitability beyond your control, then you may not bother trying. You may withdraw physically by removing yourself from the room or environment, or you may withdraw psychologically by not speaking, by ignoring, or by insulating yourself so much that what is said or suggested has no penetrating power.

2. Winning. If your self-concept is threatened, or if you feel strongly that you must look after your own interests, then this method may be your choice. If you have a position of authority and it becomes threatened, winning is a counterattack. Regardless of the cost, winning is the goal.

3. Yielding. We often see yield signs on the highway; they are placed there for our own protection. If we yield in a conflict, we also protect ourselves. We do not want to risk a confrontation, so we give in to get along with our partner.

4. Compromising. You are giving a little to get a little. You have discovered that it is important to back off on some of your ideas or demands to help the other person give a little. You do not want to win all the time, nor do you want the other person to win all the time. This approach involves concessions on both sides and has been called the "horse trading" technique.

5. Resolve. In this style of dealing with conflicts, a situation, attitude or behavior is changed by open and direct communication. The couple is willing to spend sufficient time working on the difference so that even though some of their original wants and ideas have changed, they are satisfied with the solution they have arrived at.

Let's evaluate the results of each.

When you use *withdrawal* as your normal pattern of handling conflict, the relationship suffers and it is difficult to see needs being fulfilled. This is the least helpful style of handling conflicts. The relationship is hindered from growing and developing. This method is often employed out of fear—fear of the other person or of one's own abilities.

Winning achieves your goal but at the same time sacrifices the relationship. You might win the battle but lose the war. In a marriage, personal relationships are more important than the goal, and winning can be a hollow victory.

Yielding has a higher value because it appears to build the relationship, but personal goals or needs are sacrificed in yielding, which can breed resentment. Yielding may not build the relationship as much as some believe, because if the relationship were that important, a person would be willing to share, confront and become assertive.

Compromising is an attempt to work out the relationship and the achievement of some needs. The bargaining involved may mean that some values are compromised. You may find that you are not satisfied with the end result, but it is better than nothing. This could actually threaten the relationship. There may be a feeling of uneasiness following the settlement.

Resolving conflict is the ideal toward which I would encourage you to work. The relationship is strengthened when conflicts are resolved and needs are met on both sides. It takes longer and involves listening and acceptance but it is worth it.

Some wives complain that their husbands won't engage in discussion to resolve conflicts. Remember that the struggle with handling conflicts in a relationship is also tied into gender differences. A wife is much more likely to confront her husband with her dissatisfaction with the marriage or a problem than a husband is to confront his wife. A man is more likely to withdraw and avoid. Perhaps one of the reasons is that in conflict men experience more physiological arousal than women, which actually allows a woman to tolerate longer escalating bouts of conflict. It also takes men longer to recover from the physiological arousal of a conflict and this is discomforting to a man.[9]

Structured Disagreement Sessions

If you and your husband have repeated quarrels and conflicts over the same issues, one of the problems could be that you are more intent on being heard than in listening to each other. It may help to *structure* disagreement sessions. If you decide to have disagreements, why not be in control of them?

Here are several steps.

1. Begin by reading the following Scriptures out loud: Proverbs 18:13; Proverbs 25:11; Proverbs 16:32; Proverbs 14:29; Proverbs 17:14; Proverbs 20:3; Proverbs 26:21; Ephesians 4:31.

2. Set a time limit of 10 to 20 minutes to begin with; you can increase this later.

3. Toss a coin to select the first one to talk.

4. The winner takes three to six minutes to present his or her side of the problem, stating what is wanted and how it will benefit both of them. The partner listens.

5. The partner summarizes what he or she heard and then pre-

sents personal perspectives in the same way. If there is still a deadlock, each suggests two or three alternatives or variations of what they presented.

The fact that this is structured and time related can interrupt the negative pattern that has developed.

What else can I suggest? Three things:

1. Find out if your conflicts are basically a power struggle. The books *Making Peace With Your Past* and *Happily Ever After* will help.

2. Discover the uniqueness of your personality and your husband's and many conflicts will be cleared up. The book *Type Talk* will help.

3. Learn to speak one another's language. The chapters in *Holding on to Romance* will assist you. If none of these suggestions help, go for counseling immediately.

Recommended Reading:

Harley, Willard F. *His Needs, Her Needs.* Tarrytown, NY: Fleming H. Revell, 1986.

Helmering, Doris Wild. *Happily Ever After.* New York: Warner Books, 1986.

Kroeger, Otto, and Thuesen, Janet M. *Type Talk.* New York: Delacorte Press, 1989.

Tannen, Deborah. *You Just Don't Understand.* New York: William Morrow and Co., 1990.

Wetzler, Scott. *Living with the Passive Aggressive Man.* New York: Simon & Schuster, 1992.

Wright, H. Norman. *Holding on to Romance.* Ventura, CA: Regal Books, 1992.

Wright, H. Norman. *Making Peace with Your Past.* Tarrytown, NY: Fleming H. Revell, 1980.

Notes

1. Dan Kiley, *What to Do When He Won't Change* (New York: Fawcett, 1987), pp. 88,89, adapted.
2. Steven Naifeh and Gregory White Smith, *Why Men Can't Open Up* (New York: Warner Books, 1985), pp. 70-115, adapted.
3. Deborah Tannen, *You Just Don't Understand* (New York: William Morrow and Co., 1990), pp. 76,77,236,237, adapted.
4. Aaron T. Beck, *Love Is Never Enough* (New York: HarperCollins, 1988), pp. 74,75, adapted.
5. Herb Goldberg, *What Men Really Want* (New York: Signet, 1991), pp. 61,62, adapted.
6. Ibid., pp. 117,186,187, adapted.
7. Ibid., pp. 117,186,187, adapted.
8. Adapted from the author's procedures and David Viscott, *I Love You, Let's Work It Out* (New York: Simon and Schuster, 1987), p. 85, adapted.
9. Michele Weiner-Davis, *Divorce Busting* (New York: Simon and Schuster, 1992), p. 51, adapted.

Chapter 13

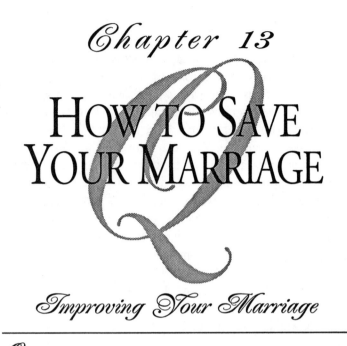

HOW TO SAVE YOUR MARRIAGE

Improving Your Marriage

Q. HOW CAN I IMPROVE MY TROUBLED MARRIAGE? HOW CAN WE MAKE OUR RELATIONSHIP MORE FULFILLING?

A. I believe any marriage can be improved and most marriages can be saved. The efforts of one partner can improve a marriage but it is difficult for one person to bear the full responsibility of "saving" a marriage. To improve your marriage, just start. That is all. Begin the change process yourself. Some steps will work. Some won't.

If your marriage has deteriorated, seek out a professional Christian marriage counselor. If your spouse refuses to go, then go by yourself. You do not need anyone's permission to get the help you need. It is an act of strength to admit you need help and to find it.

If one or both of you engage in self-defeating and negative behaviors, remember, you probably learned these behaviors prior to marriage. Because they were learned behaviors, they can be unlearned and replaced with positive behaviors. Look in the book of Ephesians and Colossians and practice the behaviors we are called to practice to reflect the presence of Jesus Christ in our lives.

Now for the big step. If you came to my office, I would ask you to tell me what you want to accomplish in your marriage rather than what your husband is doing wrong. For example, if you want your husband to be less insensitive to you and less rude, describe specifically what it is you want from him. Make it reasonable. Make it measurable. Make it attainable. Make it attractive to him. Make it a goal you are working toward. Always look forward in trying to improve your relationship. Do not put your energy into what is wrong. It will also help to read the other sections in this book pertaining to changing and encouraging your partner.

You can take several steps that will lessen the difficulty in your marriage relationship and help improve your marriage. All it takes is a willingness on your part to take these steps, regardless of how your husband responds or what he says. Please keep in mind a statement that I say again and again to those I counsel: If what you are doing now is not working, you do not have anything to lose by trying this, do you?

Behavior Traps to Avoid

Now, let's consider some of the most frequent traps that couples fall into and what you can do about them.

1. Tunnel vision. This trap is deadly. It is limiting. You focus on one minute detail as the foundation for your perspective of an entire event or situation. You return from what was supposed to be a weekend away for romance and say, "We quarreled the entire time." But is that really true? Put the quarrels in context and you will probably be able to say, "Yes, we did quarrel but not the entire time. We had some enjoyable moments too." Expand your vision! And let your husband know you recognized the positive.

2. Negative focus. This killer is also very limiting. You pay attention to only the negative and critical comments from your husband. When positive statements are made, you ignore or misperceive them. For some reason, the loving, supportive and encouraging comments do not register because of the times your spouse was negative or critical. You empower these times and use them as a giant eraser. But you can choose to recognize, reinforce and draw out the positives. Let them erase the negatives. It is possible. Write down the positives and thank your husband whenever he is positive.

3. Personalization. In this trap, you arbitrarily decide your husband is trying to hurt you, even with the absence of evidence. Perhaps this is the time to take 100 percent responsibility for the way you are feeling. Have you ever said, "I feel hurt but I know that isn't your intention. Could you share that in a different way for me?" It can't hurt to try this method.

4. Overgeneralization. This is a great way to create chaos within a marriage. All you do is take one or two incidents and conclude that your husband's behavior at those times is the way he usually behaves. Such overgeneralizations are typical such as, "He always criticizes me." You could also choose to draw a reasonable conclusion such as, "He doesn't always criticize. He builds me up and when he is critical, he's often right and I can learn from him." Perhaps putting into practice these passages will help: Proverbs 25:12 and 28:13, *TLB*.

5. Color thinking. Color thinking is actually not color but black and white. Perfectionists are good at this kind of thinking. You see either events in your marriage or behaviors of your husband as positive or negative—no in-betweens. When your husband's performance is not perfect (though it may be good) you see him as a complete failure. Your expectations for him are rigid and he cannot make one slip or it negates all of his positives. But giving credit for the positives and paying less attention to the negatives will help you accept his humanity as well as your own.

6. Magnification. This is looking at one's partner or a situation through distorted lenses. It is also called exaggeration. You may tell your husband, "I can't handle your rudeness and you'll never change." You tend to see the problems as unresolvable and also catastrophic. What would happen if you chose to recognize the difficulties but then focused on the solutions? Why not put your desires into positive requests and believe that in time the other person will hear you and respond. It works better.

7. *Negative expectations.* This trap works against you in more ways than one. You simply assume that your husband is going to respond or behave in a negative manner. You expect the worst from him and see his responses through this filter. And naturally you do discover it! Pessimism colors your expectations so you end up not being disappointed. But if you were to become vulnerable and expect the best of your husband, perhaps your belief in him would help him to respond differently. Scripture talks about this idea. It is called encouragement. And if your partner were responding in a positive way, how would you be behaving? Perhaps that is what will make a difference.

8. *Labels.* We seem to live by them—but most labels within a marriage are negative. Negative labeling of a partner's behavior or qualities seems to brand him forever as this kind of person. Labels such as "flaky," "undependable" or "spendthrift" prompt you to believe he can never change. He is imprisoned by the labels. Why not evaluate his qualities for what they are, identifying both the positive and negative? You may not like what he says or does but his behavior does not make him flaky or undependable! Give him the opportunity to be different!

9. *Feelings are not facts.* Too often we draw the conclusion that if we feel strongly about some issue between ourselves and our spouse, it is a fact. We tack on a statement of fact about our feelings such as, "I feel rejected. My husband deliberately tried to make me feel that way," or "I feel angry. My husband deliberately did something to make me feel that way." Feelings are important and need to be expressed, but we cannot draw conclusions from them. We need to remember that we are responsible for our feelings regardless of the way our partner behaves.

10. *Mind readers.* They do not just exist in a small, dimly lighted room with burning incense. Unfortunately, we all tend to engage in

mind reading from time to time. Especially in marriage, we often believe we know what our partners believe, what they are thinking and what they will do in any given situation. And we base our responses, actions and feelings on this private knowledge we own. The problem is no one has the ability to be a mind reader. If you had this ability you would be rich. Basing our perceptions on what and how a person has been in the past condemns him to a life of sameness, with little possibility for change. Listen to your husband with your eyes and your ears and with the expectation that what you will discover might be new.

11. Moralistic thinking. This is a coercive way of attempting to control a husband. It is reflected in words such as, "You should..." or "You must..." or "You just have to..." It is the belief that you know what is right for yourself and for him as well. But it won't work. It won't change your husband nor will it draw him toward you. However, it will push him farther away. It is all right to make preference statements. At times we all prefer different responses and behaviors from our partners, but they will be the ones to decide if they will respond.

12. Negative perspective. One of the most destructive traits in a marital relationship or even a dating relationship is a negative perspective. I often hear negativism in counseling. A counselee comes in and all she can see in the relationship are the problems and the negatives. One little upset during her day unleashes a memory of negative tape. If the evening has been going well and her husband brings up a problem it negates all the positives of the day.

Change will occur only when a person decides to focus on the positives and builds on those. A negative could also be perceived as a challenge and an opportunity, could it not? But after all, that is your choice.[1]

Do you get the message from these suggestions? It begins in your thought life. Eliminate the negatives and focus on the positives. That is the foundation.

Obedience in Marriage

Q. HOW CAN I OBEY, SUBMIT TO AND LOVE MY
HUSBAND WHEN HE IS TAKING LITTLE OR NO
INITIATIVE TO ASSUME A SPIRITUAL ROLE
IN OUR LIVES? THE BIBLE DOES
SAY "OBEY" YOUR HUSBAND.

A. I have been hearing questions about obedience toward a husband for the past 30 years. And they will continue to be asked in future generations as they have for the past 2,000 years. Not all of you will agree with what I will say. You may not even like it. But it may cause you to think. I hope some of the information may serve to answer some of your other questions.

First of all, obedience is not to be confused with submission. Although some of the traditional wedding vows have the word "obey" in them, the word is not found in Scripture. Obey is used in reference to slaves and children, not wives. Scripture does not teach a one-way submission; it teaches mutual submission.

The Word of God calls for mutuality in marriage, not one dominating over the other. It teaches that both the husband and wife are to live in a daily, individual, personal and voluntary submission to Jesus Christ as Lord and Savior (see Eph. 5:21).

Behind all decisions and plans in a marriage relationship, love is to be the guiding principle as taught in 1 Corinthians 13.

Both the husband and wife need to be aware of their status as "heirs together" in Christ (1 Pet. 3:7, *NKJV*) and as equal members of the body of Christ (see 1 Cor. 12). The purpose of these gifts is to build up, through mutual submission, the Body of Christ as well as their own marital relationship. They are to recognize that they are incomplete without one another. This is how the various roles and responsibilities are to be delegated within a home, not arbitrarily or on an "I'm a man and you're a woman" basis.

Marriage is built upon a healthy, interdependent relationship and not on prescribed, arbitrary roles or tasks, which each personality is forced to fit. This allows the uniqueness of each person's personality to flourish and expand. Decision-making is a process that involves time and a willingness to arrive at a solution that is acceptable to each person. The goal is consensus in important areas and neither person uses manipulation or power tactics to get their way. When there is no consensus, then the decision should be delayed. Each partner should pray honestly before the Lord for His leading and a decision is not made until there is agreement. This means that initial desires and plans will alter but there will be agreement.[2] Those who are insecure and have a need for power will not agree with what I have stated here.

Scripture shows us an order of responsibility. The husband is the head but a wise husband discovers that he leads by love rather than by demand. Paul gave us a new understanding of leadership in marriage. He assigned leadership responsibility rather than rank, sacrifice rather than selfishness, and duty rather than demands.

The husband is never to demand, unless it is a life and death decision and someone has to make an immediate decision. A wise husband seeks his wife's opinion; he realizes he needs her perspective. And he puts into practice sacrificial action in following, "Let us not love with words or tongue but with actions and in truth" (1 John 3:18). The servant role is not very popular today with either men or women; some people equate it with being a codependent, which is far from the truth. The husband is to lead by serving. This is how good leaders lead.

Perhaps Dwight Small sums it up best. He says the Greek word used here means "to voluntarily complete, arrange, adapt, or blend so as to make a complete whole or complete pattern." Donald Grey Barnhouse said, "Both the Greek and Latin carry the idea of throwing oneself under, as a foundation, as an assistant, or to use the biblical phrase, 'a helper *fit for him.*'"[3] I like Barbara Rainey's comparison showing the world's view of submission versus Scripture's view.

World's View of Submission	Scripture
Non-resistant	Loyalty
Unassertive	Completing
Bowing	Allegiance
Cowering	Faithful
Subservient	Obliging
Second-class	Willing
Lower/inferior	Flexible
Sweet-talking	Adaptable
No initiative	Blending
No backbone	Consent to
Agree to	Defer to[4]

"But," you say, "my problem isn't submitting. I just wish he would take some leadership and not dump it all on me."

What *do* you do if your husband won't lead? Has he given up leading in all areas or just some? Does he feel insecure in those areas? Do you create an atmosphere in which he can tell you about it? Find areas in which he is leading and affirm him on those. He needs your appreciation.

Do you follow when he tries to lead or fight him every inch of the way? I have talked to some women who say they like to discuss and debate everything. That can turn off a man quickly, because he does not see the need for talking about the issue. And some things do not need to be analyzed to death. Some women overpower their husbands and then complain that he does not lead. If you take over, why should he lead?

A husband is not a skilled leader to begin with. It takes time for all of us to grow and develop. As well, how many role models did your husband have to show him a skilled leader? Most men lack this training.

Your leadership style and personality will probably be different from your husband's. Realize that most of the differences you see in him are personality differences. As you learn to understand him and work with his personality you will see a difference in his response.

If your husband is very unresponsive, continue to encourage and believe in him. It helps if you have another older woman who can listen and guide you during this difficult time. She may help you to keep things in balance. How does your husband see the problem? Or would he call it a problem? What does he want from you? Sometimes it helps to enlist other women to pray for an unresponsive husband but they need to be trusted, nongossiping women. Do not talk critically about your husband to others—especially your own parents or in-laws. See this area as a yet undeveloped area of his life. See him having the potential to lead.

Disillusionment

Q. I HAD THE EXPECTATION THAT I WOULD EXPERIENCE A LOVE RELATIONSHIP IN MARRIAGE. DOES EVERYONE PUT UP WITH AWFUL TREATMENT 90 PERCENT OF THE TIME AND CALL THAT "MARRIED LOVE"? AT THIS POINT I'M THINKING, WHO NEEDS IT! I AM DISILLUSIONED.

A. Disillusionment can set into any marriage. Lack of love feelings can occur for a multitude of reasons. When you were dating, you possibly experienced some infatuation; it is a strong magnet that draws two people together. But during this phase you exaggerate qualities that are there or see potentials that do not exist. If you never passed from that to a deeper level of sustaining love and commitment, disappointment will occur. It is difficult to sustain the infatuation level of excitement and mutual gratification, and if you use that as a standard of love for your marriage you will be disappointed.

What originally attracted you to one another in the first place is not usually enough to sustain your love and marriage. Each must grow and develop within the relationship. The expectations you have for your marriage often feed the problem. The more extensive and unrealistic (or inflexible) they are, the greater the level of disappointment. And then the expectations turn into demands.

Many women fall in love with a man's potential more than the man himself. They see what he can become or how he needs to be fixed and base their response upon that. I have heard women say they go on "resource missions" when they are looking for a man. Sometimes this is reflected in statements such as, "He just needs a little more time," or "No one has loved him as much as I have and that will help him change," or "Everyone misunderstands him except me."

Commitment Is Needed

What is needed in a relationship even more than love is commitment; it is the glue that holds you together during a love recession. Commitment is a sense of dedication to the other person and his welfare. It is the model of servanthood we see in Scripture. This issue is touched on in *Holding on to Romance*.

> Some time after the honeymoon, many married couples ask, "What happened to the magic? It's disappeared. We were romantic at one time—where did it go? It's almost like an illusive dream. Does this happen to everyone?" Yes, all marriages change with time and courtship-level romance often fades. Depending on the couple, romance can either disappear completely or it can change with the marriage and be expressed in new, more creative ways.
>
> For many of us, romance and marriage was the pot of gold at the end of our childhood rainbow of grown-up fantasies. Most marital journeys begin with some romantic intentions. Some of these intentions are sky high while others are just a bit above the horizon. And in some marriages, each partner has different aspirations for romance; this difference can create strain on the marriage and disappointment in one or both partners.

As most of us moved toward marriage, our sense of reality was distorted by wishfulness and fantasy. Often this intense romantic illusion can neutralize the positive development of the marriage. The fantasies and unrealistic expectations brought to marriage can create a gulf between the spouses as the disappointments mount up.

If you married in your early 20s, as most couples do, you married at a time when most individuals are in the midst of developing their own personal lives. You are still in the process of establishing your own identity. You are still trying to discover "who you are." Your self-discovery can often be overshadowed by the attraction you and your loved one feel for each other and your desire for marriage.

Think back to your courtship for example. What thoughts and feelings went through your mind and heart? Most of us started our marital journey by falling in love. And if you think back to determine how it happened, you might be hard pressed to come up with an answer. You just know that it *did* happen. Do you remember when your thoughts strayed all day long to your loved one and your pulse quickened when you saw him or her? For some, love and romance was a growing process and for others it was like a jolt of electricity.[5]

Love is not something that just happens; it must be cultivated so it can grow. As I work with couples in premarital counseling, one of my goals is to discover the quality of love they have for one another. If it is too idealistic or has a shallow base, I try to bring a sense of reality into their relationship. Occasionally couples do not want to hear the questions I ask. Sometimes they wonder why I do not accept their cliché-type answers, which do not always have the sense of realism that is needed.

Love Recession

Perhaps you are experiencing a love recession in your marriage.

Sometimes marital love is intense, strong and vibrant. But there are also times when you begin to question your love for your spouse or your spouse's love for you. For some reason, love recedes from a previously higher and more fulfilling level. Sometimes this occurs at predictable stages in marriage, such as after the honeymoon, during childbearing, when the empty nest occurs and so on. It can happen after 2 years of marriage, 20 years, or 40 years. Yes, just like a financial recession, a love recession can even happen to Christians who think their marriage will only climb upward.

When people feel that their love (or their partner's love) is weakening, they experience a multitude of feelings. A love recession can be frightening, frustrating and even depressing. Anxiety rises and you look for an answer. It can be threatening for a couple to face up to a sense of diminishing love, but it can also become a time of positive growth. It is like a financial crisis in which the way you respond can have a large bearing on your survival. Unlike the victim of a financial recession, however, you are never bankrupt of currency in a love recession. You never run out of love. You just need to look for it in some new places so you can grow and develop new love in your relationship. (See *Holding on to Romance,* for a complete discussion of this issue.)[6]

Six Styles of Love

People love and express their love in various ways. Are you aware of your style? Here are six basic styles of love.

1. Best Friends Love style is a comfortable intimacy that develops over a period of time. Two people have a close association and share mutual interests. Their love grows through companionship, rapport, mutual sharing and dependency and, over a period of time, self-revelation. It is rare at the beginning of the relationship for either person to believe their friendship will develop into love or marriage.

The love that does develop and is expressed is more of a thoughtful, warm response and not romantic or passionate. Intensity of feeling is a bit foreign to this relationship. Intense arguments or displays of emotion are lacking. When there is a difference of opinion, rational discussions prevail because the couple can draw upon a depth of warm and mutual affection.

2. Game-playing Love is a second style of love. To the game-playing lover, an emotional relationship is a contest to be won. Even when married these people seek a challenge to add spice to their relationship. Some even create risks to keep the marriage from becoming boring. Fighting and flirting are common.

3. Logical Love is a style in which a person concentrates upon the practical values that can be found in the relationship. These people are very pragmatic and often have a list of what they are looking for in a mate. Romance does have some place in the relationship, but love to the logical lover should be an outgrowth of a couple's practical compatibility. Their love is stable as long as they perceive the relationship to be one of a fair exchange.

4. Possessive Love is the most unfulfilling and limiting type of love. The possessive lover has a frantic need to know that he or she is loved. These people have frequent and intense emotional swings from elation to despair, and from devotion to jealousy. They have a driving need to possess and be possessed by their partner.

5. Romantic Love is best described as "two people involved in a totally emotional relationship." Romantic lovers, whose symbol is Cupid's arrow piercing a heart, are in love with love itself. Valentine's Day is as important to them as Christmas. Love at first sight is a necessity and a constant series of emotional highs are expected in the relationship. Physical attraction is very important, as are small and frequent romantic niceties and gestures.

6. Unselfish Love is a giving, forgiving, unconditionally caring and nurturing love. Self-sacrifice is involved. We love our partner even when he or she creates emotional pain for us. We respond more to the needs of our partner than to our own needs.

What is your basic style of love, as determined from the brief descriptions above? Use the chart below to rate yourself on a scale of 0-10 for each style (0 means nonexistent, 5 means average and 10 means very strong). Then do the same for your partner. Which style would you like to develop in yourself, and which would you like to see develop in your spouse?

You may discover that you are a combination of two or more styles. This is very common.

Best Friend Love	1	2	3	4	5	6	7	8	9	10
Game-playing Love	1	2	3	4	5	6	7	8	9	10
Logical Love	1	2	3	4	5	6	7	8	9	10
Possessive Love	1	2	3	4	5	6	7	8	9	10
Romantic Love	1	2	3	4	5	6	7	8	9	10
Unselfish Love	1	2	3	4	5	6	7	8	9	10[7]

Where Did My Feelings Go?

Q. I DON'T LOVE HIM ANYMORE. WHAT CAN I DO TO REGAIN MY LOVE FOR MY HUSBAND—LIKE WE HAD WHEN WE WERE FIRST MARRIED?

A. Do you feel like you do not love your husband? Describe for me in detail what love is? Can you? What are the ingredients that make up love? Before wanting something we need to know exactly what it is we want.

What Is Love?

Mature love has several ingredients:
- Feelings of warmth, which replace the intensity of infatuation.
- The feeling of caring as expressed in being concerned about your partner's welfare and being ready to respond to a need.
- Affection expressed in the way your partner prefers—anything from a note to a smile to a hug.
- Acceptance of the other person including his or her strengths

and weaknesses. It means not trying to make your spouse be a certain way in order to make up for a deficit in your past.

- Empathy, which means being able to tune in to your partner's feelings and to experience to some degree what he is experiencing.
- Mature love, which involves being sensitive to the delicate and vulnerable areas of your partner's concerns.
- Mature love also includes companionship, friendship, intimacy, pleasing and supporting the other.[8]

Rate Yourself

Now the questions:

On a scale of 0-10 (0 meaning nothing and 10 meaning "an abundance"), how do you rate your spouse for each of these characteristics?

What rating for each of these characteristics do you feel from your spouse?

What is the greatest level for each of these characteristics you have felt *for* your spouse?

What is the greatest level for each of these characteristics you have felt *from* your spouse?

Could it be that the reason you are struggling with love feelings for your spouse is that you do not feel loved by him?

One of the questions I ask those in counseling who are considering a divorce is, "Could you honestly say at this time that you have given 150 percent to loving your partner in each of these areas of love? If not, why not do that for the next three months; pull out all the stops and love him. Then if nothing happens, if you divorce, at least you can look back and say you gave it your all. At this point you can't really say that, can you?" What about you? Could you say that?

I find three common responses from people.

One is, "He doesn't love me in the special way I want him to." I understand that, but you don't want to be controlled in your love response by what he is or isn't doing, do you?

Second, some say, "I can't love until I feel like it. I'd be a hypocrite." You won't feel like it until you do it! People fall in love by doing things for and with another person and that is how they stay in love as well. Loving another does not depend upon our feelings.

Third, some have said, "If I do this my feelings might change somewhat and then I'd feel obligated to stay. I'm not sure I want to stay, especially if he doesn't change."

If you feel you do not love your partner, what have you done with that love energy? I often find that it still exists but has been directed elsewhere. It could be drained off by romance novels, soap operas, or even an imaginary involvement in your mind with another man; or you could even be on the verge of an affair because of your actual closeness with another man. It is difficult to generate love for your spouse when he has competitors who have no negative history like he does. Emotional deadness and coldness toward a spouse is reinforced when someone else enters the picture—either in your mind or in reality. I would encourage you to read the enlightening book by Lois Mowday entitled *The Snare* (NavPress). It has kept many women from straying.

Your Love Language

One reason why people feel their partners do not love them is that they have never fully clarified what their needs are and how their partners can specifically meet those needs. Everyone is unique and we each must learn to love the other in a way that registers. I have seen many who try to love their partner but keep missing the mark. In a simple way, each person must learn to speak a partner's love language. Do you know what I am talking about? If not, I would encourage you to read chapter 8 of *Holding on to Romance* for a full explanation.

But, you say, "You don't know how many times I've told my husband. It just won't work. He won't respond and I can't learn to love him." If you have done the following, then I'll keep quiet!

  1. Was it shared as a loving, healthy request or a nagging demand?

  2. Did you vary your presentation of requests or was it done in

the same predictable way each time? Was your request based on what you wanted rather than the specific negative action exhibited by your spouse?

3. Did you share your request in a communication style that matched his personality? More is said about this elsewhere in this book. Instead of ignoring his uniqueness, discover what his characteristics are and what they mean, and then adapt your responses to him.

4. Did you acknowledge the times that he did respond, affirm these episodes and describe the positive effect they had on you?

5. If it was not shared with him in writing, it has not been shared! As men tend to be single-minded and visually oriented, requests need to be shared in writing in order for them to register.

I know of one creative wife who sent her written list of ways in which she wanted to be loved to her husband at work in a certified letter. Enclosed in the letter was the key to a hotel room outside of town where she was waiting for him that evening. That got his attention!

Evaluate Your Behavior

You can allow a love recession to devastate you or you can respond to it as a time of growth and change. If and when a love recession hits, accept what you are experiencing and feeling as something that is quite normal. Do not deny your feelings. Instead, write them down—both positive and negative. Set up a convenient appointment to communicate your feelings. Then lovingly share the entire range of your thoughts and feelings with your partner, not as an ultimatum for him to change but as a point of information, signaling your interest in making your marriage stronger.

Evaluate your thought life toward yourself and your partner over recent months. Evaluate your behavior and your partner's behavior over that time and be sure you give yourselves credit for the positives.

We all have a tendency to focus on defects, failures and negatives rather than on the positives, even though the positives often outweigh the negatives. When our perspective is out of balance it often leads us to talk ourselves out of being in love with our partners!

Consciously try some new, loving behaviors toward your partner. Make a special effort to act out your love even if the feelings of love are not as strong as they once were. Consider the various ways of expressing your love to your partner that are suggested in this book.

Steps to Improve Love— and Stay in Love

Q. HOW DO I STAY "IN LOVE" WITH MY HUSBAND?

A. Let's consider some steps you can take to build and enhance the love in your marriage. The initial step is to identify the termites that might be weakening the structure. The contaminators in a marriage can subtly and steadily eat away at the foundation of a relationship.

Forgiveness

One of the worst contaminators in marriage is *unresolved anger,* which leads to resentment and eventually marital failure. Before you proceed it is essential to extend forgiveness; then you will have an opportunity to rebuild your love. Forgiveness is possible. I would encourage you to read chapter 6 of this author's book *Holding on to Romance,* Lewis Smedes' excellent book *Forgive and Forget,* and a helpful secular book called *The Forgiving Marriage* by Dr. Paul Coleman.

Just think about these words describing forgiveness:

> In forgiveness, you decide to give love to someone who has betrayed your love. You call forth your compassion, your wisdom, and your desire to be accepting of that person for who he

or she is. You call forth your humanness and seek reunion in love and growth above all else.

Forgiveness is the changing of seasons. It provides a new context within which to nurture the relationship. The changing of the seasons allows you to let go of all that has been difficult to bear and begin again. When you forgive, you do not forget the season of cold completely, but neither do you shiver in its memory. The chill has subsided and has no more effect on the present than to remind you of how far you've come, how much you've grown, how truly you love and are loved.

When forgiveness becomes a part of your life, little resentment is left. Anger may not vanish immediately, but it will wither in time. The hot core of bitterness that was embedded firmly in your being burns no more.

Forgiveness comes first as a decision to act lovingly, even though you may feel justified to withhold your love.[9]

Reflect on Your Courtship

One way to rebuild love is to *reflect upon your courtship*. It was during courtship that you probably experienced some of your most intimate and romantic feelings toward each other. This is the time when hopes, dreams and expectations for marriage are most intense. Because most couples build their relationship on romance, they rarely articulate what they expect in a relationship. What were your expectations during your courtship?

Remember the intense feelings of love you had toward each other. By reviewing your courtship, you can help establish hope for what can occur in the marriage now. If you were romantic during courtship you may now feel led to exert more effort to commit yourselves to redevelop your relationship.

Here are some questions to help you reflect on your courtship:

1. When was the last time you touched each other affectionately?

2. When was the first time you held hands? What was the setting? Do you remember how you felt?
3. What did you think of your partner the first time you kissed?
4. What attracted you to your partner?
5. In what way were your personalities alike then?
6. Recall your courtship—where and when did you meet? What
   did you most enjoy doing?
7. What were three of the most delightful experiences of your
   courtship?
8. What were your hopes and dreams for your marriage then?
9. What would it take for this to become a reality now?
10. If you were courting your partner now, how would you
    respond? Perhaps that's the answer!

Bless Your Husband

A unique way to keep love alive and fight recession is to *bless your
spouse*. The word "blessing" in the New Testament is based on two
Greek words that mean "well" and "word." Blessing your spouse lit-
erally means to speak well of that person.

You can bless your partner by what you say to him and how you
say it. You should speak lovingly and encouragingly in order to make
your mate's life better and fuller, not out of a sense of duty. Sincere
compliments, words of encouragement and "sweet somethings"
thoughtfully spoken are romance builders and love enrichers. Your
verbal response to your partner's words is important. Saying thank-
you, expressing appreciation and offering requested information or
opinions with kindness will bless your mate. Perhaps the ultimate
way of verbally blessing your partner is to lift that person to the Lord
in prayer and intervene on his behalf.[10] Verbal expressions of grati-
tude and affirmation cannot be overstressed.

Edify Your Husband

Another biblical approach to keeping love alive that parallels blessing is *edifying*. To edify means to build up another (see Rom. 14:19; 15:2; 1 Thess. 5:11). You can edify your husband by becoming his greatest fan. You are in the front row of the grandstand for your partner's every endeavor, cheering, "Go for it! You can do it! I believe in you!" You are the president of your spouse's fan club, encouraging, "You have the capability, value and worth regardless of the task. I'm praying for you."

As you edify your spouse in this way you will increase his sense of self-worth. The result will be an increase in your spouse's capacity to give of himself to you in love.

I like the ways Dr. Ed Wheat suggests for building up partners:

1. Make a decision to never again be critical of your partner in thought, word or deed. This should be a decision backed up by action until it becomes a habit that you would not change even if you could.

2. Spend time studying your spouse so you develop a sensitivity to the areas in which the person feels a lack. Discover creative ways to build up your spouse in those weak areas.

3. Spend time daily thinking of positive qualities and behavior patterns you admire and appreciate in your spouse. Make a list and thank God for these.

4. Consistently verbalize praise and appreciation and do this in a specific and generous manner.

5. Recognize what your spouse does, but also who your spouse is. Let him know that you respect him for what he accomplishes.

6. Husbands, publicly and privately show your wife how special she is to you. Keep your attention focused on your wife and not on other women.

7. Wives, show your husband how important he is in your life. Ask his opinion and value his judgments.

8. Respond to each other physically and facially. Our faces are the most distinctive and expressive parts of us. Smile with your total face. Your spouse needs to receive more of your smiles than others.

9. Be courteous to each other in private and in public. Each of you should be a VIP in your home.[11]

Recommended Reading and Listening:

Beck, Aaron T. *Love Is Never Enough*. New York: HarperCollins, 1988.

Coleman, Paul. *The Forgiving Marriage*. Chicago, IL: Contemporary Books, 1989.

Lewis, Robert, and Hendricks, William. *Rocking the Roles*. Colorado Springs, CO: NavPress, 1992.

Rainey, Dennis. *Staying Close*. Dallas, TX: WORD Inc., 1989.

Smalley, Gary. *If Only He Knew*. Grand Rapids, MI: Zondervan, 1979.

Smedes, Lewis. *Forgive and Forget*. New York: HarperCollins, 1984.

Wheat, Ed. *How to Save Your Marriage Alone*. Grand Rapids, MI: Zondervan, 1983. (Chapter 15)

Wheat, Ed. *Love Life*. Grand Rapids, MI: Zondervan Publishing House, 1980.

Wheat, Ed. "Love Life" two cassette tapes. (Available from Christian Marriage Enrichment, Tustin, CA.)

Wright, H. Norman. *Holding on to Romance*. Ventura, CA: Regal Books, 1992.

Notes

1. Doris Wild Helmering, *Happily Ever After* (New York: Warner Books, 1986), pp. 14,15, adapted.
2. Margaret J. Rinck, *Christian Men Who Hate Women* (Grand Rapids, MI: Zondervan, 1990), pp. 84,85, adapted.
3. Dennis Rainey, *Staying Close* (Dallas, TX: WORD Inc., 1989), p. 158.
4. Ibid., p. 158.
5. H. Norman Wright, *Holding on to Romance* (Ventura, CA: Regal Books, 1992), pp. 87-89.
6. Ibid., p. 118.
7. Marcia Lasswell and Norman N. Lobsenz, *Styles of Loving: Why You Love the Way You Do* (New York: Doubleday and Co. Inc., 1980), pp. 167,168.
8. Aaron T. Beck, *Love Is Never Enough* (New York: HarperCollins, 1988), pp. 185-189, adapted.
9. Paul W. Coleman, *The Forgiving Marriage* (Chicago, IL: Contemporary Books, 1989), pp. 22,23.
10. Ed Wheat, *Love Life* (Grand Rapids, MI: Zondervan Publishing House, 1980), pp. 177,178, adapted.
11. Ibid., pp. 178-191, adapted.

Chapter 14

ANGER AND CONTROL IN MARRIAGE

Coping with a Husband's Anger

Q. HOW CAN I COPE WITH MY HUSBAND'S ANGER?

A. Anger is one of the emotions that disrupts many marriages. Your question implies that your husband's anger is something to be tolerated and allowed to continue. The problem with anger is that it pushes people apart and furthers the distance between them.

To allow continual anger to run unchecked is destructive to a relationship. Anger is a God-given emotion and has a purpose, but it is to be controlled. Time and again in Scripture we read about being slow to anger (see Prov. 16:32 and Jas. 1:19).

Your first step is to determine if your husband's response is really anger. Sometimes men speak loud or with great intensity; if you came from a quiet, mellow background it is easy to interpret this as anger. The dictionary defines anger as a sense or response of displeasure. Is this what you are hearing?

Second, why do you want to reduce the amount of anger in your husband? You may simply find it distasteful or you might be fearful that it could get out of hand. You might also feel that it extends your disagreements rather than resolves them. When you discover what it is that bothers you about his anger, explain this to him verbally or in writing during a calm time. Express how you feel rather than attack him.

What is his anger saying? Sometimes a wife is able to determine this by using the following questions: "When you are angry and upset, is it because (1) you are frustrated? (2) feeling afraid? or (3) because you have been hurt? Perhaps you could consider these possibilities and talk about it later." These questions reflect the three underlying causes of anger, as it is a secondary emotion and does not usually reflect the true feeling or response.

For a man, anger feels stronger than hurt and fear, and thus safer. Many men work hard to cover their pain by shielding it with anger. Regardless of how intense and destructive your spouse's anger is, it is an expression of hurt, fear or frustration. But too often we all react to the camouflaged response, which is anger. If you can give your husband permission in your own heart and mind to be angry, it will be easier for you to handle his response.

Approach your husband by asking, "When you are angry, how do you want me to respond? Should I say nothing, leave the room, hold you, reflect back what I hear you saying, ask questions, or get angry back at you? Perhaps you could think about that for a while and we can discuss it when it's convenient for you." Hopefully he will respond in time and then you can ask, "What can I do to bring resolution? What suggestions do you have?"

Other statements some wives have made to their angry husbands are similar to this, "I understand there are times when you are angry. I would appreciate your working on conveying this anger in a way that doesn't push me away so much. I want to be close to you but this makes it difficult. Either write me a note telling me about your anger or take some time to diffuse it. When you are upset please tell me what you would like me to do differently and I will be happy to listen to what you have to say. It would also help if you would let me know if you're feeling frustrated, hurt or afraid so I really know what is going on."

Be sure you are doing nothing to contribute to or reinforce your husband's frustration or anger. I would encourage both you and your husband to read the book, *When Anger Hits Home* by Gary Oliver and this author, and *The Angry Man* by Dave Stoop (Word Books).

Releasing Your Anger

Q. HOW DO I RELEASE THE ANGER I FEEL? WHY CAN I FEEL DEPRESSED BUT NOT ANGRY?

A. Consider this fact: From childhood, most women are discouraged from expressing anger. They are taught to be the nurturers, soothers, peacemakers and stabilizers. The motto they learn is please the world and hold relationships in place. In an unspoken way, displayed anger in women is unladylike, unmaternal and even unattractive. It is not feminine to be angry.

Thus, many women are stuck with their anger and have nowhere to take it. And many learn to experience hurt rather than becoming angry in certain situations. The anger builds up over the years and when it is released it carries with it the accumulated residue. The result is overreaction.

When a woman expresses her anger toward her spouse, it creates distance and she does not feel much like a wife. She has a feeling of isolation. This is not comfortable; which is why when expressing anger, many women also express tears, guilt or sorrow. But this contaminates the expression of anger and confuses those around them. Many women quickly shift their feelings of anger into hurt. It is safer. And when you learn to bottle up one emotion, it sometimes causes emotional repression in other feelings.

When a woman cannot express either anger or tears, I would be concerned about a severe dysfunction that may have existed in her home. The deadening of feelings is both unhealthy and a sign to take action and discover why it occurred.

Many men and women experience depression when they bottle

up their anger. In fact, repressed anger is one of the major causes of depression. It is a dangerous way to handle anger because the anger remains alive inside us, churning around and looking for a way to come out. For many women, this is a learned response because of a lack of encouragement to experience anger.

When you do feel anger, admit it to yourself and perhaps even to someone else. Discover the cause. Is it frustration, hurt or fear? Listen to the message your anger is telling you. If you are concerned about overreacting with your anger, write it out in detail. Describe your feelings. Write an unmailed angry-letter and read it out loud. Look through the book of Proverbs and identify all the passages that talk about being "slow to anger." Visualize how you will be slow to anger.

When you express your anger, do it assertively rather than aggressively. Do not yell, blame or attack. Do not say, "You make me angry." Take responsibility for your anger. State that you are angry, why you are angry, and what you would like to see happen at this time. Practice doing this with a good friend so you can become comfortable. Do not apologize for your anger. It is there. It is yours. God created you with the capacity to be angry. Direct it toward injustices.

Dealing with Your Frustrations

Q. HOW CAN I HANDLE EMOTIONS THAT ERUPT FOR NO APPARENT REASON? (THESE ARE NOT PMS RELATED.)

A. Your question implies there is no cause for your emotions. But the causes are there. Sometimes our emotions are triggered by some small incident but are hooked into our historical reservoir of accumulated hurts. All it takes is some small stimulus to set them off. It could also be that we are sensitive in a certain area and other people's behaviors or statements cause us to react. Frustration can often be the trigger.

Frustration often happens when we are not getting our needs or expectations met. Sometimes we have shared these clearly with others, but often we have not and we expect them to know or automatically comply. Here are several questions that may help you get a handle on these unexplained emotional responses.

When are my emotional responses most apt to occur? Is there a pattern? Do particular situations contribute to these reactions? Do these reactions happen more in the morning, afternoon or evening? With whom do they occur? What do I say or do to express these emotions? How do they affect others?

Perhaps it would help to keep an emotions diary to chart your progress with this difficulty. Include in your diary:

1. The date and time my last emotional reaction occurred was...
2. The level of my feeling on a scale of 0 (none) to 10 (intense) was...
3. My emotional reaction was directed toward...
4. The way I felt inside was...
5. What I was saying to myself at this time was...
6. My outward response to others was...
7. Was there any difference in my response this time compared to the time before?
8. What would I like to feel and do the next time?
9. What improvement will I make the next time?
10. The way I will pray about this situation is...
11. The person I will enlist to assist me with this problem is...

Controlling the Controller

Q. HOW CAN I STOP LETTING MY HUSBAND CONTROL ME?

A. You may find it difficult to be open in the presence of a controller. You are always afraid that what you say will be used as ammunition against you. And controlling spouses usually do not respond openly. Their defenses have been honed to avoid openness. They are skilled at projecting onto you their own problems. The information given by a controller is usually slanted to show that he is right and the rest of the world is off base.

Do not be intimated. Do not try to fight fire with fire; it won't work. You cannot control a controller. Instead, give him permission from your heart and mind to be a controlling husband. Tell yourself it is okay for him to be this way. Assure yourself that you do not need to be intimidated by his controlling behavior.

Do not be negative. Let me ask you some questions. Do you talk with yourself about your husband and how you feel about his behavior? Do you focus on his unpleasant behavior and how you wish he would change? Or do you rehearse previous encounters with him and anticipate the worst scenario each evening? If you keep these negative "instant replays" and "previews of coming attractions" rolling in your mind, you will become physically drained and anxious.

Respond calmly. If you want to enter the mental film business, create some new films to project in your mind that show you responding in a healthy, affirming, nonintimidating manner toward your husband. See yourself responding calmly to him instead of resisting. It is possible.

Accept an insecure husband. One of the saddest statements I hear in the counseling office usually comes from a wife who is the victim of a dominating spouse: "It is so peaceful when my husband is gone. The family all gets along so well when he's away. But when he's at home we all tense up waiting for his outbursts. I know I shouldn't say this, but we're happier when he's away. We're tired of being ruled and controlled. That's not the way a family is supposed to live."

The control described by this woman reflects the insecurity that drives her dominating husband. Keep in mind that the roar of the dominator is usually just a shield covering up a frightened, insecure person.

Be in control. Do not allow your husband to sidetrack you from what you want to say to him. When he interrupts you, come back to what you want to say, although you may need to start your sentence several times. This is a variation of the broken-record technique, which involves making the same statement again and again in order to stay in control and get your point across.

When your husband insists on making a point, acknowledge what he says, then offer your alternatives. But remember, the way you share your ideas is very important.

Introduce alternatives. Years ago, one of my counselees shared how she had learned to introduce alternatives to her controlling husband. This is what she said:

> For years I was just overwhelmed by him. I cared for him, but his tendency to control me and dominate our social relationships was alienating me from our friends. I have learned to do three things which soften his tendency to control.
>
> First, I ask questions to encourage him to fully explain his controlling actions. One question I always ask is, "What will be the benefits of this action for you and what will be the benefits for me?" That question has stumped him a few times.
>
> Second, I've learned to say, "Jim, you know me. I always like to hear two good ideas instead of one. Give me one good alternative to what you are suggesting that we do." Now and then he actually comes up with two workable alternatives.
>
> Third, I request a delay in Jim's decision making. I simply say, "I would like some time to think this over." I know it frustrates him at times, but he's learned that I can't be hurried into a decision. He knows I need time to sort through his argument and he is more willing to give me the time I need.

I have seen this technique work in marriage situations in which one spouse is constantly oozing criticism in order to wrest control.

Look to God. When you discover you are acceptable to God, you will look to Him for direction and approval. And by being acceptable to yourself, you take ownership of your feelings, attitudes and behavior. If you are aligned with God and with what He wants you to be, you do not need to be afraid of criticism or try to justify your position. You have the power to make your own choices and to grow through an experience.

Be nondefensive. As a nondefensive wife, you will respect and feel good about yourself. You will believe in your worth and your capabilities. You will possess your own identity and sense of security. Being nondefensive, you can listen to others more objectively and evaluate better what your husband is saying, even when he expresses himself in a negative manner. You can accept him for who he is, even if you do not agree with him.

Identify the cause of attack. Ask yourself, "What can I learn from this experience? Is there a grain of truth in what I am hearing to which I need to respond?" Asking these questions will shift you from the position of a defendant in the relationship to that of an investigator. Your spouse's attack may be grossly exaggerated, unreasonable and unfair. Disregard the false statements. Give him permission to exaggerate and blow off steam. Eventually the exaggerated statements will drift away like chaff and only the truth will remain. Keep searching for the grain of truth. Try to identify the real cause for his critical attack.

Determine the issues. Try to determine precisely what it is you do that bothers your husband. If he behaves like this every day, you probably already know. Ask specific questions such as, "Will you please elaborate on the main point?" or "Can you give me a specific example?"

Use a checking-listening technique to verify what the critic is saying. Statements that begin, "I think you might be saying..." or "Are you suggesting that..." will help you further clarify the point of contention and move the issue toward resolution.

You might say, "I'm going to take a few minutes to think this over," or "That's an interesting perspective you have given. I need to think about it." Then ask yourself, "What is the main point he's trying to make? What does he want to have happen as a result of our discussion?" Sometimes it is helpful to clarify that point with him by asking, "What would you like me to do differently as a result of our discussion? I'm really interested in knowing." Men usually do not expect this approach.

Explain your position. Once the central issue has been identified, confidently explain your position rather than withering under the attack.

Regardless of how hostile or destructive your husband's criticism may be, perhaps there is some truth in what he is saying. If you are able to acknowledge any true issues, you will communicate to your husband that he has been heard and that you are not defensive. You can say, "You know, there could be some truth in what you say." You have not admitted to anything, but you are leaving the door open to the possibility. Your response will disarm him and he may have to reconsider his approach. In doing this you will retain your dignity, feel better about yourself and model a biblical pattern of responding to criticism.

> It is a badge of honor to accept valid criticism (Prov. 25:12, *TLB*).
>
> What a shame—yes, how stupid!—to decide before knowing the facts! (Prov. 18:13, *TLB*).
>
> Don't refuse to accept criticism; get all the help you can (Prov. 23:12, *TLB*).
>
> A man who refuses to admit his mistakes can never be successful. But if he confesses and forsakes them, he gets another chance (Prov. 28:13, *TLB*).

Recommended Reading:

Oliver, Gary, and Wright, H. Norman. *Pressure Points: Women Speak Out on Anger and Other Life's Demands.* Chicago, IL: Moody Press, 1993.

Oliver, Gary, and Wright, H. Norman. *When Anger Hits Home.* Chicago, IL: Moody Press, 1992.

Lush, Jean. *Emotional Phases of a Woman's Life.* Tarrytown, NY: Fleming H. Revell, 1990.

Chapter 15

ABUSIVE HUSBAND

Abuse Defined

Q. HOW DO I LOVE AND FORGIVE MY HUSBAND
WHEN HE ABUSES ME?

A. Whenever the issue of abuse is raised in my counseling office, I need to have the word "abuse" defined. Sometimes what we call abuse is not abuse but a form of expression different from our own. In other cases it is abuse! Verbal, emotional and physical abuse occur far too often in our Christian families. An estimated one out of every two families in our country experience some form of domestic violence *every year.* Abuse is any behavior designed to control and/or subjugate another person through the use of fear, humiliation, and verbal or physical assaults. Humiliating, making fun of and putting down a child or even a spouse can be abusive.

Physical Abuse
Physical abuse refers to brutal, deliberate physical contact rather than accidental occurrences. This can include any behavior that either

intends to inflict or actually does inflict physical harm. Primarily, it consists of pushing, grabbing, shoving, slapping, kicking, biting, choking, punching, hitting with an object, or attacking with a knife or a gun.

Emotional Abuse

Emotional abuse has a multitude of expressions. Scare tactics, insults, yelling, temper tantrums, name-calling and continual criticism fall into this classification. Some people point out the defects of their family members in a way that makes the members feel as if they had been stabbed with a serrated knife. Threatened violence is a form of emotional abuse, too. Holding up a weapon, swinging a fist near a person's face, destroying property or kicking a child's pet falls in this category. Withholding privileges or affection or constantly blaming one family member for the family's difficulties is abuse.

I have heard some people defend their shouting pattern of behavior as normal. They say, "That's just the way we did it in our family. Everyone shouted and we accepted it. That isn't abuse." But in their new family it may become abuse because of the sensitivity of the other family members. Shouting can become terrifying if it is consistent, intense and very loud.[1]

Verbal Abuse

If verbal abuse is constant, seek counseling immediately. If you (or your children) are being verbally abused, confront your husband directly at a calm time. Explain what you have experienced, how it affects you and the children, and what you would appreciate your husband doing instead. Then thank him for both listening to what you have said and for considering it.

When you see your husband responding more positively, reinforce what he is doing. But when his anger turns to physical abuse and violence is the time to protect yourself and the children. The best—and really only—way this works is to immediately separate, and seek a restraining order. If there is physical harm, you may need to report him to the authorities. Definitely do so if he has harmed your children.

Seek the help and support of an abuse center and encourage your spouse to seek counseling. Do not listen to those who tell you to stay, be submissive and change him through your response. Too many women have sustained permanent physical and emotional damage—some have lost their lives.

Many engaged women believe they are marrying a caring, loving man because he acted loving and caring during courtship. But they soon discover they have actually married a misogynist—a woman hater. Author Dr. Susan Forward suggests the following checklist about your relationship with the man in your life.

- Does he assume the right to control how you live and behave?
- Have you given up important activities or people in your life in order to keep him happy?
- Does he devalue your opinions, your feelings, and your accomplishments?
- Does he yell, threaten, or withdraw into angry silence when you displease him?
- Do you "walk on eggs," rehearsing what you will say so as not to set him off?
- Does he bewilder you by switching from charm to rage without warning?
- Do you often feel confused, off-balance, or inadequate with him?
- Is he extremely jealous and possessive?
- Does he blame you for everything that goes wrong in the relationship?[2]

If you answered yes to most of these questions, you are involved with a misogynist. And if so, you would benefit by becoming much more aware of this kind of man and how you can learn to respond.

Abusive Husband

Read the books in the recommended reading section at the end of this chapter.

Changing a Husband's Abusive Behavior

Q. HOW CAN I CHANGE MY HUSBAND'S ABUSIVE BEHAVIOR? WHY DO I STAY WITH A MAN WHO IS ABUSIVE?

A. Some time back a woman made an appointment to see me. When she came in, part of her problem was apparent. One eye was blackened and patches of hair were missing from her head, the result of her husband pounding her head against the bathroom floor. Needless to say, she was terrified of her husband.

The couple had been married for 10 years and had 2 young children. He was fairly well known in the community and was a Sunday School teacher at their church. He was respected by others and had served on the church board at one time. Once a month he exploded with no visible provocation or warning. The beatings had become more frequent and violent and were physically apparent on the victim. Shortly before her visit to my office, she had experienced bruised ribs, which hindered her ability to do the housework. In time, her husband became irate over this, which had caused the latest incident.

When the husband was willing to discuss the problem, he blamed his wife. Most of the time he refused to talk about these incidents and demanded that she do as he said.

As she talked, she cried in frustration. He had been beating her for three years, and no one else knew about it. "He's like a Dr. Jekyll and Mr. Hyde," she said to me. "When he's nice, he's nice. But when he's mean, watch out. I shouldn't be here today. He'll flip when he finds out! I'm afraid for the children as well. What should I do? I want my marriage. I do care for him but I can't take the violence any more. I don't believe in divorce but I don't believe in this either. I'm tired of doing his bidding, and it doesn't keep him from becoming angry. So, now what?"

Taking Charge of Abusive Behavior

This counselee had several options and the consequences of each needed to be considered carefully.

1. She could continue as she had been doing and allow the situation to exist. But this would increase the possibility of being beaten again. Without realizing it, allowing the situation to continue merely encouraged her husband to continue his violence. He was not the one experiencing negative consequences. *Being passive will not work.*

2. She could divorce him. This was not an option for her and thus was not the answer.

3. She could emotionally insulate herself. Without realizing it, she may have already started the process. In most cases, emotional insulation creates an emotional divorce so the psychological pain can be blocked out. But the physical abuse will continue and emotional insulation carries the risk of deadening oneself emotionally to everyone—not just one's husband. As well, this type of insulation makes an individual more vulnerable to an affair.

4. The counselee could take charge of the situation and create a crisis. No guarantee exists, but an approach like this has worked for many. At the time of our appointment, the counselee was allowing herself to be both abused and controlled. Also, her husband was learning that he could get away with it. No woman should ever subject herself to *any* abuse.

I suggested she plan in advance a statement she would make to her husband about the situation. It would be simple and factual in stating her intentions. I encouraged her to first write it out and rehearse it verbally, perhaps with another person. Then, either at a time when her husband was demanding that she do something unreasonable or at a calm moment, she should make her statement. This would probably upset him and throw him off balance, but the crisis it precipitated might change the destructive marital pattern.

Here are the steps to follow if you find yourself in a similar situation:

- Let a trusted friend, relative, or counselor know about the problem and what you intend to do. Stay away from those who disagree with this approach or give a lot of unsolicited advice.
- If necessary, arrange for a safe place to stay for yourself and your children. Make financial plans for this step as well.
- Be committed to follow through once this procedure is started.
- Make a statement to your spouse along these lines:

I have something I need to share with you and I want you to hear me out. Because I care about you, myself, and our marriage, I am going to make some changes. First of all, I will no longer be doing everything that you demand of me. We will discuss the issues as two adults. You may become upset at this but that is your choice.

Second, I will no longer submit to nor tolerate any physical violence on your part. If you ever lay a hand on me again, I will take two steps. I will call the authorities and press charges and I will separate from you and take the children with me. And because I care about you, myself, and the children, we will stay separated until you have begun professional help for yourself and we both enter into marriage counseling.

Third, I feel that in order to overcome what causes you to respond with such anger and violence, I want you to seek professional help at this time. I have discussed this concern with others and they agree with me. I have the name of a professional counselor and I am willing to go with you if you so desire. And I will continue to make this latter request of you each week until you go for help.

- When you decide on a time to share this with your spouse, ask those who are aware of the problem to be praying for you.
- Your statement should be presented calmly, slowly and with confidence. But, what happens if he interrupts, goes into a rage, stalks out, or becomes violent?

If he interrupts, lean forward or stand up and use hand motions to indicate that *you* are interrupting *him* and say, "Please wait until I've finished" in a calm, directive voice. Then start over.

If he raises objections, argues, or becomes angry, use the broken record approach and repeat word for word what you have said. If he starts to become violent, take the children and leave. Put your statement into action.

You can employ other alternatives to this approach as well. If your spouse tends toward excessive violence, enlist the support of a minister or of family members to be present when you make your confrontation. But remember, you are the spokesperson and they are there for physical support and protection.

If your church has a couple in which one spouse is a reformed abuser, enlist their support for the confrontation.

Either write out your statement word for word or make a cassette tape and send it to your husband at work by certified mail. State that you will meet him at a specific time for dinner at a quiet restaurant to discuss the situation. Get a baby-sitter to take care of the children for the evening.

These are all unexpected, unpredictable, different forms of behavior indicating that you mean business. They may sound like radical suggestions, but destructive behavior calls for radical changes. No one can guarantee the outcome but if some new approach is not employed, either the marriage or a life will be destroyed.

Why would a woman want to stay in an abusive relationship? Many of them tend to be tolerant of abuse because they came from violent homes. Often the woman blames herself and holds herself responsible. She also tends to make excuses for her husband. Battered women also tend to grow up with low self-esteem, which makes them more vulnerable to attacks. They also tend to put others' needs before their own and they are rescuers. Their hopes are unrealistic because they believe a husband when he says he will change.

Most battered women tend to be socially isolated. They do not have any social support and this tends to reinforce their lack of resources to deal with the problem. Many of them are also emotionally and economically dependent.[3]

Handling a Husband's Defensive Behavior

Q. WHEN WE HAVE A PROBLEM IN OUR MARRIAGE, WHY DOES MY HUSBAND ALWAYS SHIFT THE PROBLEM TO ME AND BECOME DEFENSIVE?

A. Most men are defensive because they do not like to admit or acknowledge when they are wrong or have made a mistake. Even properly worded suggestions can be received as if they had done something wrong. And they often feel that to respond to the suggestions would actually be an admission of guilt. I have talked to some men who told me they were willing to consider what their wives suggested but the suggestions never ended. When they complied with one item, another seemed to take its place.

The more stressed out a man is, the more he may tend to react in a defensive manner. When any suggestion directly indicates or subtly implies that he has failed in some way, he will experience stress. The *fear of failure* and *being out of control* are two of the major stressors for men.

So what can you do about it? First, identify what you have been doing that has not been working. Too often we use the same approach over and over and become predictable, making it easy for our spouse to remain defensive.

My Personal PJ Episode

I remember a time when my wife used a positive shock experience to help me change. Several years ago I had the habit of not hanging up my pajamas in the morning when I got up and dressed. I would toss them toward the hook on the door—where they belong. Sometimes my basketball shots landed, but most of the time I missed. And from time to time, Joyce suggested that it might be nice if I would hang them up myself each day. But nothing seemed to change.

I will never forget the day I was sitting on the couch reading the paper when Joyce came up and sat next to me with my pajamas folded neatly on her lap. She put her arm around me, smiled, and said, "Norm, you are a man of excellent organizational ability and deep concern for being precise, accurate, in control, and orderly. I just know you would delight in knowing that when you left for work each morning, you could reflect back and remember that when you arose and started the day, you had taken off your pajamas, walked over to the hook on the closet door, and carefully hung first the tops and then the bottoms on the appropriate hook. I'm sure that would really help make your day. Thank you for listening." And with that she stood up and left the room.

I was taken totally off guard. I had listened a bit shocked at this unusual approach and I sat there grinning. But little did I know what had been done to me because about a month later I realized that since that day I had been hanging up my pajamas. I was hardly aware that I was changing but she certainly got my attention.

How to Have a Creative Crisis

Another approach is again quite direct but sometimes effective.

Whenever behaviors within a marriage or family relationship are destructive and detrimental, such as infidelity or abuse, one of the best approaches is to create a major crisis. This approach will not be easy because it goes counter to many years of reinforcing patterns of behavior and response. This is where Dr. James Dobson's book title, *Love Must Be Tough,* is so appropriate. You must be tough but loving. You must take a stand. A person who is an abuser, adulterer, alcoholic or gambler is helped the most by being confronted with his behavior and given a loving ultimatum. The person is not helped by being allowed to continue his behavior and having his spouse cover for him.

Before you confront your husband about a major marital problem, you need to take several steps.

1. You need to prayerfully consider what to do and spend lots of time seeking God's will.

2. It may be helpful to discuss the problem with a qualified person who believes in the confrontational approach.

3. Spend time writing down the typical ways you respond to your spouse's bad behavior, including the specific statements you make. Then write out and rehearse out loud what you will say instead of your usual responses. Try to anticipate your spouse's response so you can prepare yourself for his reply.

Be sure you are familiar with the use of the broken record technique in case you need to use it. It has proven to be very effective. The broken record technique entails being persistent and saying over and over again what you want without becoming angry, obnoxious, irritated, loud or out of control. You stick to your point as though you were a record with the needle stuck. You ignore all side issues that are raised and also ignore a request for reasons behind the confrontation (Why are you doing this to me?). You are not thrown by what the other person says and you continue to be persistent.

For example:

Joan: Jim, I'm concerned about the amount of time you've been gone and I thought it might be helpful for us to look over our schedules.

Jim: Oh, good grief! There you go again, griping about my schedule. You like the money I bring home, don't you?

Joan: I understand you're making good money but I am concerned about the amount of time you're gone and would like to talk about it.

Jim: Well, my schedule is set and that's that. What about you? What do you do with all the time you spend around here? The house could use some cleaning.

Joan: You could be right about the house and I will work on it. I am concerned about the amount of time you're gone and feel it would be good for both of us to look at our schedules.

Jim: Look at what? Why should I be here more? We don't do anything!

Joan: Jim, I am concerned about your time away and would really like to discuss this with you.

Jim: (pause) Well, what's there to discuss?

When you are repetitive and persistent, the other person often realizes he cannot sidetrack you and perhaps reluctantly begins to discuss the issue.

The attitude in which you create a crisis is the main element to consider. A timid, pleading approach, or a hostile, angry tact is not the answer. Becoming angry with a child is not effective; nor is it with a spouse. Action is needed. A calm, serious confidence must be expressed.

It is important to rehearse and practice what will be said in advance. Do not share all the pain and hurt you have experienced. Do not share all of what you are thinking or plan to do—and above all do not be predictable. The crisis could include changing your daily routine, the way you fix meals or do tasks around the home, altering your time table, how much you talk, and so on. Show that you are strong and in control. But you do need to act in love. Do not do anything that might undermine your husband's relationship with other members of the family who do not know what is happening. Your goal is to build a new relationship.[4]

Recommended Reading:

Forward, Susan. *Men Who Hate Women and the Women Who Love Them*. New York: Bantam Books, 1986.

Rinck, Margaret J. *Christian Men Who Hate Women*. Grand Rapid, MI: Zondervan Publishing House, 1990.

Notes
1. Gary Jackson Oliver and H. Norman Wright, *When Anger Hits Home* (Chicago, IL: Moody Press, 1992), p. 199.
2. Susan Forward, *Men Who Hate Women and the Women Who Love Them* (New York: Bantam Books, 1986.
3. Grant Martin, *Counseling for Family Violence and Abuse* (Dallas, TX: WORD In., 1987), pp. 35-41, adapted.
4. H. Norman Wright, *How to Have a Creative Crisis* (Dallas, TX: WORD Inc., 1986), p. 149.

Chapter 16

MARRIAGE HOT BUTTONS: FINANCES, ALCOHOLISM, IN-LAWS

Husband's Financial Irresponsibility

Q. HOW CAN I DEAL WITH MY HUSBAND'S
FINANCIAL IRRESPONSIBILITY?

A. Money conflicts in marriage are common, but it is the emotional significance attached to money that makes it such a volatile issue. When money differences occur, perhaps the underlying questions are, "Don't you trust me? How much can I trust you?"

In most relationships, money has several meanings. Finances can be a symbol of trust and security, a means of control, a reflection of wanting to be dependent and independent. Money can also be a means of status and esteem. What were the beliefs and concerns that you brought with you into marriage? What were your spouse's? Are you a spender or a saver? What is he? What does money mean to you and to him? These underlying questions and issues need to be clarified.

How do you approach your husband about your concerns? Do you call his behavior "financial irresponsibility"? If so, do not expect much of a response except for defensiveness or anger. Share your feeling of concern or insecurity in a loving way so he can understand what it is that concerns you. If you see a spending pattern that spells trouble, be precise and specific about your concerns so that you convey a clear message to your husband. Document specifically what you see as well as the consequences of any financial irresponsibility.

Do you have money for all the monthly obligations or are you going deeper into debt each month because of your husband's spending habits? Do you have a budget with a personal allotment for each person to do as he or she wants? Who established the budget and do you both agree with it?

Have you ever sought counsel from a competent Christian financial advisor? That may be the next step. And if money is just one of several conflicts in your marriage, seeking counseling for all your issues may need to be next on the agenda.

Sometimes the problem is that each of you places a different value on money. If this is the case, be sure you do the following:

1. Develop a set routine for paying the fixed monthly expenses the first of each month. If one tends to be a spender, this will guarantee that the essentials are paid first.

2. Keep some money separate for each of you so that neither feels confined or controlled by the other's habits.

3. If one person tends to build up debts, a strong confrontation may be necessary because *you* may be mutually responsible for the person's debts. Work toward depositing all paychecks in the bank and have a limit on how much cash each one has per week. Keep all checks and credit cards at home and work toward an agreement that any purchase over $50 must be discussed together.

4. Discuss your financial priorities so each of you understands the other.

Planning and Keeping a Budget

Q. HOW DO I GET MY HUSBAND TO HELP PLAN A BUDGET
AND STAY WITHIN IT? HE SAYS HE WANTS A BUDGET, BUT
THEN HE GOES AND SPENDS AND SPENDS.

A. Do you currently have a budget? You want to work toward a mutually agreed upon budget, as well as a commitment to follow it. Ask your husband, "What can we do to make sure we follow this budget?" Then make a plan. Every two weeks meet together to discuss how the budget is working. If you already have a budget, but your spouse refuses to stick to it, his spending habits could have another meaning. Does your husband have self-control in other areas of his life or is irresponsibility a consistent pattern throughout? If so, money problems are another manifestation of impulsiveness and there are other reasons for his irresponsible behavior.

If your husband has agreed to a budget and then violates it you may want to say, "We need help. We have agreed to a budget and then the agreement is broken. I don't fully understand why this happens but it is affecting our financial status and my trust for you. Perhaps we need to be accountable to someone else, such as a group of other couples who have worked through this, one of our ministers or a financial advisor. I am getting desperate and am scared of what might happen to us financially. I love you and want the best for us. What do you suggest we do?"

If your husband says he will stick to the budget, follow up with, "What is your plan for sticking to it? What is going to make this work this time and how can I help you with your plans to follow through?" You will need to be clear, specific, persistent and supportive. And if this does not work, go for assistance yourself and let your husband know that you are going.

Dealing with an Alcoholic Husband

Q. HOW CAN I DEAL WITH MY ALCOHOLIC HUSBAND?

A. When one person in a family is an alcoholic, everyone suffers. Most of us have suffered from this problem in one way or another. You may feel as the psalmist felt: "You have shown your people desperate times; you have given us wine that makes us stagger....Save us and help us with your right hand, that those you love may be delivered" (Ps. 60:3,5).

One of the raging questions today is whether alcoholism is a sin or a disease. To sum up the discussion and controversy—it is both. Alcoholism is a disease but an alcoholic is still accountable for deciding whether or not to drink and whether to accept or reject assistance in overcoming this problem.

How to Help Your Husband

The first step for you to take is to become an expert on alcoholism through extensive reading and by going to an Al-Anon group or an Overcomers Outreach group. There are no shortcuts. You have a major problem in your family and you have probably tried to handle it in many ways. You may have thrown out all the alcohol around the house, begged, nagged, yelled, reasoned, bargained, asked others not to give him drinks, threatened to separate or divorce, kept track of how much your husband drinks, gone looking for him and cut him off from the finances. And nothing worked. These methods do not help.

The three most important steps you can take are *confrontation, detachment* and *intervention.* Confrontation has nothing to do with judgment. It points out facts and deals with your relationship to your husband; its purpose is to salvage love, heal the relationship and help it grow.

Certain things need to be avoided in helping your husband. As you make changes, do not explain why, do not try to be his therapist, do not ask him why he does what he does and do not make ultimatums you are not ready to keep. Confront him whenever you feel his drinking is affecting you or your children. Morning is usually the best time. Do not ever try to talk to him when he is under the influence of alcohol. Be factual and to the point—immediately. Tell him what he did and how it made you feel.

Do not moralize, preach or give any predictions for the future. Leave out your own opinions and conclusions. Do not repeat yourself. It does not matter whether your husband acknowledges whether he heard you or not. Your tone of voice is the key. If it is moralistic and judgmental, you have lost him. Do not express anger or fear. Keep it as neutral as possible. Use "I" messages.

If your husband accuses you or becomes angry, stay out of an argument. That is not your purpose. Do mention promises he has made to remind him that you expect him to follow through. You can recommend Alcoholics Anonymous (AA) or Overcomers Outreach, but do not nag about it. Be sure you have the information handy if he happens to respond to your suggestion. When he does something you appreciate, affirm him. He needs your compliments and reinforcement. If his drinking has created a conflict or problem, do not rescue him. Stay out of it and let him handle the consequences.[1]

Tough love. Detachment is part of the process of changing yourself, and this must occur. This involves disengaging your emotional overinvolvement with your husband and the situations he gets you into. It does not mean you stop loving and caring for him, even though he may interpret what you are doing as exactly that. It means you allow him to fully experience the negative consequences of his drinking behavior. This is compassion, not cruelty.

In a sense this is a form of tough love. It is reflected in your refusing to cover for him anymore. Let him find his way home at night. Do not call his workplace for him and say he is "sick." Do not bail him out financially. If he is picked up for drunk driving, let him stay in jail for a while. I have seen this work wonders. Do not put up with any physical or verbal abuse.

Intervention. Years ago the thinking concerning alcoholics was that they had to "hit bottom" before they would ever go for help. The advent of the intervention process, however, helps you to raise the "bottom" and make it occur sooner. Here is a description of what an intervention is as described by Pauline Bartosch, cofounder of Overcomers Outreach Inc., which is one of the finest ministries available to help with alcoholism and other addictive problems.

Intervention is usually successful only when carried out with the help of a professional counselor who is specially trained in intervention techniques. Family members should NEVER think they can pull this off by themselves. Emotions are too involved, making objectivity next to impossible. Although pulling the rug out from under a chemically dependent person is difficult, it is often the best favor we could do for him and may well save his life. You can no longer afford to make idle threats that are never carried out. You must ask yourself, "What am I willing to risk to save this person's life?" Then you offer your addicted loved one the CHOICE of either getting help, or possibly forfeiting his job, his home, or even his family.

Concerned family members, close friends, and hopefully the alcoholic's employer meet together with the professional interventionist, usually at a treatment facility or hospital program. The confrontation is carefully planned and rehearsed during several sessions without the alcoholic's knowledge. Together they plan the strategy for helping the alcoholic recognize how his disease has affected him and his loved ones. Then, at a later designated time, the alcoholic is invited by a loved one to go along to just one counseling session with the professional counselor.

Meanwhile, the significant people in his life have already gathered at the agreed location. In this surprise encounter, the alcoholic is greeted by the people who are closest to him. A concerted effort is made, at just one sitting, to make the evidence so overwhelming that the alcoholic will become fully aware of the sum total of his true condition. During these sessions, each person has come prepared with a list of specific instances during which he has been hurt, embarrassed or upset by the alcoholic's behavior. All during this strategic meeting, angry, hurtful words must be replaced by bare, factual statements spoken kindly. Whatever it takes to get the alcoholic in the door of this first encounter is truly worth the effort. Sometimes it works to invite him to come just to listen "this one time."[2]

Mother-in-law Problems

Q. HOW CAN I HANDLE MY RELATIONSHIP WITH MY MOTHER-IN-LAW? SHE SEEMS TO INTERFERE IN OUR LIVES SO MUCH.

A. This is not just your problem. It is also your husband's problem. You and your husband need to identify exactly what it is that bothers you (and realize it may not bother your husband as much as it does you). Then decide what you would like to have change. It may take the two of you sitting down with your mother-in-law and clarifying what bothers you and what you would appreciate from her in the future. Expect your mother-in-law to be offended, surprised, sad, to cry, be angry and maybe not get in contact with you for a while. These are normal reactions. But in time the relationship can become much stronger. For this to happen, however, it takes planning on your part.

Do Plan

If you want a change in a relationship with your mother-in-law, begin by establishing what has been called a "Do Plan." This approach always focuses upon positive behavior and positive changes. In implementing this plan, you consider the behavior of your mother-in-law as well as your own responses to her. Look at yourself, for you can control only what you do, not what others do. Because you are younger than your mother-in-law, you also have greater flexibility in making changes. It would be nice if your in-laws would make the necessary behavioral changes you want. But if they cannot, it is up to you to either learn new ways of responding to them or decide not to see them as often.

In creating your plan, first ask yourself if what you are doing in response to your mother-in-law is really helping you and the relationship. Do not be concerned about the past or the future right now, just the present. If you find some aspect of your in-law relationship is troubling to you, select a small area of the relationship that you would like to change. Write down what you want to change and the way you will go about making this change. What you write down must be detailed and specific. Do not leave anything to chance.

Again it must be emphasized that your plans must focus only upon the positive. Negative plans will not work as well. For example, if you often get into a quarrel or argument with your mother-in-law, do not write in your plan, "When I see her I will not argue or quarrel with her." It would be better to say, "When I get together with my mother-in-law, I will be friendly and warm, and ask her positive questions. I will thank her for her suggestion but clearly let her know that I'm doing it a different way. If she suggests it again I will say, 'Mother, what did I say a few minutes ago about how I would do it? I did hear you.'"

If your mother-in-law usually drops in unexpectedly, ask her to always call first. It is your home.

One couple visited their in-laws or was visited by them only once a year because of distance and travel expense. But beginning two weeks prior to their visit the couple spent several hours planning how they wanted to respond to their parents and in-laws. They rehearsed ways of responding to what they knew might arise as minor irritations. The visits were always enjoyable. Could you and your husband do this?

As you plan, it is important that you see yourself as the active person. Success does not hinge upon what any other person does.

Husband Not Getting Along with In-laws

Q. HOW CAN I ENCOURAGE MY HUSBAND TO GET ALONG WITH MY PARENTS?

A. The old adage, "You don't marry a person, you marry a family," was meant to be humorous and yet it is true. But not everyone is willing to accept this truism. Getting along with difficult in-laws takes time, patience and effort.

Here are some suggestions. Decide to yourself what you mean by "not getting along." Do you mean they argue and quarrel or they do not spend time together? Or do they just not have very much in common? It is important to specifically define what you see as the problem, but then be open to hearing how your spouse feels and how he sees the issue. Does your spouse get along with his own parents? If not, he could be projecting this problem onto your parents.

Sometimes our parents can be offensive but because of our own loyalty we overlook what others won't tolerate. Often in-law conflicts occur because we want to spend more time with our own parents rather than with our in-laws. When parents live close by, it is often easier for an adult child to visit them more frequently than the spouse is willing to visit. And nothing is wrong with such solo visits. When parents live far away, it takes some creative adjustment to visit them. And if your parents do live far away, are your yearly vacations spent in visiting in-laws? This may be satisfactory for one spouse but not for the other. Splitting up your holiday or alternating where you go on vacation may be the answer.

Above all, listen to how your partner feels and together brainstorm some alternatives to what you are doing now. Sometimes it could be an act of love on your partner's part to spend time with in-laws who have nothing in common with him. He feels a sense of obligation. Sometimes your parents feel obligated, too, and both parties feel the strain of having to make small talk. Be patient, keep the visits brief and it may work better for everyone.

Putting Own Family Before His Parents

Q. HOW CAN I GET MY HUSBAND TO PUT ME BEFORE HIS PARENTS IN MATTERS OF DECISION MAKING AND TIME?

A. It is difficult when a sense of competition begins to develop between a spouse and in-laws. Does your husband put his own parents first? If so, does he put both parents ahead of you, or just his mother? This is much more common. More conflicts occur between the mother-in-law and the son's wife than any other in-law relationship. The two women seem to create conflict between themselves.

Are your husband's parents putting the pressure on him or does he volunteer to become more involved? Sometimes parents do not let go of a son when he marries. Or is your husband still trying to please his parents? Talk with your husband about your concern and ask him what he thinks are his parents' expectations of him. Then ask what his expectations are for his relationship with his parents. Asking for a response in writing may be helpful. I have asked some counselees how their parents would survive if they weren't around to help them. When the adult child says, "They would do fine," I suggest they begin to allow them to do fine now.

Are you pressuring your husband not to be involved with his parents? If so, you may actually be pushing him closer to his parents! Sometimes husbands use their parents to escape from their own marital unhappiness. Are you involved with your husband when he visits them or do you separate yourself from him and his family? Perhaps participating and being more involved will help. Let your spouse know that you will look forward to knowing his plans to visit his family. As well, you will appreciate knowing how he wants to spend time with them, and if he wants to involve them in personal family decisions. This approach has been known to work.

Recommended Reading and Resources:

Belofsky, Penny. *In-laws/Outlaws.* New York: Copestone Press, 1991.

O'Connor, Karen. *When Spending Takes the Place of Feeling.* Nashville, TN: Thomas Nelson, 1992.

Overcomers Outreach, Inc. Bob and Pauline Bartosch. 2290 W. Whittier Blvd., Suites A/D La Habra, CA 90631. Phone: (310)697-3994. Fax: (310) 691-5349.

Parker, Christina B. *When Someone You Love Drinks Too Much.* New York: HarperCollins, 1990.

Notes

1. Christina B. Parker, *When Someone You Love Drinks Too Much* (New York: HarperCollins, 1990), pp. 51-54, adapted.
2. Bob and Pauline Bartosch, *Overcomers Outreach Inc.*, La Habra, CA: 1986.

Section Three

FAMILY ISSUES

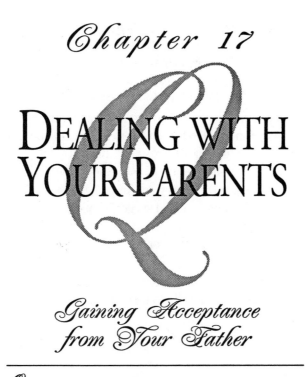

Chapter 17

DEALING WITH YOUR PARENTS

Gaining Acceptance from Your Father

Q. HOW CAN I TELL MY FATHER THAT ALL I WANT
FROM HIM IS HIS ACCEPTANCE FOR WHO I AM
AND NOT FOR MY ACCOMPLISHMENTS?

A. Have you asked your father for acceptance before? If so, and he did not respond, why do you think that is? Did he hear the request? Was it presented in language that he connected with? Does he ever give acceptance to anyone without it being tied into how they have performed? I ask this because many men do not really know how to say, "I value you just for who you are and not for what you do." They build their own value on how they perform and then transfer this to others around them. This does not excuse them from giving you what you need. However, I believe any man can learn to respond differently.

Many women counselees have shared with me what they have done in their relationships with their fathers to make acceptance without performance a reality. I will list their insights for you:

1. They modeled what they wanted for their fathers. They gave him affirmation and acceptance, which were not based on what he did but just for who he was.

2. They verbally or in writing thanked him for the affirmations he gave and said, "Dad, on a scale of 0 to 10, those compliments or affirmations register at about a 5 for me. If you would like to hit a 9 or a 10 here is what you could say..."

3. One woman gave her father a list of the kinds of affirmations she would appreciate and suggested he consider them, perhaps even practice them and then try them out on her. She said that either a verbal or written form would be all right with her.

No matter what you try, remember that your attitude, tone of voice and positive reinforcement will make a major difference.

Dealing with Domineering Parents

Q. HOW DO I PLEASE (OR BREAK AWAY FROM!) A
CONTROLLING, POSSESSIVE PARENT? (IN MOST
CASES THIS REFERS TO THE MOTHER.)

A. It would be nice if all parents were healthy emotionally and were able to do the job of parenting perfectly, including releasing us when we get to be adults. Many parents are, and fortunate is the child who has had such positive experiences. But such is not always the case. Healthy parents do not have to control their adult children. But many parents are dissatisfied and are afraid of what we call abandonment. They cannot tolerate the loss of their children, and the older the child is the more important it is for them to remain attached to that child. They try many ways to accomplish this, which could affect the child in various ways including blurring the child's identity. The child may have difficulty seeing who she is as a separate person.

The mother-daughter relationship is charged with emotion. You and your mother have the potential to be close friends or intense, alienated enemies. I like the following quote:

> No relationship is as highly charged as that between mother and daughter, or as riddled with expectations that could, like a land mine, detonate with a single misstep, a solitary stray word that, without warning, wounds or enrages. And no relationship is as bursting with possibilities of good will and understanding.[1]

A woman can be dominated in many ways by her parent. Some women are dominated by what we call *default*. Sometimes a woman feels weak and insecure and relies on her parent's control to serve as a camouflage for her own weakness. She does not like it but she is not sure she can live without it.

Some women are dominated by the *negativism* of a parent whereas others are dominated by an apparent *weakness* on the part of the parent. Some disabilities may be genuine and others faked. Fear of a parent's disapproval or rejection feeds the domination other women experience. Do any of these feel like your situation?

Some parents control by *smothering*. They do and do and do for you. They slave for you without you asking them to do so. But they use it to manipulate you. They say they have your best interest at heart and just want to help but there is a price to pay. Other mothers respond like an avenging angel against you. They heap shame upon you. Do any of these sound familiar?

There are no easy ways to change these types of relationships with your parent. You have to take charge and initiate any changes you want. The initial step is to determine who in your family is controlling and in what way. Determine the reason you continue to respond to his or her control efforts.

What style of response does your mother use? Some are critics. They throw verbal hand grenades. They look for opportunities to be displeased with you.

Handling Confrontation

A confrontation is in order with your controlling parents. Hints or subtleties won't work. If you are like many women, your first reaction might be, "It will never work." "It will cause more problems than I've got now." "I could never do that." "Maybe someday I'll do it." "Maybe it will work." I hope your response is the latter.

Here are four things to consider before you plunge ahead with confronting your parents:

1. You need to feel strong enough to handle your parent's response whether it be rejection, anger, denial or personal attack against you to create shame.

2. You need a support system of friends to help you plan for this, deal with it, pray for you and believe in the steps you are taking.

3. Then either write a letter or rehearse what you want to say. Anticipate how your parent might respond and practice non-defensive responses.

4. Finally, give them permission not to accept what you are doing and to be hurt and withdraw for a while. Keep in mind that for most people, the anticipation of a confrontation is usually worse than the actual confrontation itself.

Be sure you have envisioned exactly what you want your relationship with your parents to be like in the future. Give specifics when you talk with your parents. Affirm them for the positives that do exist and then focus on what you would like them to do differently and how this is going to affect you. Some women share their confrontation in person, some in writing and often more than once. You will need to be consistent in requesting what you want from your parents and then behave as though it is going to occur. Use a friend to support you, especially when you feel it is not going to work.

I have talked to some women who in preparing for a confrontation imagine the worst possible scenario. They see their parents angry, tearful or fainting, and still envision themselves being calm and continuing to state how the relationship will be different. Some women have asked their spouse or friend to role-play this situation with them so they can become comfortable.

But what if it does not work? It may not. But at least you have let it be known to your parent that you are no longer a willing player for their game. And then continue responding the way you said you would. Sometimes it helps to let your parent know you can understand their feelings of being hurt and rejected, and if it helps them to respond this way it is all right with you. This might break their pattern of games and manipulation. You are not doing this for the sole purpose of having your parent change. You are taking this step to show that you will be different.

I have also seen some women actually tell their mothers that they want a trial separation from them to see if the problems could be lessened by not having contact for a time. Often this gets the parent's attention. And in a few extreme cases a permanent separation has occurred because of the severe pathology and inability to change on the part of the parent. But in most cases, positive changes can occur.

Handling a Critical Mother

Q. WHAT WILL HELP ME DEAL WITH THE HURT AND REJECTION I FEEL FROM MY MOTHER? SHE IS CRITICAL AND I CAN'T SEEM TO PLEASE HER REGARDLESS OF WHAT I DO.

A. A woman who has a critical mother ends up feeling hurt and rejected. We seem to take on the responsibility for changing the situation; we feel we are to blame in some way.

The best plan is to put the responsibility back on the person who is creating the problem—your mother. Do you believe the criticism you hear from your mother? If so, you probably dwell on it and spend inordinate amounts of time trying to figure out how to please her. You may also live in dread of talking with her or seeing her. If you are like most of us, you have probably imagined scenarios of pleasing your mother and having her praise you. It won't happen unless you help to make it happen.

Now, if you were seated in my office you would probably say, "How in the world can that ever happen?" It goes back once again to what you will probably consider a confrontation. Let me suggest some questions or statements you can share with your mother, following the guidelines from previous questions.

"Mother, I'm interested in knowing what it is that I do that pleases you. I would like you to be specific."

"Mother, can you tell me how I would know that I please you. What do you usually say that would let me know that?"

"Mother, some of the things that I will do and say will please you and some will not. Tell me how you are going to handle what doesn't please you and what you will say to me. Then I want to tell you what I would appreciate you saying."

"Mother, in the future I would appreciate it if, when I please you, you would say so and if I do something that doesn't, just let it go, since it doesn't have the effect that you want. If I want your comments or suggestions, I will ask you. But if I hear that coming unsolicited, I will simply interrupt you and ask you to stop."

Do these sound radical? Perhaps. Do they work? In time, yes they do. And that is really all you can expect.

Remember, a critical woman is usually an unhappy woman and just as critical of herself. Perhaps as your relationship begins to change you can talk with her about what she could do to deal with her own unhappiness. And keep in mind you may never please her, but that is not your calling in life, is it? You have been called to glorify God and enjoy Him forever. That is a far cry from being consumed by trying to please a mother who has a defective perception of you. You will gain your unconditional acceptance from God and that is a good place to direct your energy. By doing this, you will also help to keep yourself from becoming like your mother. Often the pattern we dislike in others begins to seep into our own lives—something you could be praying about. Also consider how you could pray about your mother that would help both her and your perception of her. Prayer does make a difference.

Extending Forgiveness

Q. HOW DO I FORGIVE MY PARENTS? DO I STILL HAVE TO HONOR AND OBEY MY PARENTS?

A. Forgiveness—the step that brings healing. Forgiveness is the basis for our relationship with our heavenly Father. We have been declared "no longer guilty." It does not mean we ignore what another person has done. We do not pretend it never happened. If you owed the bank a thousand dollars and they called you and said, "We're going to pretend that you never borrowed the money so you don't have to repay us," that is not forgiveness. But if they said you borrowed the money and you owe us but...we are going to cancel the debt—that is forgiveness. It also means to quit punishing or seeking revenge or holding a grudge against another person—or even yourself. Scripture tells us to forgive:

> And forgive us our debts, as we also have forgiven (left, remitted and let go the debts, and given up resentment against) our debtors (Matt. 6:12, AMP).
>
> And become useful and helpful and kind to one another, tenderhearted (compassionate, understanding, lovinghearted), forgiving one another [readily and freely], as God in Christ forgave you (Eph. 4:32, AMP).
>
> Be gentle and forbearing with one another and, if one has a difference (a grievance or complaint) against another, readily pardoning each other; even as the Lord has freely forgiven you, so must you also [forgive] (Col. 3:13, AMP).

Forgiveness begins with an act of the will. You must make a decision to forgive not because you feel like it, but because you know it is the healthiest step for you to take. Why? Because it frees you from the emotional effects of what was done to you. And remember, it can be a slow process to see your hurt and resentment diminish.

Forgiveness involves letting go. Did you ever play tug-of-war as a child? As long as each participant is tugging, you have a "war." But when someone lets go, the war is over. When you forgive your father, you are letting go of your end of the rope. No matter how hard he may tug on the other end, if you have released your end, the war is over for you.

Letting go is not always easy, as Dwight Wolter explains:

> Letting go is not always easy. When we live in a dysfunctional home, we are afraid to leave the security of the situation, bad is it is. We have become childlike and are unprepared for the real world. The possibility of letting go means change and we cannot relax enough to take off on our own. The child in us needs to be taken out of the driver's seat. We need to trust that our adult self is capable of taking us to our desired goal. To forgive, means letting go and being willing to let go of our unforgiving attitude. We need to admit that the events and feelings of our childhood happened. We need to stop blaming ourselves for what is a family problem. We need to admit to ourselves that, regardless of how much we try, the past cannot be undone. We cannot change what happened in the past, but we can have a better tomorrow.[2]

Forgiveness means identifying and facing each objection you have to forgiving the other person (or yourself). Identify each of these in writing and then release each one to the person of Jesus Christ and thank Him for taking this from you.

Your answers to the following questions will indicate whether or not you have forgiven.

1. Have I stopped secretly hoping that the person gets what he deserves?
2. Have I quit talking about this individual to others?
3. Have I quit replaying my revenge in my mind?
4. Do I frequently think about the person and what he did to me?

5. Am I glad when something good happens to him?

6. Am I more open and trusting toward other people?

7. Am I less angry, depressed, resentful or bitter?

8. Have I quit blaming this person for how my life has turned out?

9. Do I feel sorry when this person has problems?

10. Do I feel more comfortable with my feelings?

11. Am I praying that God will bless this person?[3]

Holding resentment toward anyone will keep you living in the past, contaminate the present and limit the possibilities of the future.

One of our problems is that most of us have a better memory than God does. We tend to cling to our past hurts and nurse them, and in so doing we experience difficulty in the present with others. We are actually attempting to pull rank on God when we refuse to forgive a person or ourselves—something He has already done. Our lack of forgiveness not only fractures our relationship with others but with God as well.

I like Lewis Smedes' insight:

> Is it fair to be stuck to a painful past? Is it fair to be walloped again and again by the same old hurt? Vengeance is having a videotape planted in your soul that cannot be turned off. It plays the painful scene over and over again inside your mind. It hooks you into its instant replays. And each time it replays, you feel the clap of pain again. Is it fair?
>
> Forgiving turns off the videotape of pained memory. Forgiving sets you free. Forgiving is the only way to stop the cycle of unfair pain turning in your memory.[4]

Can you accept whatever the offending person may have done to you in the past? Acceptance means forgiving to the point that you no longer allow what has occurred in the past to influence you anymore. Only through complete acceptance can you be free—free to develop yourself, to experience life, to communicate openly, to love yourself entirely.

Forgiveness means saying, "It is all right; it is over. I no longer resent you nor see you as an enemy. I love you even if you cannot love me in return." When you refuse to forgive, you inflict inner torment upon yourself, and that makes you miserable and ineffective. But when you forgive someone for hurting you, you perform spiritual surgery on your soul. You cut away the wrong that was done to you. You see your "enemy" through the magic eyes that can heal your soul. Separate the person from the hurt and let the hurt go, the way children open their hands and let a trapped butterfly go free. Then invite that person back into your mind, fresh, as if a piece of history between you has been erased, its grip on your memory broken. Reverse the seemingly irreversible flow of pain within you.[5]

One of the delights of counseling is to witness the reconciliation of a parent and an adult daughter. I have seen an emotionally distant adult woman develop a caring relationship with her aged parent. I have seen an abused daughter develop a healthy relationship with her parent through the forgiveness that Jesus Christ allows us to experience. Some of you, when you forgive your parent or whoever it was that hurt you, will move into a closer relationship with God. Remember: When you acknowledge and release your anger, and forgive your parents for anything and everything they have done, you have let go of your end of the rope and the tug-of-war is over.

Recommended Reading:

Leman, Kevin. *The Pleasers.* New York: Dell Publishers, 1992.

Reed, Bobbie. *Pleasing You Is Destroying Me.* Dallas, TX: WORD Inc., 1992

Secunda, Victoria. *When You and Your Mother Can't Be Friends.* New York: Delecorte Press, 1990.

Smedes, Lewis. *Forgive and Forget.* San Francisco: HarperSan Francisco, 1984.

Stoop, David. *Forgiving Our Parents, Forgiving Ourselves.* Ann Arbor, MI: Servant Publications, 1991.

Stoop, David. *Making Peace With Your Father.* Wheaton, IL: Tyndale House Publishers, 1992.

Wright, H. Norman. *Always Daddy's Girl.* Ventura, CA: Regal Books, 1989.

Wright, H. Norman. *Holding on to Romance.* Ventura, CA: Regal Books, 1992 (chapter 6).

Notes

1. Victoria Secunda, *When You and Your Mother Can't Be Friends* (New York: Delacorte Press, 1990), p. 5.

2. Dwight Lee Wolter, *Forgiving Our Parents* (Minneapolis, MN: CompCare Publishers, 1989), pp. 55,56, adapted.

3. Lynda D. Elliott, *My Father's Child* (Brentwood, TN: Wolgemuth and Hyatt, 1988), p. 62, adapted.

4. Lewis B. Smedes, *"Forgiveness: The Power to Change the Past"* p. 26, Christianity Today, January 7, 1983.

5. Lewis B. Smedes, *Forgive and Forget* (San Francisco: HarperSan Francisco, 1984), p. 37.

Chapter 18

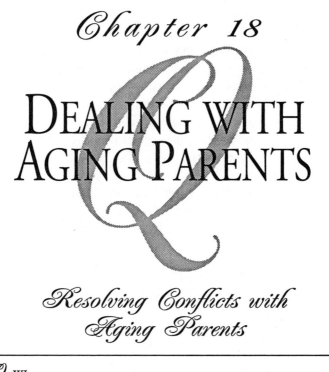

DEALING WITH AGING PARENTS

Resolving Conflicts with Aging Parents

Q. WE ARE RUNNING INTO CONFLICTS WITH OUR PARENTS AS THEY AGE. IT SEEMS LIKE THEY MAKE MORE DEMANDS ON OUR TIME AND SOMETIMES THEY SEEM TO TRY TO CONTROL US BY USING GUILT OR OUTRIGHT PRESSURE. AND THEN WE WONDER, WHAT WILL BE BEST FOR THEM WHEN THEY ARE OLDER AND CAN NO LONGER TAKE CARE OF THEMSELVES?

A. Sometimes our responses and feelings will vary because of the quality of the relationship we have had with our parents. For some, that relationship is close, for others, distant. We may want to help them because of feelings of love, guilt or obligation.

At some point, your parents will not function as well as they once did and some of the negative traits that bothered you earlier may become even more pronounced. You and your spouse will need to decide what you are capable and willing to do to care for your parents and present a united front. You won't be able to change your parents nor all of their responses toward you. You can learn, however, not to let them push the buttons that upset you.

I would encourage you to talk with others who have experienced this stage of life, and gain from their experiences. If you have brothers or sisters, talk together as a family to see how you can best help your parents at this stage of life. And by all means be sure everyone reads *Caring for Your Aging Parents* by Barbara Deane and *Eldercare for the Christian Family* by Timothy S. Smick.

Whether your parents live on their own, in a retirement facility, nursing home, or with you, here are some questions for you to consider. These questions are related to your parent living with you but are applicable to other situations as well. If your parent(s) are still young, it is not too early to begin reflecting upon their future as it will involve you.

- Does she accept your spouse as head of the house? Is there anyone in your household that she doesn't get along with—including pets?
- Are there differences in lifestyles that will cause conflict—e.g., she loves television and you hate it; she goes to bed and gets up early and you're a night owl?
- Will she be bringing any pets? Who will care for them?
- Will she share in performing household tasks such as cooking and cleaning? How will these responsibilities be decided?
- Will she parent your children, if any are living at home?
- Will she have her own room? Her own furniture and television?
- Will your home require modifications to make it safe for an elderly person—e.g., grab bars in the shower, well-lighted stairs, and no highly waxed floors and throw rugs to cause falls?
- Is she able to take care of her own personal needs—bathing, dressing, toileting, and taking medications—or will she require help?
- Does she like the food you serve or does she require a special

diet? If the latter, will you be expected to cook two menus, one for her and one for the rest of the family?

- What will she do all day long in your home? Does she have interests she can continue to pursue? If you are a full-time home-maker, will she expect you to be her companion? If she has to be alone, will she become isolated, bored, and depressed?

- Will her family and friends be able to visit? Will she be able to visit others; attend church services and functions, social events, and senior activities; do volunteer work?

- Will she maintain her car and driver's license? If not, is other transportation available, or will you have to become her driver?

- Will she contribute to household expenses? Will anyone else in the family assist financially?

- Is she able to manage her own financial affairs? If not, now or in the future, who will take over this responsibility?

- Will you have time alone for you and your spouse, and for you and your children? How will this be managed without making her feel "left out"? Will you be able to take vacations without her? What about her vacations?

- Is she able to stay by herself while you're away? Is she willing to?

- If respite care is needed so you and your spouse can get away, is there anyone in the family who will provide it? If not, how will you manage to get respite? Does she understand your need for it, and is she willing to cooperate so you can have it? If you become ill, who will take over?

- Is there a will and a safety deposit box? Where does she keep important papers?

- Will she continue with her present physician, or will you have to find a new one for her? Are she and her doctor willing to discuss her medical care with you? Do you know how she feels about life-prolonging treatments? Has she communicated her wishes to her physician?

- Who will care for her if she becomes ill? Will insurance cover medical and home health care costs and, if necessary, long-term care costs?
- Do you know her wishes in regard to disposition of her belongings? What about funeral arrangements?[1]

Physical and Mental Deterioration of Aging Parents

Q. HOW CAN I COPE WITH THE PHYSICAL AND MENTAL DETERIORATION OF MY PARENTS?

A. Physical and mental deterioration of our aging parents is a difficult adjustment for most of us. One reason is that we do not really anticipate this stage of our adult life nor do we plan for it. Not only is it a time of loss for your parent(s) but for you as well. The parents you knew as a child and young adult are now functioning and perhaps behaving in a new way. And often they look to us to help or rescue them. I know. My wife, Joyce, and I have been involved in this process for several years with one mother in her late 80s and the other 92.

Strange as it seems your task now will be three-fold: (1) grieving over the losses you see happening before your eyes in the life of your parent; (2) accepting the level of ability that your parent has at this point in life; and (3) loving them in a balanced way.

It may help you to make a list of the changes you see in your parent and then say good-bye to each loss you are able to identify. This helps you accept this transition in their lives. You will be confronted with forgetfulness, repeated statements and stories, perhaps not being appreciated for what you do, frequent phone calls and so on.

In the past few years, I have made it a practice to call my mother each day just for a few minutes. I know that what we will talk about is what we talked about yesterday and the day before that. What has helped me is to frequently say to myself, "Mom is doing the best she can with what she has at this point in life. It's all right for her to repeat." Perhaps if we give our parents permission to respond in the way they do, it will make it easier on us.

Sometimes you have feelings of frustration because you remember your parents when they were alert and functional and caring for you. Now that is history. You cannot fix old age. You may feel anger because you feel powerless. Another reason for being bothered is because this is a preview of what will occur in your own life and again you can do nothing to change that. Do not dump your frustrations on your parents. Talk with a friend or write out your feelings.

What you can do is reach out in love in a tangible way, pray for your parents and guide them to the comfort of God's Word. Listen to them. Do not try to correct what they say or argue them out of their feelings. Do not judge them, do not give an abundance of unsolicited advice and do not feel you have to solve their problems. Help them find a solution. Do not make them dependent upon you because that will make them feel even worse about themselves. It is possible to teach an elderly parent to be dependent upon you by doing too much for them. This is not healthy.

What the elderly need are smiles, a lot of touching, listening and the knowledge that even if you are miles away they are thought of and loved. You are now their parent in many ways. The roles have just reversed. Encourage them with passages from God's Word such as, "Even to your old age and gray hairs I am he, I am he who will sustain you. I have made you and I will carry you; I will sustain you and I will rescue you" (Isa. 46:4).

Responsibility Toward Aging Parents

Q. WHAT IS A CHRISTIAN'S RESPONSIBILITY TOWARD AGING PARENTS? I FEEL GUILTY. AM I SUFFERING FROM JUSTIFIED GUILT OR AM I BEING MANIPULATED?

A. We have a calling to love and care for our parents but it is to be a balanced style of caregiving. You will need to be the one to decide what you are able to give. It may not be sufficient for your parents and they may try to manipulate you. Perhaps they want to come live with you or want you to drop by every day or phone them four times a day. You will need to set your own schedule and limits and in a nondefensive, nonangry way let them know both that you love them and that there is a limit to what you will be able to do for them.

Steps to a Balanced Life as a Caregiver

What are some of the steps to take to help you live a balanced life at the same time as you are caring for a parent? Be sure you have your own separate life from them. Ask for help from other relatives, friends, your church or community resources. Asking for help does not mean you are abandoning your parent. Do not feel as though you have to be in control of every phase of your parent's life. Set limits regarding which of your parent's needs (not wants) you can meet. Get away as much as you can. Have fellowship with others and if possible find or begin a support group of others in your same situation.

This can be a time of rich growth for you as a person and for your own immediate family. You can develop a closer relationship with the Lord, and because of this time of testing, a more mature faith. You may also have an opportunity to face many of your feelings this experience generates. For some it is a time of healing past hurts. Perhaps Paul summed it up best in Romans when he said, "Suffering produces endurance, and endurance produces character, and character produces hope, and hope does not disappoint us" (Rom. 5:3-5, *RSV*).

Many caregivers have told me they have learned to (1) be more compassionate; (2) take one day at a time; (3) take more responsibility for their health now as they prepare for old age; (4) be more loving now so others will want to be around them when they are old and; (5) become a role model for others to emulate. Old age is hard work for the aged and is difficult for those who care for them as well.

If you are currently a caregiver or will be facing it in the near future, be sure to prepare by reading the two recommended books.

Recommended Reading:

Deane, Barbara. *Caring for Your Aging Parents—When Love Is Not Enough*. Colorado Spring, CO: NavPress, 1989.

Smick, Timothy S. *Eldercare for the Christian Family*. Dallas, TX: WORD Inc., 1990.

Note

1. Barbara Deane, *Caring for Your Aging Parents—When Love Is Not Enough* (Colorado Springs, CO: NavPress, 1989), pp. 168-170.

Chapter 19

CODEPENDENCY WITHIN THE FAMILY

Codependency Defined

The word "codependent" was coined in the 1970s for the treatment of alcoholism and since then has been gaining wider usage. Originally it referred to the family members of an alcoholic, as they too were affected by the alcoholism. Now it is applied to anyone in a significant relationship with a person who has any kind of dependency.

Often counselees come in and say, "I'm a codependent" or "I'm a co-ad. I'm sure you know what that is." My response is usually, "Could you tell me what *you* mean by the word as it may have a different meaning to each of us." We need to clarify what we mean by the word "codependent." One of the pioneers in describing this problem is Melody Beattie who defines a codependent as "one who has let another person's behavior affect him or her, and who is obsessed with controlling that person's behavior."[1]

I like the definition Pat Springle of Rapha gives in his book *Rapha's 12-Step Program for Overcoming Codependency:*

> Codependency is a compulsion to control and rescue people by fixing their problems. It occurs when a person's God-given needs for love and security have been blocked in a relationship with a dysfunctional person, resulting in a lack of objectivity, a

warped sense of responsibility, being controlled and control-ling others (three primary characteristics); and in hurt and anger, guilt, and loneliness (three corollary characteristics). These characteristics affect the codependent's every relation-ship and desire. His goal in life is to avoid the pain of being unloved and to find ways to prove that he is lovable. It is a desperate quest.[2]

Characteristics of Codependents

Q. WHAT IS THE DIFFERENCE BETWEEN TRUE BIBLICAL CARING AND CODEPENDENCY? WHAT ARE THE CHARACTERISTICS OF CODEPENDENTS?

A. The characteristics of codependents vary in degree of intensity. Which of these do you relate to?

Lack of Objectivity

Most people who come from dysfunctional families usually believe their family is "normal." They have difficulty seeing the unhealthy ways their family members related to one another, because they never have experienced emotionally healthy relationships. Coming to grips with the pain, hurt, anger and manipulation they have suffered can be threatening, so they tend to deny the existence of their problems and unhealthy patterns of relating. Thus they continue in their unhealthy pattern.

Warped Sense of Responsibility

The key words for codependency are: "rescue," "help," "fix" and "enable." The codependent sees herself as a savior; she is driven to help others, especially the needy people in her family. Usually at least one person in the family is unwilling or unable to take care of herself. The person may use both self-pity and condemnation to draw out a helping response from the overly responsible codependent. The codependent wants to be loved and accepted. She wants to avoid conflict, and does whatever it takes to make that person happy. The codependent is so busy taking care of others, however, that she neglects to care for herself by making her own decisions and determining her own identity and behavior.

Controlled and Controlling

Like everyone else, codependents need love and respect. Having been deprived of these precious commodities, she determines to do whatever it takes to win the affirmation she craves. Her means to that end is to make people happy, as her chief fear is that people will be unhappy with her. Those around her often learn how to use praise and condemnation to manipulate her.

Hurt and Angry

Dysfunctional families often foster a system of communication that may include words of love and acceptance. The actions, however, demonstrated by family members often hurt deeply. Hurt and anger go hand in hand.

Guilty

Codependents often feel guilty. Why?—for what they have done and have not done; for what they have said and have not said; for what they have felt and have not felt. You name it, they feel guilty for just about everything. Often such guilt produces feelings of worthlessness and shame.

The codependent gets her worth—her identity—from what she does for others. She rescues, helps, enables, but regardless of how much she does for others, it is never enough. That is the trap of living in a dysfunctional family. She rescues but is rejected. Lacking objectivity, she concludes: "It's my fault; if I were a better person, they would love me." She spends her life trying to be good enough to earn the love and acceptance she so desperately wants, but fears she never will. And she ends up haunted by the shame of feeling that she has not—or cannot—measure up.

Lonely

Codependents spend their lives giving, helping and serving others. They may appear to be the most social people in the world, but inside they are lonely. They hurt. Their attempts to please others by helping and serving are designed to win affection. Though they may occasionally see a glimpse of love and respect, it usually fades quickly. Then, thinking they have been abandoned by both people and God, they feel empty and companionless. They distrust authority, believing that anyone above them is against them, and they build elaborate facades to hide their painful feelings of loneliness.[3]

There are exceptions. I have seen people with these characteristics who have come from healthy families and I have seen healthy people who have come out of unhealthy environments. I say this so we do not fall into the trap of categorizing and stereotyping everyone.

Codependents are not living a New Testament model of loving, helping or serving. We are called to love from a pure heart, not manipulate to fill our own needs. We have not been called to be a slave to the whims of others but to respect ourselves and create a healthy interdependence within relationships.

Reflect on the specific behaviors of codependency in the chart below and either indicate a situation or a person in your life that reflects each behavior.

BEHAVIOR   **PERSON OR SITUATION**
- feel responsible for others'
  behavior, but often don't
  take responsibility for our own.

BEHAVIOR   **PERSON OR SITUATION**

- need to be needed.
- expect others to make us happy.
- can be demanding or indecisive.
- can be attentive and caring or
  selfish and cruel.
- often see people and situations as
  wonderful or awful, "black or
  white," with no room for
  ambiguity, or "gray."
- often overreact to people or
  situations which we can't control.
- seek affirmation and attention
  or sulk and hide.
- believe we are perceptive, and
  sometimes are, but often can't
  see reality in our own lives.
- see others as being "for us" or
  "against us."
- get hurt easily.
- use self-pity and/or anger to
  manipulate others.
- feel like we need to rescue
  people from themselves.
- communicate contrasting
  messages, like "I need you.
  I hate you."
- don't say what we mean and
  don't mean what we say.
- are deeply repentant but commit
  the same sins again and again.[4]

Recovery from Codependency

Q. HOW CAN I GAIN RELEASE FROM MY CODEPENDENT PATTERNS OF NEEDING TO PLEASE OTHERS IN ORDER TO FEEL GOOD ABOUT MYSELF?

A. What can you do at this point? Here are some suggestions, keeping in mind that these recommendations are basic and will take time and effort to implement.

Read resource material. We have a wealth of material available and you do need to be selective. One of the best resources I have used is *Rapha's 12-Step Program for Overcoming Codependency.* Working through this book with another person or in a group is helpful.

Recovery group. It is vital to determine the philosophy of the recovery group you join. Will you recover to the point of not needing to be involved in the group anymore? I have seen many who have traded their codependent behavior with people for a recovery group. They attend several group meetings each week, believe that everyone must be in a group and that they will be there forever. This is not healing and recovery. This is just another dependency. Our sufficiency is in Jesus Christ and not in a group. Groups can simply be a means to an end.

Read Scripture. The next step is to believe you can be a different person. Dwell on these Scripture verses to help you believe change is possible: Isaiah 26:3; John 8:32; 2 Corinthians 1:3,4.

Respond properly. Each day identify a misbelief and a behavior pattern that fits the descriptions of what we have been talking about. Then detach yourself from the behavior or person you are responding to in a dependent manner. Then decide exactly what you are and are not responsible for in each situation or with that person. An important step is to identify what will be a healthy response rather than what you did. Set a goal of how you want to respond. Share it with another person. Write it out in detail. In your heart and mind see yourself responding in this way.

Repair fences. Boundaries are one of the main issues that could be a problem for you. If you grew up with unclear or inappropriate boundaries, remember that these fences can be repaired. The initial step is to take a personal inventory of the symptoms in your life at the present time. Here are some of them:

- feelings of obligation;
- hidden anger/resentment toward others' demands;
- inability to be direct and honest;
- people-pleasing;
- life out of control;
- no sense of identity or "who I am";
- inability to fulfill work demands;
- blaming others or circumstances too much;
- excusing/denying failure;
- depression;
- anxiety;
- compulsive behavior (eating, substance abuse, sex, money);
- chronic conflictual relationships.

Reject requests. Reflect on where and how you might have learned these symptoms. Sometimes it helps to discuss this with other siblings who might be struggling as you are. In which area of your life do you need to set some boundaries? The steps you take will be small ones. For some, it is as simple as saying no to small requests instead of, "It doesn't matter to me." Hearing yourself say no can become comfortable.

The "Messiah" Complex

Some codependents end up feeling like a messiah and behaving like one. Another word for them is a "helpaholic." In her book, *When Helping You Is Hurting Me,* Carmen Berry has given the best description of this person. Messiahs have been taught that their main purpose in life is helping. Their motto is, "If I don't do it, it won't get done!" They feel responsible for making sure everything turns out all right and everyone is happy. They feel indispensable. Their second main characteristic is, "Everyone else's needs take priority over mine," and they operate in that manner. There is no balance to their love or the area of need fulfillment.[5]

Specifically, a messiah behaves in the following manner. She tries to earn her sense of worth by behaving in a worthy manner. She lets others determine her actions, has a need to overachieve, and is attracted to others who have the same kind of pain. She has problems in establishing and keeping both personal and intimate relationships. She ends up being caught in a cycle of isolation, feels driven to endless activity and only stops when she drops. Does this sound like anyone you know?[6]

How to Protect Personal Boundaries

Q. HOW CAN I LEARN TO SET EFFECTIVE BOUNDARIES THAT WILL BE EFFECTIVE BUT NOT CONTROLLING?

A. One of the problems that occurs in codependent relationships is boundary violation.

Perhaps the best way to describe what we mean by boundaries is to call them "property lines." When Iraq invaded Kuwait in 1990, the boundary lines were violated. Our states and the property on which our houses are built are all demarcated by clear boundaries, which are elaborately specified in the written property titles. At one time I requested that a city employee survey my lot so I would be clear about my property lines. I did not want to infringe upon my neighbors if I built a structure or planted some trees.

People with clearly defined boundaries fence off certain areas of their lives with a "KEEP OUT! NO TRESPASSING!" sign. Intimacy is by invitation only to certain trusted people. Others find their private territory constantly invaded and wonder why. Without realizing it, these people may have posted a sign saying, "TRESPASSERS, WELCOME!" Many people allow others to invade by not taking any action, not stating what they prefer, by explaining too much, or by living in fear of offending someone.

A woman who has never learned how to say no feels endless confusion about her boundaries. In describing some of the sources for this confusion in children, Dr. John Townsend has suggested that parents who are confused about boundaries tend to produce children who are also confused.

Source Points of Confusion

We can identify several source points of confusion concerning boundaries. Consider these in three ways. First, does this situation sound familiar in the family from which you came? Second, does it sound familiar in your current family situation? And third, if so, what steps can you take to change this situation?

- Parents who feel abandoned when their children begin to make autonomous choices. These parents respond to autonomy in their children by conveying guilt or shame messages about their lack of love and loyalty to the family or to the parents.
- Parents who feel threatened by their increasing loss of control over the children. These parents use anger or criticism, not guilt or shame messages, to convey their unhappiness over the children's new-found separateness.
- Families which equate disagreement with sin.
- Parents who are afraid of the anger of their children.
- Parents who are hostile toward the anger of their children.
- Families which praise compliance in the name of togetherness over healthy independence.
- Families in which emotional, physical, and sexual abuse occur. These kinds of abuse cause severe damage to the children's sense of ownership of their bodies and themselves.

- Families in which the children feel responsible for the happiness of the parents.
- Parents who rescue children from experiencing the consequences of their behavior.
- Parents who are inconsistent in setting limits with the children.
- Parents who continue to take responsibility for the children in adulthood.[7]

Love Gone Wrong

Someone summed up the codependent problem by saying it's a case of "love gone wrong." The last thing you want to do is move from misguided love to being uncaring and unloving. When we love others the way Scripture calls us to love, there will be sacrifice and involvement in others' lives. You will sacrifice but you will be able to be strong and tough when necessary. You will know where the boundaries are and when to detach. When you experience hurt, you will let the other person know. You will feel responsible for your own behavior but not the other person's. You will be able to empathize without becoming enmeshed.

Building Healthy Boundaries

What can you do in your marriage or family to encourage healthy boundaries for yourself and others? Here are several positive steps you can take:

1. Allow freedom for other members to state their opinions and state your own.
2. Make it safe to disagree without fear of recrimination. Be willing to disagree yourself.
3. Encourage every person in the family to think for himself or herself and show that you believe in his or her ability to decide. Model this for others.

4. Assist each person in discovering his or her talents and spiritual gifts and in developing and using them to the fullest. What are yours?

5. Allow the expression of all feelings—including anger. Express yours in a healthy way.

6. Set limits with natural and logical consequences, but not fear or guilt.

7. Allow age-appropriate choices if you have children.

8. Respect others when they say no.[8]

Recommended Reading:

Berry, Carmen Renee. *When Helping You Is Hurting Me*. New York: HarperCollins Publishers, 1988.

Springle, Pat. *Rapha's 12-Step Program for Overcoming Codependency*. Dallas, TX: WORD Inc., 1990.

Notes

1. Melody Beattie, *Codependent No More* (New York: Hazeldon Foundation, 1987), p. 31.

2. Pat Springle, *Rapha's 12-Step Program for Overcoming Codependency* (Dallas, TX: WORD Inc., 1990), p. XIII.

3. Ibid., pp. 12,13, adapted.

4. Ibid., p. XIV.

5. Carmen Renee Berry, *When Helping You Is Hurting Me* (New York: HarperCollins Publishing, 1988), pp. 6,7, adapted.

6. Ibid., p. 32, adapted.

7. H. Norman Wright, *Family Is Still a Good Idea* (Ann Arbor, MI: Servant Publications, 1992), p. 114. And Dave Carder, Earl Henslin, Henry Cloud, John Townsend and Alice Brawand, *Secrets of Your Family Tree* (Chicago, IL: Moody Press, 1991), pp. 173,174.

8. Carder, Henslin, Cloud, Townsend, Brawand, *Secrets of Your Family Tree*, pp. 172,173, adapted.

Chapter 20

DYSFUNCTIONAL FAMILIES

Dealing with Feelings of a Dysfunctional Family

Q. HOW CAN I DEAL WITH MY FEELINGS CAUSED BY COMING FROM A DYSFUNCTIONAL FAMILY?

A. The legacy of feelings you are left with from a dysfunctional family are often tied in to your beliefs. If you were in my counseling office over a period of weeks, I would ask you to keep a daily listing of your thoughts and feelings to discover the linkage between the two. The more you identify your thoughts, the more intense some of your feelings may be and this could be bothersome to you. That is all right; it is a sign of progress. Give yourself time, expect small improvements, look for them, isolate and build upon them.

As you replace old messages with new, accurate information, your feelings may begin to subside. As you change, you may experience guilt as you give up your old roles. Challenge your guilt for there is no need or place for it now. At a point in the change process you will discover you have choices in your life. You are not locked into where you are now forever.

In the book *Love Is a Choice,* by Dr. Robert Hemfelt, Dr. Frank Minirth and Dr. Paul Meier, part 5 takes you through the 10 stages of recovery and has been beneficial to many women. The authors describe the process as a roller coaster ride:

> It's a classic, one-of-a-kind, that's been thrilling people for over half a century. It's the grandpa of all roller coasters, the jackrabbit at Hershey Park. And you've just climbed into its end car. The car catches into the chain drive with a jerk and you begin the long, slow grind up the trestled hill. You wonder, as the expectation builds, whether this silly little bar across your lap is going to be worth beans, if you *really* need it.
>
> For half an eternity you poise on the brink. You're never quite prepared for that first screaming swoop straight down. Your head reverses directions before your stomach reaches the bottom and you're clattering up the next hill—and down—and up....The humps and hills get lower, the right-angle turns become negotiable. The first wild plunge far behind now, you coast casually into the unloading shed, and lurch to an anticlimactic stop.
>
> That's just about the way recovery will go. In our recovery model, the first steep drop will provide the impetus and the wherewithal for the uphill healing. There will be other hills in your future, but none will be as high, and you'll be equipped with the means to roll up over them.[1]

One of the most significant steps of recovery is when you can create a new self-perception. I believe this is easier for a Christian than a non-Christian because of who we are in Christ.

Create a Support System

Part of your recovery and growth process involves a supportive person or persons in your life. I have had people ask, "Why? What difference will it make having others as a support?"

Let's consider the functions of a support system. For one thing, it makes you accountable and thus you will be more honest. Manipulation and rationalization won't work as well. The system will provide accurate information and help you stay in touch with reality. It will help you evaluate what is important and what is not by setting priorities. One of the real benefits is providing you with others who care about you, who help "bear your burdens" so that you realize you are not isolated and alone. A support system will assist you in feeling better about yourself and help to build your self-esteem.[2]

As you look for a supportive person or group, keep in mind they have many responsibilities. They are there to nudge you to fulfill your responsibilities, to help you become what you want to become, to listen to you objectively, to help you set priorities and goals, and help you stay focused on reality.[3] They function as a sounding board and a friend. They are also a daily contact, which is vital for you to develop consistency in your growth. They can help take some of the pressure off by providing a variety of healthy distractions.

Dealing with an Unloving Father

Q. HOW DO I DEAL WITH THE FACT THAT MY FATHER WAS DISTANT AND COLD AND UNLOVING? I HAVE A HARD TIME SEEING GOD AS MY FATHER AND PRAYING TO HIM!

A. Your question about your experience with your father and relating to God is not an uncommon struggle. Often we create our image of God based upon our fathers. Many people struggle to experience God's love and grace because the concept is buried by the rubbish of our relationships at home. A passage in the book of Jeremiah speaks to this issue: "Can men make God? The gods they made are not real gods at all" (Jer. 16:20, *TLB*).

What can you do? Tell God and another person how you see Him at this time in your life. It helps to tell Him. After all, it won't be any surprise to God. Each day read aloud the Scriptures listed in the section under self-esteem. I also suggest you read two books as a corrective process: *The Knowledge of the Holy* by A.W. Tozer is a devotional presentation of the attributes of God. J.I. Packer's book, *Knowing God*, expands our knowledge and understanding of God's attributes in yet another way. Dwell on these truths and the truths of Scripture. Write an unmailed letter to your earthly father, stating the discoveries you have made about God and declaring that no longer will his experiences with you dictate your perception of God. If your father is still living, pray that he would come to make the same discovery about God that you have made.

Breaking the Dysfunctional Chain

Q. IS IT POSSIBLE TO BREAK THE CHAIN OF FAMILY DYSFUNCTION? I FIND MYSELF RESPONDING TO MY CHILDREN THE SAME FRUSTRATING WAYS MY PARENTS RESPONDED TO ME.

A. As you seek to be a different kind of parent to your own children from the parenting you received, you will experience conflict. Your parents gave you messages about being a child and your own children also give you messages.

Your parents said: "Children? They're unreliable, powerless and demanding."

Your children say: "We are powerful and simple and innocent."

Your parents said: "Children are bad and uncontrollable."

Your children say: "We can be good."

Your parents said: "If we love you it means we have to sacrifice and be martyrs."

Your children say: "Loving children can be fun."

Your parents said: "You as a person are helpless and inadequate and can't make it on your own."

Your children say: "You are too powerful. You're also gifted and awesome."

Your parents said: "Life is tough, difficult and a mixed bag."

Your children say: "There is joy in life."

So...who are you going to listen to?[4]

What can you do specifically to help break the chain, to not make the same mistakes and to become a transition person?

Decide how you want to be different.

Some of the most common responses that those from dysfunctional homes want to avoid with their own children are (1) inconsistency; (2) irrational, arbitrary or excessive rules; (3) emotional distance; (4) nonlistening; (5) preoccupation with and insufficient attention toward the child; (6) and either misinformation or lack of information.

Counter each untrue parental message with the truth. Focus on how God views you in Scripture. Forgive your parents for what they did and for the untrue messages they gave you. Forgive yourself for hanging on to these falsehoods for so long. Forgive yourself for blaming them for their lacks and deficits you did not know about for so long. Redevelop the thoughts you want to have about yourself and your children and read them over each day.[5]

On a day-to-day level, watch out for a tendency to be hypercritical of your children if you were criticized a lot as a child. It is easy to do because you may feel they need your advice, they need to be put in their place, or you may live in the fear of others criticizing you through what your children do.

Respond to each child as a unique creation. Their accomplishments and abilities need to be evaluated on an individual basis.

Evaluate your expectations for each child. They might need to be lowered. Build your children's self-esteem through their identity in

Christ. Arrange small successes, give them respect and an abundance of praise and affirmation. When they do something you don't like, let them know you still love them as a person. When you make a mistake as a parent (and you will) admit it, apologize and forgive yourself immediately.[6]

Communication is a big part of the process. Some responses can serve as barriers to the development of a child and some responses are builders.

Communication Skills

BARRIERS

1. ASSUMING: If we assume our child will have the same reaction to a stimulus as they had last time, and act accordingly, we are ignoring the individual's ability to change.

2. RESCUING/EXPLAINING: If we step in and explain things or intervene so our child does not experience the consequences of his or her behavior, we deprive them of the opportunity to learn from their experiences.

3. DIRECTING: If we direct our children's every move we are likely to be met with resistance and hostility and defeat our children's initiative.

BUILDERS

1. CHECKING: By checking with the child each time we want them to attempt a behavior, we allow them to show how much they have grown since they last faced such a request.

2. EXPLORING: By exploring various solutions with our child, by asking leading questions and allowing them to think about the answers, we help them develop problem-solving skills.

3. ENCOURAGING/INVITING: By inviting participation and contribution instead of directing, we convey a feeling of respect for our child.

4. EXPECTING: If we expect perfection in the beginning, we will interfere with the important little steps our children take toward mastery of a task and we will discourage them unnecessarily.

4. CELEBRATING: By praising small steps in the right direction, we affirm the child's progress and show our confidence in their potential for growth.

5. ADULTISMS: If we forget what it is like to be a child and expect, demand, or require the child to think like an adult, we produce feelings of impotence, frustration, hostility, and aggression.

5. RESPECT: By understanding that attitudes and behaviors come from perceptions and beliefs, we can recognize our child's different way of seeing the world and affirm his or her right to be a child.[7]

Adult Children of Alcoholics

Q. MY PARENTS WERE ALCOHOLICS. HOW CAN I UNDERSTAND IF THIS AFFECTED ME OR NOT?

A. Perhaps the best way for you to understand what is occurring in your life as an adult child of an alcoholic is through some extensive reading or perhaps a Christian recovery group experience. But for the purpose of introducing you to some of the characteristics, consider these concerns.

There are approximately 30 million ACOAs in our country. And in spite of the devastation and pain of their alcoholic background, they are at a high risk of marrying an alcoholic or even becoming one themselves. Those who grow up in alcoholic homes have common symptoms and behaviors as a result of their common experiences. And the family system establishes rules of behavior and roles so the family can handle having an alcoholic as a member.

An alcoholic family is inflexible and cannot adapt easily to change nor does it allow family members to willingly change. You do learn to adjust to the unpredictable behavior of the alcoholic, and in the process rigid rules are imposed on the others.

Alcoholic homes follow a rule of silence that states, "Don't talk about what's happening in our family to outsiders or even those within our family." Conflict between family members is denied. In order to keep the family system intact and functioning, it is necessary to keep silent. Children learn to keep silent about what they see and feel as well. The fear, anger and hurt an ACOA feels stems from an inability to cope and process these feelings as he or she was growing up.

An alcoholic's family members cling to each other but they rarely become intimate. And they do not let others into their system or let anyone out. The members are isolated and end up being codependent as well. Most ACOAs were either physically or emotionally abandoned or both.

In order to survive the crazy rules in this type of family, the members take on a series of different roles. Various roles exist but the most common are:

The *Hero*—You try to make your family look good by achieving in school or work.

The *Scapegoat*—You direct attention from the family by getting into trouble.

The *Lost person*—You hide, avoid making waves and get attention by your isolation.

The *Clown*—You are funny or cute and release tensions in the family by cutting up.

The *Placater*—You try to smooth things over in the family to reduce conflict.

The *Enabler*—You prevent the drinker from experiencing the consequences of his alcoholism.

Do any of these sound familiar? Please look into this issue in more depth as there is not enough room in this short section to do more than simply define ACOA tendencies. Help is readily available and change is possible.

Recommended Reading:

Packer, J.I. *Knowing God.* Downers Grove, IL: InterVaristy Press, 1979.

Tozer, A.W. *The Knowledge of the Holy.* San Francisco, CA: HarperSan Francisco, 1978.

Woititz, Janet G. *Adult Children of Alcoholics.* Deerfield Beach, FL: Health Communications Inc., 1990.

Notes

1. Robert Hemfelt, Frank Minirth, Paul Meier, *Love Is a Choice* (Nashville, TN: Thomas Nelson, 1989) pp. 178,179.

2. Joel Robertson, *Help Yourself* (Nashville, TN: Thomas Nelson, 1991), p. 164, adapted.

3. Ibid., p. 179, adapted.

4. Randy Colton Rolfe, *Adult Children Raising Adult Children* (Deerfield Beach, FL: Health Communication Inc., 1989), p. 19, adapted.

5. Ibid., p. 19, adapted.

6. Claudette Wassie-Grimm, *How to Avoid Your Parents' Mistakes When You Raise Your Children* (New York: Pocket Books, 1990), p. 181,182, adapted.

7. Ibid., p. 199.

Chapter 21

DEALING WITH CHILDHOOD SEXUAL ABUSE

Handling Feelings of Unworthiness

Q. AM I LESS OF A PERSON BECAUSE I WAS
SEXUALLY ABUSED? I FEEL SO UNWORTHY.

A. Feelings of being dirty or unworthy are often a struggle. Are you less of a person because you were abused earlier in life? The strong and emphatic answer is NO! You are not unworthy, you are not soiled or damaged goods even though you may feel this way or you may have been told this by someone. Your worth, value and dignity is a fact. It still exists and it is a gift from God. People may tear you down and degrade you but the defect is in them and not in you. I would suggest that you read and study the chapter on self-esteem and identity as the information there may help you begin to counter the negative perception you have about yourself.

The Abused Victim Is Innocent

One of the most common ways perpetrators of sexual abuse deny the seriousness of what they have done is to blame the victim. They do this to deceive themselves and avoid the truth about what they have done. And if you were told this as a child you probably believed it because adults are supposed to tell us the truth. As a child, you were innocent and you carry no responsibility for the abuse. You could not have stopped it because a child is not physically strong enough to stop an adult, or emotionally or intellectually mature enough to cope with the tactics of an adult abuser.

You probably lived in fear, which kept you from telling others, and felt you would be blamed or punished, or it would not have accomplished anything. Some women carry a load of guilt because their own bodies responded to the sexual onslaught. You may have resisted it in your mind but your body responded. This does not mean you enjoyed it or were a willing participant. Our bodies are constructed in such a way that they can respond without our consent.

Handling Feelings of Blame

Q. WAS I TO BLAME BECAUSE I WAS ABUSED?

A. If anyone ever told you, either as a child or an adult, that you were at fault for your abuse, you have been told a lie. No one ever deserves abuse from an adult and you did not bring it on. And if you believe that you deserved it, you may also believe you deserve to be punished and you might be behaving in a way that is consistent with that belief. Your behavior could reflect your low opinion of yourself. Challenge this lie. Let your anger be directed toward the offender.

Perhaps it would help if you wrote out something such as the following and read it aloud several times a day, "I was not and am not responsible for what this person did to me as a child. They have to carry the full responsibility for their sin and for how they abused me. I will not accept nor carry any responsibility for this. I was the victim and I am now going to be moving on with my life and become a whole person through the strength of Jesus Christ and His healing presence in my life."

Share the above statement with others. Encourage them to encourage you in this process. I know of some women who take out pictures of themselves when they were a child and whenever they read this statement they look at the picture(s). Some have found it helpful to recall as many abusive situations or events as they can remember and make emphatic statements about each one while looking at the picture. This exercise coupled with other suggestions found later in this chapter may assist you on your journey toward healing.

Effects of Abuse on the Present

Q. CAN PHYSICAL OR SEXUAL ABUSE EARLIER IN MY
LIFE BE AFFECTING ME TODAY?

A. It *is* affecting you whether you are aware of it or not. One of the long-term effects of physical abuse is the tendency to repeat this pattern in one's own family situation. The overall results of any kind of abuse are:

1. Feelings of being "damaged goods";

2. Guilt;

3. Fear;

4. Depression;

5. Low self-esteem.

6. Repressed anger;

7. Inability to trust;

8. Blurred role boundaries and role confusion;

9. Failure to complete normal developmental tasks;

10. Problems with self-mastery and control.

Sexual Symptoms

Many sexual symptoms are evident as well. These can include the following:

1. Lack of sexual desire or inhibitions;
2. Sexual dysfunctions;
3. Painful intercourse;
4. Inability to enjoy some types of sexual activity;
5. Promiscuity;
6. Problems with sexual identity;
7. Attraction to illicit sexual activities such as pornography or prostitution;
8. Overly negative reactions to public displays of affection or nudity or even skimpy clothes;
9. The use of sexual manipulation to get what you want;
10. Sexual addiction.

One or several of these could be present.

Emotional Problems

Many emotional problems have been briefly indicated in the previous paragraph but need additional amplification. Consider these possibilities:

1. Intense anger and rage that erupts out of nowhere;
2. Swings in your mood from depression to a manic state;
3. Chronic, deep depression;
4. Forgotten periods of days, months or even years;
5. Extreme fears or phobias;
6. Sleep disturbances ranging from insomnia, nightmares, waking at the same time every night;

7. Addiction to food, drugs, alcohol;

8. Obsessive/compulsive tendencies, which could include overeating, shopping, eating, cleaning;

9. Any of the various eating disorders including bulimia and anorexia;

10. Flashbacks and hallucinations in which you are overwhelmed with memories of the abuse that are so real they seem to be actually happening to you again;

11. Self-destructive behavior including self-mutilation, suicide, overuse of substances.

And if all this were not enough, physical symptoms can also occur, including somatic symptoms and a tendency to be accident prone.[1]

Often women find themselves saying, "Yes! That's me!" in reading these symptoms. If that is the case for anyone reading this material, it is important that you find a trained counselor to help you further investigate the possibility of this having happened to you.

Physical and sexual abuse does affect us. That is the bad news. The good news is that recovery is possible!

Recovering from Effects of Sexual Abuse

Q. HOW CAN I RECOVER FROM THE EFFECTS OF SEXUAL ABUSE? HOW CAN I EXPRESS THE ANGER I FEEL?

A. Recovery from the effects of sexual abuse is similar to grieving over a loss in your life. Part of the process is deciding to say good-bye to something in your life. Prior to this though, you have to (1) give up all elements of denial; (2) face the fact that what happened happened and; (3) decide to break free from that trauma and move forward in your life. It is a commitment to begin and continue your journey. You need to face your feelings and release them so they no longer dominate you.

Dealing with Your Anger

As you face what happened, your anger toward the perpetrator will emerge. It is all right to be angry; it is normal. You need to be angry about the violation. Sometimes as the memories emerge, your anger is such that you may find it best to reconcile with some people from your past and perhaps separate from others. You may develop the strength to confront the abuser for the first time in your life. The value of this is not in his response but the fact that you have done it. Sometimes other people need to be warned so he does not have an opportunity for further abuse.

You may also be angry at those who did not protect you, who did not listen to you, or who exposed you to the abuser. Usually this is the mother. The anger should not be suppressed, repressed or directed at something that is not the true cause. You may also be angry at God.

Sometimes counselees ask, "Where was God when I needed Him? Why didn't He protect me against the abuse?" These are honest questions. The answer is that God created man with freedom, and we are still reaping the results of the Fall. The offender was the one who abused you; not God. It was the free choice of the person who mistreated you. The offender was the one who denied you safety as a child; it was not God.

"But," you say, "because of that abuse I was cheated as a child. I missed out on joy and love and nurturing and protection." That is true. But these things are still available to you regardless of your age.

If you do not release your anger, it will churn around inside of you, interfering with your life, your personal relationships and your self-esteem. If you cannot accept that others deserve your anger, you may believe that you deserve it. Releasing it will help you affirm your innocence. Identify the fears you have about releasing your anger. It could be that you are afraid of losing control, of retaliation, of hurting others or becoming like those who abused you.

Begin by identifying exactly what you are angry about and toward whom you are angry. Create an image of how you see your anger. As a roaring lion? A steam pipe ready to burst? You will need some physical activity to help you feel your anger and release it. Stomping on the garbage sack, pounding nails and digging in the yard are some ways to vent anger. It may help to write unmailed letters to the person and/or complete the following sentence many times a day, "I am angry at you because..." You could imagine the person sitting in a chair across from you. Talk out loud telling him or her about your anger. Tell them that you have a right to be angry and you are going to learn to live free from what they did to you. Proclaim your freedom from what they did. The chapter on "Releasing Your Anger" in Beverly Engel's book *The Right to Innocence* has many helpful suggestions and guidelines.

Victims of sexual abuse, physical abuse, war trauma and disaster trauma, have found that taking the step of some formal ritual or ceremony can serve as a reminder that there is going to be an end to suffering and a beginning to recovery. You are saying good-bye to the bondage you have lived under. Identify each problem, personal behavior, characteristic, negative thought and troublesome feeling in order that you can say good-bye and release them.

You will have a time of pain and separation in this process because you are moving into uncharted waters; and though it is good, it is different. Numbness, depression, the reoccurrence of anger and guilt may be companions, but that is normal.

One daughter made a list of all the abuses the offender had done to her. She sat in a room by herself and placed a picture of her father in a chair and then took each offense and said aloud, "You did this to me. You shouldn't have but you did. I was so hurt and angry, but I am giving up my hurt and anger through the help of Jesus, I am learning to forgive you for this and from this moment in time, I am declaring an end to this chapter in my life. From this point on my focus is the future and what I am going to become in Jesus Christ.

This time of healing is what I will dwell on, rather than what you did to me."

The next step is realizing that in a sense you have discarded your old identity and you are developing a new one. You have said good-bye to the old but you are just beginning to say hello to the new. Not too much is familiar. Give yourself plenty of time. Constantly remind yourself of the changes you have already survived in your life. If you are following these steps in recovery, you definitely are a survivor. Keep your focus forward. Write out what you are planning to become.

Read the book *Chosen for Blessing* by this author so you can capture the possibilities for your future. When I learned to play racquetball a number of years ago, it was unnatural and I felt awkward. I did not see myself as a racquetball player. But in time, that changed.

Nurture yourself as though you have planted a garden. Begin to take better care of yourself in a positive way. Keep reminding yourself that what you are working toward is far superior than what your life was like before.

I have found that in all areas of counseling people do better when they add three elements to their growth process.

First, anticipate how you might sabotage yourself. It may be conscious or unconscious. But give it some consideration. If you find your progress coming to a halt, look for the points of sabotage.

Second, plan for those times when you feel weak and vulnerable. At what times might you feel discouraged? What might discourage you? What negative thoughts might you have that would cripple you? What will you say in response to them?

Third, have a plan for how you are going to make progress and determine what progress is. Dwell on the Scriptures and memorize them to give you strength.[2] Some helpful passages are:

I have strength for all things in Christ Who empowers me—I am ready for anything and equal to anything through Him

Who infuses inner strength into me, [that is, I am self-sufficient in Christ's sufficiency] (Phil. 4:13, *AMP*).

Call to Me and I will answer you and show you great and mighty things, fenced in and hidden, which you do not know—do not distinguish and recognize, have knowledge of and understand (Jer. 33:3, *AMP*).

For I know the thoughts and plans that I have for you, says the Lord, thoughts and plans for welfare and peace, and not for evil, to give you hope in your final outcome (Jer. 29:11, *AMP*).

Steps Toward Progress

What kind of steps can you take as part of your plan? Remember, you may feel as though you are in a vacuum. The anger and resentment are being evicted but what do you fill your life with now?

Learn to trust. One of the first steps may feel risky because it involves learning to trust. This involves taking others at face value, giving them the benefit of the doubt, not making negative assumptions, being more open about what you share and so on. It will be a slow process and you may want to proceed cautiously. It is not just a matter of trusting other people but learning to trust God because He is the only one who will be totally consistent.

Focus on others. To develop trusting relationships you will need to become focused more on others than yourself. Take the time to really get to know other people. Do not expect any one person to meet all your needs.

As you move toward others, consider if you have any behaviors or tendencies in your life that are detrimental to you and your relationships. (Some of the additional reading will help you identify these.)

Take inventory. At the end of each day, inventory the new and positive steps you have taken. Do not dwell on setbacks or old patterns. Look at the new and positive things you are doing and share them with a person you trust. Thank God for His working in your life.

Take the necessary time. Often when an abused person comes for counseling she asks a question I have learned to expect: "How long, Norm? How long does it take to recover?" Often it takes two to three years if you have patience and perseverance. Before you react negatively to this time period, ask yourself: "What will it be like in two or three years if I don't work on recovery?" The time it takes is tied to the severity and duration of the abuse; how open and honest you can become; the amount of support you receive from others and the amount of time you spend each day working on recovery. Those who keep a journal about their feelings each day recover the quickest. You cannot push yourself nor compare yourself with others.

How will you know that you have recovered? How will you measure progress? Like all counseling, recovery is a process. It is a slow step-by-step journey, some days you move forward smoothly and some days nothing happens and it seems like you have regressed. During the down days remember the days when it was better. In time the down days will be less frequent and less intense.[3]

If you find it necessary, seek a licensed, qualified Christian counselor who can help you recover.

Recommended Reading:

Elliott, Lynda, and Tanner, Vicki, *My Father's Child.* Nashville, TN: Wolgemuth and Hyatt, 1988.

Engel, Beverly. *The Right to Innocence.* Los Angeles, CA: Jeremy P. Tarcher Inc., 1989.

Frank, Jan. *A Door of Hope.* San Bernardino, CA: Here's Life Publishers, 1987.

Wright, H. Norman. *Chosen for Blessing.* Eugene, OR: Harvest House Publishers, 1992.

Notes

1. Beverly Engel, *The Right to Innocence* (Los Angeles, CA: Jeremy P. Tarcher Inc., 1989) pp. 12-15, adapted.
2. Lynda Elliott and Vicki Tanner, *My Father's Child* (Nashville, TN: Wolgemuth and Hyatt, 1988), pp. 66-78, adapted.
3. Engel, *The Right to Innocence,* pp. 47-52, adapted.

Chapter 22

GRIEVING A LOSS

Facing Your Losses

Q. HOW CAN I LET GO OF THAT WHICH HAS CAUSED
GRIEF IN MY LIFE AND FACE MY LOSSES?

A. Grief and loss may not be a part of your life right now. But at
some point, they will be. We all face losses in our lives. Most of us
have never been given assistance in how to handle our losses nor do
we understand the process of grieving. Our lives are a blending of
loss and gain. Many of your losses will be evident. They will be tangible, such as the loss of a person through separation. Others may be
more subtle, such as the loss of hope or a dream. You may be aware
of the pain of this loss but you may not identify it as a loss.

When you lose a spouse through death, you will experience a
closure of your grieving over a period of time. In the death of a child,
the loss lingers on for years. In the loss through a divorce, complete
closure may not come, especially if children are involved. But regardless of the loss, you need to grieve.

Over the years I have learned to ask those in counseling the
question, "What is there in your life that you have never fully grieved

over?" Amazingly, most of them in time are able to identify something in their lives in which the grieving has not been completed. And this can interfere with your current life situation. Each time you experience a new loss, it will be intensified by the unresolved loss that needed to be grieved over.

Three things are expressed through the grieving process. (1) You express your feeling about your loss. (2) You express your protest at the loss as well as your desire to change what happened and are unwilling to have it be true. And all this is normal. (3) You also express what you have experienced from the devastating effects of the loss.[1]

The purpose of grieving over your loss is to get beyond these reactions, to face your loss and work on adapting to it. You will begin with the question, "Why did this happen to me?" and eventually your "Why?" questions will change to, "How can I learn through this?" "How can I now go on with my life?" "What can I learn through this experience?" and "How can God be glorified through this experience?"

Steps to Recovery

Q. HOW DO I COPE WITH MY LOVED-ONE'S DEATH? WHAT STEPS DO I NEED TO TAKE TO RECOVER?

A. First, you need to change your relationship with whatever you lost. If it was a person, you eventually need to realize that the person is dead. You are no longer married to or dating him. You need to recognize the change and develop new ways of relating to the deceased person. You have to learn to live *without* the person the way you once learned to live *with* the person. Memories, both positive and negative, will remain with you. We call this acknowledging and understanding the loss.

The second step is to develop your life to encompass and reflect the changes that occurred because of your loss. This will vary, depending upon whether the loss involved a job, an opportunity, a relationship, or the loss of a parent or spouse to death.

The third step is to discover and take on new ways of existing and functioning without whatever it was you lost. This involves a new identity, but without totally forgetting.

The fourth and major step in recovery is saying good-bye to whatever it was you lost. I have seen people say good-bye out loud to a person (dead or alive); make a public declaration of good-bye to a group; stand in front of an office building and say good-bye to a former job; and say good-bye to drugs as the drugs were being burned. One of the best ways is to write a good-bye letter to whatever it was you lost and then sit and read it out loud.

It helps to bring home the reality that a loved person or object or relationship is gone. Saying goody-bye is not morbid, pathological, or a sign of hysteria or being out of control. It is a healthy way to transition into the next phase of life. (For additional help with this, see chapter 6 of *Recovering From the Losses of Life.*)

Fifth, discover new directions for the emotional investments you once had in the lost object, situation or person.[2]

These five steps may sound simple but they are not; all grief involves work, effort and pain. Here is how these steps can be accomplished.

How to Grieve

Acknowledge and understand the loss. This is essential to starting the grieving process. Depending upon the severity, some losses will soon be a faint memory whereas others, such as the death of a child or spouse, may never be completely settled. But this step does mean integrating the loss into your life.

Overcome your shock and denial and face the painful reality of what occurred. It means saying, "Yes, unfortunately this did happen." Facing your loss means you do not attempt to postpone the pain;

you do not deny that it actually happened; and you do not minimize your loss.[3]

You feel and face all of your emotions.

Tell others about it as soon as possible. Call it for what it is. "It was a loss and I am grieving." You may want to keep track of who you told, the date and their responses. Some women have found it helpful to tell at least one or two people each day during the first week after the loss. It means making a conscious decision: "I am going to face it and feel the pain." The best way to describe this kind of pain is intense emotional suffering. You will experience anger, denial, fear, anxiety, rage, depression and many other emotions.

Let your tears flow. Some of us have never learned to cry. We are afraid to let go of our tears. Many of us live with fears and reservations about crying. We may cry on the inside but never on the outside. A way to overcome this is through the process of developing what is called a "Programmed Cry." This is not a one-time activity but something a person might use on several occasions, especially during the first few months after a major loss.

Select a room in your house that has some sentimental value for you. You will need tissues, a stereo and photographs of the person you lost, whether through a dating breakup, divorce or death. It is best if this is done in the evening.

Turn the lights down low and take the phone off the hook so there are no interruptions. Turn on a stereo to either tapes or a radio station that plays mellow music with few interruptions. As sadness hits you, continue to think about your loss. Look at any of the photographs that help you remember what you once had or would have had. Recall the positive and intimate times. Express out loud what you are feeling; do not put a restraint on your tears.

Sometimes it helps to put an empty chair in front of you and talk to the chair as if the person were there. I have encouraged people to talk to God out loud about the loss. Tears and words can express feelings of sadness, depression, longing, anger, hurt, fear and frustration.

But remember, in the midst of your feelings and their expression, your healing and recovery are taking place. As you begin to feel better, allow that healing to occur. Focus on the positive feelings and thoughts that emerge, and say the thoughts aloud. Then put away all the reminders and symbols of your weeping. Share your experience with a trusted friend or write it in a diary.[4]

Watch out for denial. It is a common reaction. In many losses, our initial response is, "Oh no! That can't be true. No! You're wrong!" This is normal. But some choose to stay in this stage and never face their loss. Grieving involves working through several layers of denial. You will first accept it in your head, then in your feelings and finally you will adjust your life's pattern to reflect the reality of what has happened. Do not remain in your denial because the price tag is more than you will want to pay.

Moving Forward, Becoming Unstuck

Q. WHAT DO I DO WHEN I FEEL STUCK IN MY GRIEF?

A. Sometimes people become stuck in their grief. What can you do when you are stuck? The following suggestions may help because they will give you a sense of being in control of the situation. At least you can see yourself doing something about the problem.

1. Try to identify what it is that does not make sense to you about your loss. Perhaps it is a vague question about life or God's purpose for you. Or it could be a specific question: "Why did this have to happen to me now, at this crucial point in my life?" Ask yourself, "What is it that is bothering me the most?" Keep a card with you for several days to record your thoughts as they emerge.

2. Identify the emotions you feel during each day. Are you experiencing sadness, anger, regret, "if onlys," hurt or guilt? What are the feelings directed at? Has the intensity of the feelings decreased or increased during the past few days? If your feelings are vague, identifying and labeling them will diminish their power over you.

3. *State the steps or actions you are taking to help you move ahead and overcome your loss.* Identify what you have done in the past that has helped or ask a trusted friend for help.

4. *Be sure you are sharing your loss and grief with others who can listen to you and support you during this time.* Do not seek out advice-givers. Find those who are empathetic and can handle your feelings. Remember, your journey through grief will never be exactly like that of another person; each of us is unique. Do not let others box you in.

5. *It may help to find someone who has experienced a similar loss.* Groups and organizations abound for losses of all types. Reading books or stories about those who have survived similar experiences can be helpful.

6. *Identify the positive characteristics and strengths of your life that have helped you before.* Which of these will help you at this time in your life?

7. *Spend time reading in the Psalms.* Many of the Psalms reflect the struggle of human loss but give the comfort and assurance that come from God's mercies.

8. *When you pray, share your confusion, feelings and hopes with God.* Be sure to be involved in the worship services of your church as worship is an important element in recovery and stabilization.

9. *Think about where you want to be in your life two years from now.* Write out some of your dreams and goals. Setting some goals may encourage you to realize you will recover.

10. *Become familiar with the stages of grief.* Then you will know what to expect and you won't be thrown by what you are experiencing.

11. *Remember that understanding your grief intellectually is not sufficient.* It cannot replace the emotional experience of living through this difficult time. You need to be patient and allow your feelings to catch up with your mind. Expect mood swings, and remind yourself of these through notes placed in obvious places. These mood swings are normal.[5]

Factors in Length of Grieving

Q. WHEN DOES THE PAIN OF GRIEF GO AWAY? HOW LONG DOES IT TAKE?

A. "How long? How long is it going to take before I recover? When will the grief go away?" I cannot say. Many factors are involved. But we do know that in the case of a death of a loved one the following time lines can be applied. If the death was a natural death—approximately two years. Accidental death—three years. Death by suicide—four years and death by homicide—five years. In the death of a child, it takes much longer. Be aware that when the intensity of your grief begins to subside, it will return with the same intensity at about three months following the loss and at one year or the anniversary date of the loss. Again this is normal in your pattern of grieving.

Your grief will follow somewhat of a pattern. I like how Richard Exley describes the grieving process. He calls it, "The tides of grief." These tides of grief will come in and go out. You will experience times of intense grief followed by periods of relative calm. Then the tide will come in again, and once more you will grieve. Just as suddenly, the tide will go out again so that if you did not know better, you would think you were finally over your grief. Of course, you are not. This is just another "resting period" before you resume your "grief work."

"As grief does its healing work, you will begin to notice some subtle changes. When the tide of grief rolls in, it will not come in quite so far, nor will it stay as long. And when it rolls back, it will go out farther and stay out longer. Your times of grief will become briefer and less intense, while your times of rest will become longer and more renewing."[6]

Do not let others tell you that you should be done grieving by a certain time. Very few people are experts on grieving. But you can become much better equipped to both handle the losses in your life and minister to others by your own study. I would encourage you, if you have suffered a recent loss, to seek out and join a grief recovery group whether the loss has been by divorce, death or for any kind of a serious loss. If you are anticipating a loss, find support. Those who survive losses are those who allow others to help them through the process.

Ministering to Another Grieving Person

Q. HOW CAN I MINISTER TO ANOTHER GRIEVING PERSON?

A. Here are some steps you can take to minister to another grieving person.

Accept what has happened and how the person is responding. You may have your own perspective on what the person should be doing or how he or she should be responding. Revise your expectations. You are not the other person and you are not an authority on that person's responses.

Accept the grieving person and let her know her feelings are normal. She might apologize to you for her tears, depression or anger. You will hear comments such as: "I can't believe I'm still crying like this. I'm so sorry." "I don't know why I'm still so upset. It was unfair of them to let me go after 15 years at that job. I know I shouldn't be angry, but I guess I really am. It seems so unfair."

Be an encourager by accepting her feelings. Give her the gift of facing her feelings and expressing them. You can make statements such as:

"I don't want you to worry about crying in front of me. It's hard to feel this sad and not express it in tears. You may find me crying with you at times."

"I hope you feel the freedom to express your sorrow in tears in front of me. I won't be embarrassed or upset. I just want to be here with you."

"If I didn't see you cry, I would be more concerned. Your crying tells me you are handling this in a healthy way."

"If I had experienced what you have been through, I would feel like opening my eyes and letting the flood of tears come pouring out. Do you ever feel like that?"[7]

In each loss you will need to: (1) discover the grieving person's personal situation and needs; (2) decide what you are willing and able to do for them, realizing that you can't do it all, nor should you; and finally, (3) contact her and offer to do the most difficult of the jobs you have chosen. If she rejects your offer, suggest another. Specific tasks could include feeding pets, making or delivering meals, yard work, making difficult phone calls, obtaining needed information regarding support groups or new employment, providing transportation, being available to run errands and so forth. At some point in time, giving the person a sensitive, supportive book on loss and grief could be helpful.

Someone, whether it is you or another concerned person, will need to help the grieving person(s) accomplish several tasks. These tasks are especially applicable in the loss of a loved one and will be accomplished over a period of time.

Help the grieving person identify secondary losses and resolve any unfinished business with the lost person. For many, these losses are never identified or grieved over. It could be the loss of a role, the family unit, the breadwinner, social life and so on. Sometimes saying aloud what a grieving person never said or had an opportunity to say to the deceased helps to complete some of the unfinished business.

Help her recognize that in addition to grieving for the lost person, grief will need to be experienced for any dreams, expectations or fantasies she had for the person. This is sometimes difficult or overlooked, as dreams or expectations are not usually seen as losses because they never existed. Yet each still constitutes a loss because these dreams have a high value.

Discover what the grieving person is capable of doing and where she might be lacking in her coping skills. Help her handle the areas where she is struggling. Encourage positive things such as talking about the loss. If she does something unhealthy, such as indulging in avoidance, alcohol or overmedication, give her other alternatives.

Because most people do not understand the duration and process of grieving, provide her with helpful information concerning what she is now experiencing. You want to normalize her grief without minimizing it. But also let her know that her grief responses will be unique. She should not compare herself to anyone else. Do not let her equate the length and amount of grieving with how much she loved the person.

Let her know you understand she may want to avoid the intensity of the pain she is presently experiencing. Your empathy, understanding and respect will do much to assist her in knowing that her grief is normal. Encourage her to go through the pain of the grief. There is just no way to avoid it. If she tries to avoid it, it will explode at some other time. She may need reminding that even with the present intensity of her pain, in time it will diminish.

Help her understand that the grief will affect all areas of her life. Work habits, memory, attention span, intensity of feelings, response to marital partner will all be affected. This is normal.

Help her understand the process of grief. Understanding that her emotions will vary and that progress is erratic will help alleviate the feeling that there is no progress. Help her plan for significant dates and holidays in advance. Encourage her to talk about her expectations for herself and help her evaluate whether or not she is being realistic.[8]

Recommended Reading:

Chesser, Barbara Russell. *Because You Care.* Dallas, TX: WORD Inc., 1987.

Exley, Richard. *When You Lose Someone You Love.* Tulsa, OK: Honor Books, 1991. This book encompasses the entire range of losses and can be used as the basis for grief recovery groups.

Kuenning, Delores. *Helping People Through Grief.* Minneapolis, MN: Bethany House Publishers, 1987. This book will give you many helpful chapters and an extensive bibliography on how to minister to others in grief.

Wright, H. Norman. *Recovering from the Losses of Life.* Tarrytown, NY: Fleming H. Revell, 1991. This book contains a chapter on how to minister to those in grief.

Notes

1. Therese A. Rando, *Grieving: How to Go on Living When Someone You Love Dies* (Lexington, MA: Lexington Books, 1988), pp. 18,19, adapted.

2. Ibid., p. 19, adapted.

3. H. Norman Wright, *Recovering from the Losses of Life* (Tarrytown, NY: Fleming H. Revell, 1991), pp. 42,43, adapted.

4. Ibid., p. 50, adapted.

5. Ibid., pp. 76,77, adapted.

6. Richard Exley, *When You Lose Someone You Love* (Tulsa, OK: Honor Books, 1991), p. 49.

7. Wright, *Recovering from the Losses of Life,* pp. 182,183.

8. Ibid., p. 195, adapted.

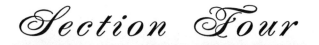

Section Four

PARENTING
ISSUES

Chapter 23

PARENTING PROBLEMS

Improving Parenting Skills

Q. MY KIDS ARE DRIVING ME CRAZY. HELP ME
IMPROVE MY PARENTING SKILLS.

A. Most parents wonder if they are being good parents. My question to you is, "What is your criteria for being a good mother or father?" What is your measure? I trust that it is not how well your children turn out in terms of morals, a college education or whether they stay married or not. That is risky as it puts you at the mercy of their behavior and free will.

What you can do to improve your parenting skills is (1) learn as much as you can about being a good mother or father; (2) face and deal with any issues in your past or your marriage that would interfere with being a good parent; and then (3) love and enjoy your children instead of worrying about your performance. Look to the Scriptures for guidelines for parenting and check out other resources.

Helping Children Become Mature

Q. HOW DO I RAISE RESPONSIBLE AND MATURE
CHILDREN IN A LOVING MANNER?

A. Our job as parents is to empower our children to become mature. Maturity can imply many things. I would define maturity as the ability to contribute to the good of other people in a positive and constructive way. Perhaps this is best illustrated in 1 Thessalonians 5:11, where we are instructed to "encourage one another and build each other up." We want our children to grow up knowing how to love and serve people and assist them in their growth.

Most children do not develop characteristics of maturity on their own. They must be empowered to maturity through the guidance of their parents. Jack and Judith Balswick describe the concept of empowering well:

> Parents who are empowerers will help their children become competent and capable persons, who will in turn empower others. Empowering parents will be actively and intentionally engaged in various pursuits—teaching, guiding, caring, modeling—which will equip their children to become confident individuals able to relate to others. Parents who empower will help their children recognize the strengths and potential within and find ways to enhance these qualities. Parental empowering is the affirmation of the child's ability to learn, grow, and become all that one is meant to be as part of God's image and creative plan.[1]

Parental love that is empowering enables rather than disables a child. When a parent holds on to a child too tightly, it is usually because he or she is trying to meet his or her own needs instead of the child's. Controlling, disabling parents jump in with "helping" comments such as, "Here, let me do that for you. It's too hard for you."

Some parents speak for a child or finish his sentences for him. But these responses handicap the child, often causing him to think, *Mom and Dad don't believe I'm capable of doing this for myself.* Parental love affirms the child's adequacy and empowers him to maturity just as God's love affirms our adequacy in Christ and empowers us to maturity in Him.

How do we empower our children to achieve maturity? We must use four techniques: (1) telling; (2) teaching; (3) participating; and (4) delegating. Each of these techniques relates to a different age level of the child and requires a different style of parental communication.[2]

How to Change Your Parenting Style

Q. HOW CAN I BE A MORE EFFECTIVE PARENT TO
MY CHILDREN? MY PARENTING STYLE IS
NOT WORKING. HELP!

A. In his excellent book, *Legacy of Love,* Tim Kimmel emphasizes the need to establish a blueprint for your child's character. His basic question is, "Do you have a plan for building your child's character?" Kimmel believes that in building your child's character you are leaving him a legacy of love.

In *Legacy of Love,* Kimmel goes into great detail exploring and expanding on each character trait. It is the best treatment of character development I have ever seen. If you want further help in this area, I suggest you work through his book.

You must use a tailor-made blueprint for each child that contains built-in flexibility for alterations along the way. And you must always remember: The same free will that allowed Adam and Eve to make wrong choices still exists within every child. Regardless of how much you do, your children may elect not to go along with your blueprint.[3]

You may be at a point right now where you would like to develop such a blueprint for your child, but some old habits stand in the way. Like many parents, maybe you have unwittingly fallen into a parenting pattern that you now understand to be less than ideal and perhaps even harmful to your child. You ask, "Where do I go from here? How do I change?" Change is possible. Here are some steps that will help you implement change in your parenting style.

1. Identify in writing what you want your parenting pattern to become and what you want to see happen in your child. This step works best when both you and your husband are united in a team effort. After you have written your responses individually, share with each other your respective plans. Commit yourselves to help each other follow this new plan, hold each other accountable and pray for each other every day.

2. Communicate your new plan to your child. Sit down with your child and inform her about your goal for her life. Explain as much as she is capable of comprehending about how she can expect you to respond to her under this new approach. Some parents have called this a "realignment session" because it gives new direction for family life.

It is important that during this session you assure your child of your love for her, and that you are committed to the best for her life. One parent phrased it this way: "I love you, and I cherish our relationship. I'm glad you are my daughter. But I also want you to know that it is very important to me to be a good parent. You deserve the best."

If you are working to change a bad parenting pattern such as being overly strict or legalistic, describe your old pattern in terms simple enough for your child to understand. You may say, "There have been times when I was overly strict with you and have not listened to what you wanted or needed. Sometimes I have been more concerned with what I thought was proper instead of what was best for your growth."

It is also important that you let your child know how you felt about how you acted in the past. Reassure your child that she was not responsible for the way you treated her. You may say, "The way I treated you was not the way I wanted to treat you. It's hard for me to admit it, but I know I probably made life hard for you the way I acted." If you need to apologize to your child or ask forgiveness for specific actions or words, now is the time to do so.

Also during the realignment session, ask your child to share with you how she felt under your old parenting style. Then ask how she might feel under the new approach you have described. Do not press your child for an immediate response; she may need time to think about it. Then ask your child to pray for you in your new endeavor.

3. Implement your new plan. To help you get started, read your new written plan aloud every morning and afternoon for 30 days. During the month, evaluate your progress at the end of each week—first by yourself, then with your spouse or a trusted friend. Do not expect instant change in yourself or your child. We all change gradually, but steady growth tends to be more permanent.[4]

Part of your parenting pattern will involve discipline and training. This should assist your child to establish a set of sound values and principles that she can use to conduct her life. Values need to be internalized.

The chart below gives three possible patterns of discipline for children. The three numbers 0, 12 and 18, indicate ages of the child as she grows into adolescence.

Pattern for Discipline

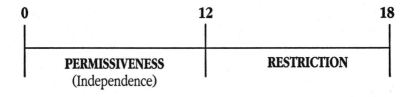

0	12	18
PERMISSIVENESS (Independence)	**RESTRICTION**	

In the first example, we see that during the first 12 years the parents have used the permissive pattern of child rearing. However, when the child becomes an adolescent the parents see the various changes and problems that occur at this age. They become alarmed and concerned and for the first time in the life of the child they begin to impose restrictions and attempt to retain control. However, they are met with resistance and conflict. Their adolescent has not been accustomed to this new pattern. It is foreign to her and she's not about to give up her freedom.

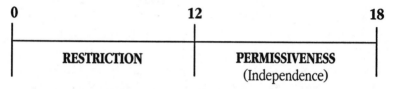

In the second example the pattern is reversed. The parents have been restrictive (in a good sense) during the first 12 years, using proper techniques and methods. When the child becomes an adolescent they allow more permissiveness and independence because the child is able to accept this and can function by herself.

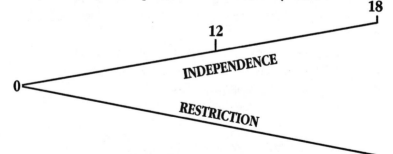

The third example gives a better explanation of this process than the second chart. Some parents follow the second chart too closely by being totally restrictive during the first 12 years and then suddenly allowing the child a great deal of freedom. The third chart indicates that this is a gradual, blending process including restrictiveness as well as teaching the child how to be responsible. Gradually the child is allowed more and more freedom and independence as she indicates that she is capable of behaving or functioning on her own. The parent, in a real sense, has learned how to "let go and let grow." But it is a step-by-step process.

Teaching Values to Your Children

Q. I WANT MY CHILDREN TO HAVE GOOD VALUES. WHAT ADVICE CAN YOU GIVE ME?

A. Your goal is to help your children establish a set of internalized values and principles. You can do this in several ways.

Responsibility. Teach your child to be responsible for what he does. The blame cannot be placed upon others. If he fails an exam because he did not study for it, it is not the teacher's fault for giving the test or asking difficult questions. If he does not carry out one of the rules of the home and has to miss his favorite television program, he is responsible for this action, not you.

Allowing your child to experience the logical and natural consequences of his actions provides an honest and real learning situation. This does not include situations that would be dangerous or injurious to the child. If he continually forgets to take his lunch to school he will learn best if he has to go without a lunch one day.

Choices. Let your child make choices. Set up situations or give instructions in which he is able to make a choice between two or three alternatives. This allows you to continue to control the situation and suggest the possible choices. But it lets your child know he has some voice and choice in the matter. It also teaches him that he must accept the consequences of his choice.

Give reasons. Give him reasons for rules or standards when he is old enough to comprehend and reason. But when you give the reasons to him, do not get involved in an argument. You are still the parent. You are simply sharing with the child why he is to do what you have asked. It is difficult for him to internalize his own value system unless he knows the "why" behind rules and regulations.

Teach him that, even though he may not accept all of the reasons given to him, it is best for him and for others that he obey. He will see the value later on. But at least let him know why he should do it.

No contradictions. Ask yourself, "Do my own actions contradict what I am trying to teach the child?" If you say, "John, don't ever talk to me in that tone of voice," ask yourself if he learned to do that from hearing you? If you say, "Don't ever lie," does the child hear you bending the truth in any way?

Love. Love him when you discipline him. The child is more open to your guidance and assistance when you sit with him, loving him, after the discipline has been administered.

Setting Rules for Children

Q. HOW DO I SET LIMITS WITH MY CHILDREN? DO I NEED A SET OF RULES?

A. Regardless of the rules you set down for your children, four basic principles must be followed.

A rule should be definable. If it is well-defined, he will know instantly when he has broken it. It must be so specifically presented that both of you know what is actually meant by the rule.

Some parents are not as explicit as they should be and expect their child or teenager to be a mind reader. Many a parent has said, "Well, he ought to know that's what I meant." If you tell your daughter she cannot go outside until her room is clean, that is a poorly defined rule. Cleaning the room to her might be closing the door and shutting out the mess. But if you tell her to make the bed, empty the trash and hang up her clothes properly on hangers, you are getting closer to a definable rule. You must be willing to live with the definition of the chore and you cannot demand any more or less than the exact fulfillment of that task.

A rule should be reasonable. The rule should actually make the environment more comfortable for the child. When he follows the rule he is performing a normal, necessary function. Make sure it is a rule the child is capable of following.

A rule should be enforceable. Whenever a rule is stated, anticipate that it may be broken. Most children like to test rules. If you cannot enforce a rule consistently, you cannot expect the child to follow it. How do you know whether or not a rule can be enforced? One suggestion is: Will you know every time the child breaks the rule without depending on another person's testimony? You must be able to find out easily whether a rule has been broken.

A rule should help a person develop inner values and control. The rule will eventually help a child become an independent, responsible person. The rule should be for the benefit of the parents as well as for the benefit of the child and others.

Teaching Adolescents

Q. HOW CAN I HELP MY ADOLESCENT CHILDREN
STAY OUT OF TROUBLE WITHOUT
"CONTROLLING" THEM?

A. If you have adolescents, consider the following suggestions:

1. Regular times should be established for family discussion. These may take place at the dinner table, while driving to or from school, during a walk after dinner, or whenever you can establish a pattern. It also means being available when a person has a need to share.

2. Let your teenager know you want to hear what he has to say. This means there will be times when you *will not share* your opinion or expertise on the subject. You may consider some of their thoughts to be way off base. (They may think the same of some of yours.) You may want to "set them

straight;" but unless you let them express their ideas without fear of being jumped on, they will learn not to say anything at all.

It is difficult to remain silent when your teen holds views contrary to your own. Most parents want teenagers to accept their ideas and opinions. And yet to develop their thinking ability, they need to learn to explore ideas and beliefs. You may not agree with what they say, and you have a right to explain your opposing viewpoint. But both of you can discuss opinions calmly, in a proper tone of voice, with courtesy toward each other.

3. Set limits on behavior but not on opinions. This is perhaps the most difficult guideline for parents to carry out without becoming overly threatened. A free expression of opinion, with proper rules of courtesy, is one of the healthiest goals a family can work toward. The effort will create an atmosphere in which people learn to listen to one another.

4. Above all, encourage your teenager. We all need to be encouraged. We need to know that we are okay, that we count, and that our efforts (not necessarily results) are recognized and appreciated. Affirm him for who he is as a person.

5. Your teenager needs to be responsible for what he does. Do not let him blame others for his own actions. I remember a situation one night when a 17-year-old arrived home more than an hour late from his date. Both of his parents were still up. They simply looked at him with a wondering expression as he walked in. He started to say, "Sorry I'm late, but that dumb car ran out of gas." But halfway through he stopped, grinned and said, "Nope. I'm late because I neglected to take the time to put some gas in the car, so I'm the culprit." The parents gave a small grin and one said, "Thanks. We both appreciate your telling us that." And they said no more. They did not have to remind him to put gas in the car next time. He learned through his experience. His remark demonstrat-

ed the benefits of some well-spent discussion times with his parents as he was growing into adolescence.

6. A principle similar to the one above is that your teenager has to learn to accept the consequences for what he does. Allowing him to experience the logical and natural consequences of his actions provides an honest and real learning situation.

   A friend of mine told of a procedure that has worked well for several families with teenagers who are dating. When this man's daughter went out on a date she was expected home at a certain time. When she was 15 she had to be in at 11:00; at 16, 11:30; and at 17, 12:00. A few exceptions were made for special occasions. She knew that if she came in half an hour late, she would have to make up that half hour by coming home that much earlier on her next date. Whether it was 5 minutes or an hour it was made up on the next date, regardless of the occasion. Very little discussion was needed; the rule was established with its natural consequences and everyone knew what it was.

7. As was suggested earlier, let your teenager make choices. "John, you will have to make a decision. You can go to Jim's house this evening to work on your car and then fix the garage door tomorrow night. You make the choice and I'll go along with it." Many potentially explosive encounters between parents and teenagers can be defused if you will approach your teen with several possible choices. Sometimes the teenager may counter with an additional choice, which may be a valid possibility. You will have to decide whether to allow that alternative.

Recommended Reading:

Kimmel, Tim. *Legacy of Love*. Portland, OR: Multnomah Productions, 1989.

McKean, Paul, and McKean, Jeannie. *Leading a Child to Independence.* San Bernardino, CA: Here's Life Publishers, 1987.

Narramore, Bruce. *Help, I'm a Parent.* Grand Rapids, MI: Zondervan Publishing House, 1979.

Scott, Buddy. *Relief for Hurting Parents.* Nashville, TN: Thomas Nelson Publishers, 1989.

Simmons, Dave. *Dad, the Family Coach.* Wheaton, IL: Victor Books, 1991.

Simmons, Dave. *Dad, the Family Counselor.* Wheaton, IL: Victor Books, 1991.

Simmons, Dave. *Dad, the Family Mentor.* Wheaton, IL: Victor Books, 1992.

Wright, H. Norman. *Power of a Parent's Words.* Ventura, CA: Regal Books, 1991.

Notes

1. Jack O. Balswick and Judith K. Balswick, *The Family* (Grand Rapids, MI: Baker Book House, 1989), p. 103.
2. H. Norman Wright, *Power of a Parent's Words* (Ventura, CA: Regal Books, 1991), p. 42,43.
3. Ibid., p. 57.
4. Ibid., pp. 60-62, adapted.

Chapter 24

PARENTING HOT BUTTONS: ANGER, FRUSTRATION, REBELLION, DRUGS

Dealing with Your Anger and Frustration

Q. WHAT DO I DO WHEN I GET SO ANGRY AND
FRUSTRATED WITH MY CHILDREN THAT ALL
I WANT TO DO IS SCREAM, HIT OR
BANISH THEM FOREVER?

A. Let's face some facts. You are going to be frustrated, irritated, disappointed and angry at your children at some time in your parenting years.

In her book, *In Love and Anger: The Parental Dilemma*, Nancy Samalin describes your situation:

> Parents are amazed that they can go from relative calm to utter frustration in a few seconds. An uneaten egg or spilled juice at breakfast can turn a calm morning into a free-for-all. In spite of parents' best intentions, bedtime becomes wartime, meals end with children in tears and food barely touched,

and car rides deteriorate into stress-filled shouting match-es...Whatever its source, we often experience parental anger as a horrifying encounter with our worst selves. I never even knew I had a temper until I had children. It was very fright-ening that these children I loved so much, for whom I had sacrificed so much, could arouse such intense feelings of rage in me, their mother, whose primary responsibility was to nur-ture and protect them.[1]

Anger and frustration usually occur when your children are causing you problems or are not living up to your expectations. Accepting and recognizing your frustration and anger is healthy. Saying, "A good par-ent doesn't feel this way," is dangerous. When you are thinking of hurt-ing your child and these thoughts persist, your frustration has hit a crit-ical stage. It is a warning. It is easy to cross the line into physical abuse. You are now at a point where you definitely need professional help.

Don Westgate, executive director of For Kid's Sake, an organiza-tion dedicated to preventing child abuse, has developed this quiz to help you discover whether you should seek help for your anger.

1. Do you feel inadequate as a parent and about knowing child development?
2. Do you have low self-esteem?
3. Are you getting angry more and more often?
4. Have some people indicated your disciplinary reactions are unreasonable?
5. Do you feel your child seldom meets your expectations or wonder if your expectations are too high?
6. Do you feel isolated or depressed?
7. Have you ever left a mark on your child?
8. Were you abused as a child?
9. Do you envision any sexual fantasies about your child?
10. Do you visualize hurting your child and think it would feel good to do so?

If you placed check marks by one or two of the questions it does not necessarily mean your anger is out of control. But if you checked more than two, or if you checked any of numbers 7 to 10, it would be wise for you to talk with your pastor or a professional Christian therapist. Doing so will help you deal more effectively with your anger.[2]

You do have a choice about how far your frustration goes and how you can deal with it, just as you can choose what to do with your anger.

I hear mothers say to me again and again, "Norm, I don't want to talk abusively to my kids, but something just comes over me and I let it rip! There's a limit to what I can take from them. I really love my children, but sometimes I don't like them very much. I've even had thoughts of throttling them! That scares me. I don't know what to do to change."

I often respond with the question: "When you feel frustrated and angry with your children, what do you focus on? How they behaved and what you said or how you would like them to behave?"

The mothers usually reply, "Oh, I keep mulling over their misbehavior and my destructive comments. I relive it again and again and beat up on myself for hurting them."

"Do you realize that by rehearsing your failures you are programming yourself to repeat them?" I ask.

The moms usually respond with quizzical looks. But it is true. When you spend so much time thinking about what you should not have done, you reinforce the negative behavior. Redirecting your time and energy toward a solution will make a big difference in how you communicate with your child. Focus your attention on how you want to respond to your frustrations and you will experience change![3]

The anger you feel is a result of being frustrated. Frustration is one of the three major causes for anger, the others being fear and hurt.

The first step at this point is to begin keeping an anger log that deals only with your anger toward your child or children. Identify the frequency, intensity and duration of your anger with each child.

What you are doing is identifying some of the situations that trigger your anger. I know of a parent who forewarns her children with the phrase, "That is a trigger and I'm getting close to pulling it." When they hear that phrase, they have learned to back off. Then follow these steps:

1. Set up an accountability program. Find someone with whom you can share your parenting struggles and frustrations and develop an accountability relationship. Select a person who will be willing to pray with you and check up on you regularly to see how you are doing.

You also need to be honest and accountable to yourself and to your husband about the changes you want to make. Take a sheet of paper and respond in writing to the following questions. Then share your responses with your husband or prayer partner:

- How do you feel about becoming frustrated? Be specific. How do you feel about getting angry? Some people enjoy their frustration and anger. It gives them an adrenaline rush and a feeling of power. Do you ever feel this way?

- When you are frustrated, do you want to be in control of your response or be spontaneous? In other words, do you want to decide what to do or just let your feelings take you where they want to go? If you go by your feelings, how will you be able to change

- If you want to stay in control, how much time and energy are you willing to spend to make it happen? For change to occur, the motivational level needs to remain both constant and high.

- When you are bothered by something your child does, how would you like to respond? What would you like to say? Be very specific.

2. Use God's Word to stabilize you. Write out each of the following verses on a separate index card: Proverbs 12:18; 14:29; 16:32 and Ephesians 4:26. Add to your card file other Scriptures you discover that relate to frustration and anger. Read these verses aloud morning and evening for one month. Be prepared for a change.

3. Plan in advance. You will only be able to change if you plan to change. Your intentions may be good, but once the frustration-anger sequence kicks into gear, your ability to think clearly is limited.

Identify in advance what you want to say to your child when you begin to feel frustrated. Be specific. Here are some possible statements you can use:

"I am very angry right now."

"I need to take time out to think and pray about what I am feeling before I decide what I'm going to do."

"It's hard for me to concentrate on my driving when you are yelling and throwing things."

"I'd like you to be quiet."

"I'm disappointed and hurt that you lied to me."

"I'm exhausted, and I need some peace and quiet now."

"I'll be glad to help you with it after dinner."

"I don't like it when you talk to me like that."

Write out your responses and read them aloud to yourself and to your prayer partner. In my counseling office I often have clients practice their new responses on me, and I attempt to respond as the other person. By practicing on me they are able to refine their statements, eliminate their anxiety or feelings of discomfort and gain confidence for their new approach. Your husband or prayer partner could assist you this way.

4. Delay reacting. Begin training yourself to delay your verbal and behavioral responses when you recognize that you are frustrated with your child. Proverbs repeatedly admonishes us to be slow to anger. You must slow down your responses if you want to change any habits of angry words you have cultivated over the years. When we allow frustration and anger to be expressed unhindered, they are like a runaway locomotive. Catch them before they gather momentum so you can switch the tracks and steer them in the right direction.

One helpful way to change direction is to use a trigger word. Whenever you feel frustration and anger rising within you, remind yourself to slow down and gain control by saying something to yourself such as "stop," "think," "control" and so on. Use a word that will help you switch gears and put your new plan into action.

5. Does it have to frustrate you? One of the approaches I often suggest to parents to diffuse a frustrating power struggle with their children is this: Mentally give your child permission to be involved in the behavior that frustrates you. For example, your little Susan always leaves the back door open when she goes out to play—and it drives you up the wall. More than once you have angrily shouted after her, "Susan, come back here this instant and close that door! You were not raised in a barn!" Often the skirmish over the back door has ruined the morning for both you and Susan.

The next time Susan leaves the back door open, say to yourself, "I don't know why Susan leaves the door open, but I'm not going to let it ruin my day. It's not the worst thing she could do. If she wants to leave the door open, I give her permission to do so. I know there is a reason for it, and it's important for me to discover that reason. It will be a learning experience for Susan and me as we try to resolve this behavior."

The permission-giving approach defuses your frustration and gives you time to implement a level-headed plan.[4]

6. Discover your child's unique learning style and personality and adapt your responses accordingly and your level of frustration will diminish. You cannot respond to each child the same way and even if you have just one child, your responses need to be honed and refined to fit that child. This is the meaning of Proverbs 22:6: "Train up a child in the way he should go [and in keeping with his individual gift or bent], and when he is old he will not depart from it" *(AMP)*.

Be sure to read *The Power of a Parent's Words,* which goes into great detail in a practical way on this issue.

7. When you talk with your child about the problem, do not be predictable. If you usually shout, speak softly. If you usually stand, kneel down. Be sure you have their attention. Speak softly, put your hand gently on the child's shoulder, look in the child's eyes and speak slowly and gently. Be specific. Focus on the essentials. Make the expression of your anger descriptive, accurate and to the point; not several points but one point. What is the bottom line? What is negotiable and nonnegotiable? Do you know? Do your children know? Furthermore, keep consistent your rules, standards and expectations. If you change back and forth your child will be confused.

Ask yourself, "What's my motive?" What do I want to accomplish? How can I use this situation to communicate my love and concern, draw us closer together, strengthen the bonds of trust and help my child learn? Your goal should be to communicate your anger in such a way that your children know they are still loved, valued and significant in your eyes. Parents who react aggressively to their children's anger are more likely to make negative and critical statements that communicate to their children that they are unworthy and unlovable. Before responding ask yourself, "How can I acknowledge my child's rights, values and concerns? How can I respond in a way that will encourage him? How can I help him become more responsible?"[5]

7. *Take breaks from your children.* Every mother needs breathing time. Enlist your husband to baby-sit so you can get out by yourself or with your friends. Or if you are a single mother, ask a friend to relieve you once in a while. Find another mother and take turns baby-sitting one another's children.

Dealing with a Rebellious Child

Q. I JUST DON'T KNOW HOW TO HANDLE MY CHILDREN'S BEHAVIOR. THEY ARE CONSTANTLY ACTING OUT.

A. The reasons for a child's or an adolescent's misbehavior are abundant. Too often the blame is laid on the parents. Regardless of the deficits in a home, a child is responsible for his or her behavior. You can take action about the problem by doing some things prior to and during the difficult times.

I am assuming you are endeavoring to create a healthy, loving, stress-free atmosphere in your home. I am also assuming you have ruled out any physical basis for these problems.

Establish Rules

The rules you set down need to be clearly defined and expressed in the language of a child at her level of understanding. From early on, it is helpful to have Mom, Dad and the child sit down and go over the rules, explaining the purpose and clarifying any misunderstandings. Tell your child you believe she is capable of following through. Put the rules in writing and have everyone sign them, indicating their understanding and agreement. If there is a violation, then you can all look at the rules again.

You can approach violations in two ways. (1) You can handle an infraction at the time it occurs by saying, "I'd like you to take some time and consider what you believe the consequences ought to be." Get the child involved in this process. (2) Or you can discuss in advance the benefits of following guidelines. A child who acts out can soon learn there are more benefits from complying than from disobeying. He may not like it but the purpose is not for him to enjoy the rules.

Regardless of the approach you take, consistency on the part of both parents is important. Immediate action and a minimum of talk is required.

Teach Responsibility

At an early age, teach your child the concept of personal responsibility. Whatever situation he creates, let him experience the consequences and be responsible for solving the problem. Many parents act as enablers and reinforce behavior they do not want. If their child or adolescent leaves the bathroom in a mess, the parents clean it up. So the child learns not to bother cleaning up after himself. Instead, make the child responsible. If he leaves dirty clothes in the closet, he can go without clean clothes. If his clothes are not available when the washing is done, he can wait until the next week for clean clothes or he can wash the clothes himself. If the child creates a mess, the child cleans it up.

Harsh? Not at all. It is simply teaching the child to be responsible. I know of wealthy families with maids who employ such rules for their children. Each family member needs to learn the art of giving and taking. One of the reasons parents have problems with their children is that too often the parents are the givers and their offspring are only takers.

If your child abuses his privileges, he will lose them as part of the natural consequences. If your teenager abuses the traffic laws and piles up violations, she quickly loses the privilege of driving. The state will take away her license. If she misuses the car, phone or TV, she loses her accessibility to these items until trust is rebuilt.

Be sure to establish the guidelines in advance. Give your teenager time to consider what he thinks should be contained in the agreement and then have him submit his suggestions to you. When it has been finalized, both parents and teenager sign and date the form, indicating their willingness and commitment to follow the covenant.

Here is a sample agreement that was worked out with a 15-year-old girl and her parents. I am not saying every parent should use this agreement, it is merely an example. You may agree with some of its provisions and disagree with others.

The agreement contains both restrictions and freedoms. Such agreements should be reviewed every six months to see how they are working and to determine which areas should be revised.

Over half the items on this list were suggested by the daughter. The word "thoroughly" was added to number two by her parents. Dad added number three, which was her least favorite rule, but one the daughter said she could live with. The reason for the rule was that too many times a radio is distracting and often played too loudly. Rule eight indicates a latitude and freedom for her driving experience. This family traveled a great deal in the summer and her parents wanted her to have the experience of driving under varied highway, traffic and weather conditions so she would be better equipped when on her own.

Driving Agreement

1. Before using either car I will ask either my mom or dad if I can use the car and explain the purpose.

2. If I want to go somewhere, my homework and piano practicing must have been completed thoroughly.

3. During the first six months of driving with my own driver's license, the radio will not be used while driving.

4. During the school year I will be allowed to drive to church on Wednesday nights but cannot take anyone home with out prior permission.

5. I will not allow anyone else to use the car under any circumstances.

6. I will be allowed up to thirty-five miles a week and after that I must pay for any additional mileage.

7. I will not carry more than five passengers at any time in the Plymouth nor more than three in the Audi.

8. Upon receiving my driver's permit I will be allowed to drive to church and run local errands when either Mom or Dad is along. I will assist in driving for extended periods of time on our long vacations under all types of driving conditions.

9. I will not give rides to hitchhikers under any conditions nor will I accept any ride if I should have any difficulty with the car.

10. I will either wash the car myself or have it done once every three weeks.

11. I will pay half the increase of the insurance costs and in case of an accident I will assume half the deductible cost.

Even before this covenant was agreed upon, the daughter had earned half of the increase of the insurance rate by helping paint the family home.

Some have asked about the consequences should these rules be broken. The father said that for two reasons nothing had been agreed upon. They as parents were willing to invest trust in their daughter to the extent that they would expect her to live up to the agreement. If, however, there was a violation, the consequences would be discussed with her and she would be asked three questions: (1) "Why do you think you did what you did?" (2) "What will you do next time?" (3) "What do you think should be the consequences for this violation of the covenant?" She would be asked to make two or three suggestions and would have sufficient time to think these over, then one of them would be selected.

Sometimes your child or teen will make threats to try to manipulate you. Such as, "I'm going to quit school," "I'm going to run away," "I'm going to commit suicide," "I'm going to do something you'll be sorry for." Above all, do not challenge them to go ahead and do it. You could say, "I love you and trust that you wouldn't go ahead and do that but you still cannot do what you've been doing. If you do take such action or continue to do this, you are choosing for us the following action..."

Do you see where the responsibility is being placed? Not on you. On them!

Learning from Your Children

Q. MY KIDS WON'T OBEY OR RESPECT ME. WHAT CAN I DO?

A. When your children won't obey or respect you, consider a new approach by listening to what they have to tell you. I have been impressed by a book titled *Relief for Hurting Parents,* by Buddy Scott. One of his concepts is that our children teach us what to do and how to respond by their actions. This may be a new thought to you. Here are some examples, and notice how the consequences fit the offense:

Children *who teach us* that we cannot trust them out of our sight must remain in our sight (grounded and more closely supervised).

Children *who teach us* that they will throw a party in our home when we parents are out of town must no longer be trusted to stay by themselves.

Children *who teach us* that we cannot trust what they say must understand that we'll be checking almost everything they say.

Children *who teach us* that we cannot trust them to remain sober must no longer be allowed to drive the family car (or the car for which we have cosigned).

Children *who teach us* that they will let their grades fall must be more closely supervised in their studying, must watch TV and play video games less, and must be checked on at school more frequently.

Children *who teach us* that they will use their privacy to plot things against the family's moral values must have their privacy interrupted so that they can be watched more closely.

Children *who teach us* that they will use the phones in their rooms to converse with the wrong crowd will have their phones removed from their rooms.

Children *who teach us* that they need counseling will be provided with counseling.

Children *who teach us* that they aren't putting forth an effort to remember to get their lunch money must solve their own hunger pangs without mom or dad making a trip to the school.

Children *who teach us* that they aren't putting forth an effort to put their dirty clothes in the hamper must do their own laundry that week.

Children *who teach us* that they aren't taking their chores seriously must put off their own activities (family privileges) until their chores are completed.[6]

This concept needs to be explained to your child. Children have the power to make things better for themselves and once they realize this, it could effect their acting out behavior.

An example of this follows:

> Dave, your mother and I have figured out how to label what's been going on in our home. You are a teacher, and we are responders. We are responding to what you've been teaching us with the attitudes and actions you've been showing us.
>
> Now, we both want the same thing. You want more freedom and privileges, and we want those things for you. We want to be able to trust you enough to give you more independence. Our dream all these years has been to raise children worthy of trust.
>
> As the teacher, Dave, it's up to you. If you choose to teach us to trust you, we will respond by trusting you.
>
> If *you choose* to teach us to be suspicious of you, we will respond by asking you a lot of questions and checking up on things. If *you choose to* teach us not to trust you, we will respond by grounding you so that we can supervise you more closely and give you the opportunity to teach us to trust you again.
>
> We will do whatever you teach us to do. We will be responsive.[7]

Running with the Wrong Crowd

Q. WHAT CAN I DO ABOUT MY CHILD WHO IS RUNNING WITH THE WRONG CROWD?

A. If your child is running with the wrong crowd, read chapter 8 in

Buddy Scott's book, *Relief for Hurting Parents*. One of Scott's suggestions is to use the following statements, "If you are involved with a friend, our whole family is involved with that friend. We have a family-style family. Therefore, we can have something to say about who your friends are."[8]

If your child is running with the wrong crowd, require an immediate, complete, clean break with this person or group.

You have to deal with the rebellious attitude and the crowd that feeds it. This is not easy but it is possible.

Handling a Child Who Lies

Q. WHAT SHOULD I DO IF MY SON DOESN'T COME
HOME AT NIGHT AND LIES ABOUT WHERE HE HAS BEEN?

A. If your child does not come home at night, take immediate action. Do not ever hesitate to talk to other parents to discover who is lying to whom. Find out where your child was, who he was with and what went on. I know of some parents who immediately take their adolescent to the juvenile division of the police department. The parents have the authorities talk with their teen, telling of the legal consequences and sharing some of the horror stories of their experiences. I am all for an immediate shock technique such as this. Read *Relief For Hurting Parents* by Buddy Scott; the author suggests a unique approach to lying, which is applicable to other problems.

The Adolescent Drug User

Q. MY SON IS DOING DRUGS. WHAT CAN I DO?

A. Any time a son or daughter is involved in drugs, the plan you pursue is for the goal of total abstinence. Since you are already aware that your child is using drugs, we won't look at the usual indicators. (However, if you are not certain if your child is using drugs, I strongly recommend you read *Help Kids Say No to Drugs and Drinking* by Bob Schroeder, and *Drug-Proof Your Kids* by Steve Arterburn and Jim Burns.)

When as a parent you discover drug use, you feel betrayed, angry at your child and the dealers, and you probably struggle with some feelings of failure. Reacting to any of these feelings with rage does not solve the problem. Intervention and treatment are needed. Sometimes just talking with your child by yourself will work, but in many cases intervention is necessary.

In using intervention, you will need to gather with the help of a counselor everyone you know who is aware of your child's involvement with drugs (or alcohol). Such a group could include teachers, friends or other parents. Accumulate data specifically reflective of the drug use. This includes information concerning how much has been used, when, how often, and your child's behavior while under the influence. This is all necessary to determine the treatment plan to employ.

The intervention needs to be scheduled at a time when your child is least likely to be using drugs. During the intervention, ask your child to listen as each person presents the evidence of the problem. If one of the participants tells your child he must go for treatment and he refuses, the consequences need to be presented. Work out such consequences with the counselor in advance: eviction from your house; termination of financial support; unavailability of any other relative's or friend's home to live in; and any other dire consequences you can share. He needs to know you mean business and that the consequences are not pleasant.

The treatment can include outpatient facilities or an inpatient treatment program. In most cases, it is best to begin with an inpatient program at a Christian facility. One such ministry that has an excellent reputation is New Life Treatment Centers. After using such a program a strong follow-up program is needed. Check at a New Life Treatment Center for information concerning the intervention. I would also call the nearest Overcomers support group in your area. These are listed at the conclusion of this book.

Recommended Reading:

Arterburn, Steven, and Burns, Jim. *Drug-Proof Your Kids.* Colorado Springs, CO: Focus on the Family Publishers, 1989.

Samalin, Nancy. *Love and Anger: The Parental Dilemma.* New York: Viking Penguin, 1991.

Schroeder, Bob. *Help Kids Say No to Drugs and Drinking.* Minneapolis, MN: CompCare, 1987.

Scott, Buddy. *Relief for Hurting Parents.* Nashville, TN: Thomas Nelson, 1989.

Wright, H. Norman. *Power of a Parent's Words.* Ventura, CA: Regal Books, 1991.

Wright, H. Norman, and Oliver, Gary Jackson. *When Anger Hits Home.* Chicago, IL: Moody Press, 1992.

York, Phyllis, York, David, and Wachtel, Ted. *Tough Love.* New York: Bantam Books, 1993.

Notes

1. Nancy Samalin, *Love and Anger: The Parental Dilemma* (New York: Viking Penguin, 1991), p. 5.
2. Mark P. Cosgrove, *Counseling for Anger* (Dallas, TX: WORD Inc., 1988), p. 120.
3. H. Norman Wright, *Power of a Parent's Words* (Ventura, CA: Regal Books, 1991), p. 122, adapted.
4. Ibid., pp. 124-128, adapted.
5. H. Norman Wright and Gary Jackson Oliver, *When Anger Hits Home* (Chicago, IL: Moody Press, 1992), p. 186, adapted.
6. Buddy Scott, *Relief for Hurting Parents* (Nashville, TN: Thomas Nelson, 1989), p. 47.
7. Ibid., p. 50.
8. Ibid., p. 71.

Chapter 25

SINGLE PARENTING

Coping with Single Parent Pressures

Q. AS A SINGLE PARENT, HOW DO I COPE WITH ALL
THE EVERYDAY PRESSURES AND STILL DO
A GOOD JOB OF PARENTING?

A. The word "cope" seems to imply just hanging on or just surviving. And it could be that as a single parent, that is the way you are feeling. Here are a few steps you can take to feel as though you are in charge.

Accept the fact that you cannot do everything well. Identify what you can do and learn to let some things slide. You may need to accept a lower standard in some areas in which you used to be proficient. By doing so, you become more of a generalist rather than a specialist. Develop a list of other people who can help you handle tasks that don't match your skills, or for which you no longer have time. Make a list of all the tasks you have to do each day for a week. Prioritize them and then indicate which of them are essential and which are not crucial. List the jobs you can afford to hire out, and which ones your children can learn to do. Some women prepare their dinners on one day of the week, freeze them and then use the microwave each night to save time. Young teens can learn to cook and do laundry, too.

Keep track of what you do each day for a week and sit down with a couple of friends and listen to their suggestions as to how you could save time.

To help you survive, be sure to follow Gary Richmond's suggestions from his practical book *Successful Single Parenting*. You need:

1. Time for rest and relaxation, including some exercise.

2. Time away from your children (this way you won't resent them when you are with them.)

3. Time for friendship. You were not made to be without human contact—*adult* human contact.

4. Time for growth, reading, studying and special classes fall into this category.

5. Time for spiritual sustenance. You need the strength that prayer can give, and you must insist on making time for continuous nourishment from God's Word.[1]

After a Divorce

Q. I DON'T WANT TO BE A SINGLE MOTHER, AND I TEND TO TAKE OUT MY ANGER AND ABANDONMENT ISSUES ON MY CHILDREN. WHAT CAN I DO?

A. Some people plunge quickly into the single life. They go through the hassles of divorce and the adjustments afterward, and do not have the time to grieve over their losses and work through their various feelings. If you believe you were victimized in the divorce, it is normal to feel anger. Face your anger and discover the real cause. You are hurting and wish that what happened had not happened.

You would probably like your ex-husband to pay a penalty for what he did. Your anger is also a demand to be heard, understood, respected and treated fairly.

If you want vengeance on your ex-husband, make a list of all the things you want to do to him, list the consequences of what would happen to you and then tell God about your feelings of anger. Keep in mind that much of our anger is generated by what we say to ourselves in our minds. Your inner conversations feed your anger.

To keep from taking it out on your children do the following:

1. Give them a verbal commitment that you will not take out your anger toward your ex-husband on them. Give them the right to ask you (when you are angry) if your anger is based on something they have done or against their father.

2. Ask yourself what you are feeling and why when your anger begins to rise.

3. Each week set a grieving date to deal with the accumulated pain. Bring up all the painful feelings and dump them out. The Psalms are often reflections of the writer's pain. Write your own psalm expressing your pain, your desire and the comfort that God gives you.

4. Put into practice the principles for reducing anger in *When Anger Hits Home* by Gary Jackson Oliver and this author.

Overcoming Guilt

Q. HOW CAN I OVERCOME MY GUILT WHEN
MY CHILDREN FAIL?

A. Guilt can be a frequent companion during the journeys of parenthood, and many reasons cause this guilt. Some single parents feel guilty because they have set a standard of parenting they can never attain. They become victims of the "superparent" mentality. You can also feel guilty when you do not measure up to the standards of others, either real or assumed.

You might also feel guilty when you do what is right. You may say no to your child, which is the best step you can take, but if the child is upset or unhappy you may not feel so good.

One of the major reasons for guilt is the false belief that parents alone are responsible for their children's behavior.[2]

You can do the best you know how, guide your child, provide her with the healthiest atmosphere possible but she still has a sin nature as well as a free will. We cannot program a child's decisions and choices for her. I know. I have been there as a parent, wondering why my daughter took a particular direction in her life.

When you feel guilty over your child's behavior, ask yourself the question, "Where is the evidence that I am responsible for this?" Most of the time, no evidence is there. If you did do something, confess it to God and experience His forgiveness. And in some cases it is appropriate to confess it to your child.

Some single parents wallow in regret but as believers do not have to because of God's grace.

Watch out for negative thinking in your parenting. It can cripple you. Make a list of what you know you have done as a parent that is positive regardless of what others have said or implied. A friend of mine, Marilyn McGinnis, wrote a helpful book titled, *Parenting Without Guilt*. In it she describes how you can handle and challenge your negative thoughts. Read each statement and then write a positive reinforcement you could use in place of it.

NEGATIVE ACCUSATION	POSITIVE REINFORCEMENT
My son wouldn't be on drugs if I had been a better parent.	
Maybe if I'd done a better job talking about sex, my daughter wouldn't be pregnant.	
Our son's marriage would never have ended like this if	

NEGATIVE ACCUSATION	POSITIVE REINFORCEMENT

we had been better models as parents.

If I hadn't gone back to work, my daughter would probably have better grades.

Our child would never have been molested if we hadn't let him spend the night with his uncle.

I should never have let my son use the car. It's my fault he had that accident and was injured.

I should never have left my son alone in the house. If I had stayed home with him, he would never have committed suicide.

Somehow, we failed our daughter spiritually and now she's joined a cult. We should have forced her to go to church with us whether she wanted to or not.

Now compare your answers with the ones listed below.

NEGATIVE ACCUSATION	POSITIVE REINFORCEMENT
My son wouldn't be on drugs if I had been a better parent.	He's getting good treatment and it looks like he's going to be OK.
Maybe if I'd done a better	I talked about sex as openly as

NEGATIVE ACCUSATION	POSITIVE REINFORCEMENT
job talking about sex, my daughter wouldn't be pregnant.	I could with her. Now we need to focus on helping her make the right decision for the future.
Our son's marriage would never have ended like this if we had been better models as parents.	We have a good marriage. Sure we fight now and then but it doesn't last long and we always resolve the matter.
If I hadn't gone back to work, my daughter would probably have better grades.	Math has always been a problem for her. Now, we can finally afford the tutor she's been needing.
Our child would never have been molested if we hadn't let him spend the night with his uncle.	We had no reason to suspect his uncle of being anything but a loving, caring person. We have started counseling to help our child.
I should never have let my son use the car. It's my fault he had that accident and was injured.	He's got to learn responsibility. The accident seems to be making him act more maturely.
I should never have left my son alone in the house. If I had stayed home with him, he would never have committed suicide.	I know now that he had been planning this for weeks. I am grateful that he knew I loved him.
Somehow, we failed our daughter spiritually and now she's joined a cult. We should have forced her to go to church with us whether she wanted to or not.	She turned off to the church years ago. Forcing her to attend would have only made her more rebellious.[3]

Recommended Reading:

Richmond, Gary. *Successful Single Parenting*. Eugene, OR: Harvest House, 1990.

Wright, H. Norman, and Oliver, Gary Jackson. *When Anger Hits Home*. Chicago, IL: Moody Press, 1992.

Notes

1. Gary Richmond, *Successful Single Living* (Eugene, OR: Harvest House, 1990), pp. 94,95.
2. Marilyn McGinnis, *Parenting Without Guilt* (San Bernardino, CA: Here's Life Publishers, 1987), pp. 17-24, adapted.
3. Ibid., pp. 85-87.

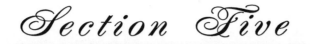
Section Five

DIVORCE AND REMARRIAGE

Chapter 26

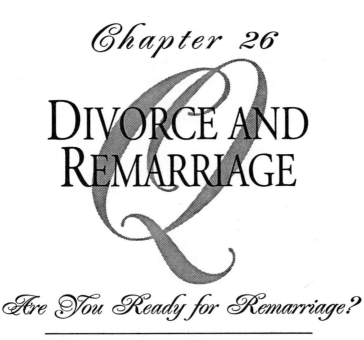

DIVORCE AND REMARRIAGE

Are You Ready for Remarriage?

Q. I AM DIVORCED NOW. HOW WILL I KNOW
WHEN I AM READY FOR REMARRIAGE?

A. When I work with previously married couples in premarital counseling, I request that both persons complete a divorce recovery program, even if the new spouse has never been married. I also recommend that a divorced person take two to three years to work through the readjustment before remarriage. Then during the premarital counseling session I give them some questions to answer.

How did you relate to your first spouse? What were the constructive and destructive ways you related? What have you learned about yourself since your divorce? A destructive pattern in a first marriage will emerge in the second unless effort has been made to identify the pattern and deal with it.

Every person who remarries has a personal history containing both hurts and sensitive areas.

Remember, some of the hurts of the past will only be healed by this new relationship. The period of recovery for a divorce usually takes three to five years. You need to have time to grieve and deal with the loss. Some of this healing occurs as you have the opportunity to relate to a new person in a new way. In what ways are you now relating differently to men and how would you like to relate differently?

How much time should be given to the former spouse and/or spouse's relatives? Ongoing contact is necessary because of finances, children, business and in-laws. In what way and how often will you be seeing your ex-spouse or his relatives? Such issues need to be identified so that both you and your new spouse will know what to expect.

The children of the first marriage will require a major portion of time and money. Two absolute guidelines to follow are: do not use the children to get back at your former spouse; and avoid criticizing the former spouse.

How will you build a world of new friends? When a divorce takes place, the loss of a community of friends occurs. Developing new friendships together will be a major task for you as a couple.

Describe how you tried to work through your problems in your previous marriage.

How did you relate to your previous spouse?

What were the constructive ways?

What were the destructive ways?

What people helped in your attempt to work through your problems? What was beneficial and what was not?

If there are children from the previous marriage, describe how you arrived at the plan of shared parenthood and how you feel about it.

Describe how much time you spend thinking about your previous spouse. List your specific thoughts.

Describe the comparisons you have already made between your former and future partner.

How often do you see your previous spouse and for what purpose? What feelings do you experience on these occasions?

Describe how you confronted and handled your feelings during the breakup of your previous marriage.

Is your former marriage over emotionally?

How have you attempted to *rebuild* yourself as an individual since the divorce? Who have you counseled with? What books have you read? What classes have you taken? Consider these other questions.

1. How long has it been since your previous marriage ended?

2. Who were the support people you developed to help you through this time?

3. How do you feel about yourself now as compared to how you felt at the end of your previous marriage?

4. What have you learned since the end of your first marriage (skills, vocational changes and so on)?

5. What have you learned from your past marriage that will help you in your new marriage? Please be as specific as possible. You might include what you have learned about yourself, your needs, your feelings, your goals, your flexibility, the way you handle stress, the way you handle another person's anger, or the ways other people differ from you.

6. In what way will you be able to be a better partner because of what you have learned? Can you think of at least six ways?[1]

The Spiritual Side of Divorce

Q. IS IT EVER ACCEPTABLE FOR A CHRISTIAN TO SEPARATE OR DIVORCE? GOD SAYS HE HATES DIVORCE, YET HE MAKES PROVISION FOR IT. IF GOD MAKES PROVISION FOR DIVORCE, WHY DO PEOPLE CALL DIVORCE A SIN? DOES GOD?

A. I do not tell counselees to divorce. Most marriages can be saved if both persons are committed to making it work. But divorce does happen. I have recommended a structured separation in some cases and in other cases talked people out of it. In some cases, separation may be beneficial for the purpose of building the marriage. But such a separation needs to have a time limit including structured dates and meetings between the couple.

The following statement is one pastor's written policy on remarriage, which I believe answers the question we are considering here. Some will feel this standard is too liberal and others will feel it is too strict.

Malachi 2:14-16 clearly indicates God is not in favor of divorce. He wants a husband and wife to be loyal, respectful and devoted to one another throughout their married life. Thus, it grieves Him and the Body of Christ when a couple decides to divorce. However, while divorce falls short of God's standard, it is no greater sin than any other. It, like all sin, is forgiven at the Cross of Calvary through Jesus Christ's atoning sacrifice. Through His grace God shows His compassion for the hurts of His people.

The Body of Christ is a gathering of forgiven sinners partaking of the grace and healing of God. We are not perfect people with perfect pasts. We are of the band of those who have been shown grace, mercy and forgiveness. Because of this, we are to be agents of mercy and forgiveness and not judgment. We seek to uphold God's standards of conduct with compassion and sensitivity rather than with legalism and insensitivity. Each situation of divorce is distinctive unto itself and must be approached with understanding and integrity.

I affirm that remarriage is appropriate in at least the following situations:

1. When the marriage and divorce occurred prior to salvation.

2. When one spouse is guilty of sexual immorality and is unwilling to repent and live faithfully with the other spouse.

3. When one of the spouses is a non-Christian and willfully and permanently deserts the spouse who is a Christian.

4. When one spouse subjects the other spouse to continual emotional, physical, and/or psychological abuse.

Other situations of divorce and remarriage would need to be discussed between a couple and me in order to decide whether or not I would marry the couple.[2]

Healing for Adult Children of Divorce

Q. HOW DO I GET HEALED FROM PARENTAL DIVORCE SO I DON'T REPEAT THE "FAILURE"? WILL I, OF NECESSITY, HAVE A BROKEN MARRIAGE IF I AM A PRODUCT OF A BROKEN HOME?

A. First, here is the *bad news* concerning the effects of divorce upon children. A 1987 study summarized the effects of divorce on grown children from broken homes. Compared to children from intact homes these adults *tended* to experience increased levels of anger, depression, sadness, sorrow, anxiety concerning future relationships, difficulty in handling memories, increased susceptibility to stress, feelings of emptiness, uncontrolled rage, worry, isolation, reduced self-esteem, bitterness and a sense that they might always be this way. They had more problems related to people, such as lower satisfaction in courtship, short-lived sexual relationships, higher divorce rates and difficulty in expressing and controlling emotions.[3]

Children of divorce experience a disruption in their lives and an abundance of losses. They lose their parental models, a safe and secure environment and the full realization of their future. As well, they can lose some of their childhood if they are pushed into adult roles and responsibilities too soon. Consequently, they are at risk of losing their ability to be close to and trust others. This is the bad news.

However, the *good news* is that hope and healing is possible. Millions of adult children of divorce are whole people who have learned from their parents' experience and have fulfilled marriages.

What can you do? First, gain more information about yourself and your situation. Read the two books recommended about adult children of divorce.

Breaking the Divorce Pattern

Decide to not let your parents' divorce dictate your life. Make a statement, "I am going to be different. My parents were divorced and it impacted me in a negative manner, but by the grace and comfort of God I will be healed." This is the initial step in breaking free from a victim mentality. I've heard many women say, "I'll probably end up divorced. After all, my parents were." Divorce for you is not a predetermined fact. You can do something about it. You can use your pain as a source of energy.

Some people enjoy remaining a victim because they gain something from it. Decide how long you will continue to think like a victim and then break the pattern. Let others know you will no longer be victimized by what happened. Declare yourself free. For many women, joining a recovery group has made a difference in their lives. Grieving over your losses is an important element of your recovery, thus a support group is valuable. Recovery is a long process and takes energy, honesty and time. Decide not to be a repeater.

Divorce: Breaking the News to Children

Q. HOW MUCH SHALL I TELL MY LITTLE CHILD
ABOUT THE REASON HIS DAD LEFT?

A. When divorce becomes inevitable, one of the toughest tasks is breaking the news to children. The ideal is for both parents to tell the child the reasons for their divorce. If both parents are present, they have a greater chance of presenting an honest objective. The child's questions can be directed to a specific parent and the united front of having both parents there makes it clear they are in agreement. But too often the ideal is not possible.

Honesty with your child is important; share as much as he can comprehend at his age level. Do not cover for your ex-spouse's faults, but do not project a bad image, either. Your child needs to be assured he is not the cause for his father's leaving.

Do not make resentful comments, attribute motives, speculate or make value judgments on your husband. Speak factually and answer any questions your child asks. Your child probably wants to know what will happen to him at this time. Tell him and reassure him as much as you know at this point. Remember—the sooner your child is told the truth, the sooner he can start to deal with the situation and begin to heal.

Dating Again After Divorce

Q. IT HAS BEEN TWO YEARS SINCE MY HUSBAND DIVORCED ME. WHY CAN'T I FEEL COMFORTABLE WITH MEN?

A. Divorce is one of the most difficult traumas a person can ever experience. As a divorcee, you have had heartbreak, disappointments, rejection, loneliness and numbness. These are the typical responses people experience when their spouse leaves. And one of the burdens that every survivor of a broken relationship carries is a residue of fear about future relationships. It is easy to allow one intense experience to contaminate and cripple future possibilities.

The trauma of a lost love relationship is one of life's most painful hurts, and the apprehension about loving again is one of life's greatest fears. Part of you says, "Let's try it again." Another part screams,

"Don't! It's not worth the risk." That painful fear of reliving the past paralyzes you from moving forward in a normal relationship. Every time you think about and relive the fear in your mind it limits you and makes you hesitant to invest energy, love and transparency in a new love relationship. Right?

So what can you do? *Grieve, recover* and *risk.*

Grieve as though it were a death.

Have you been through a divorce *recovery* program? If not, please consider doing so. If you have, perhaps a second time would help.

Risk, above all risk a new relationship. But before doing anything else, perhaps it would help to answer these questions:

Do you feel you have fully grieved over this person and released him? (If not, use the books recommended later.)

Write out your feelings about yourself and your ex at this time.

Write your response to the following sentence 10 times to identify your fears.

In a future relationship I am afraid of...

Now take each fear and describe what you will do to overcome this fear and reach out. Decide when you will do it.

Describe what it is that makes you feel uncomfortable with men. Is it something about you or something about them that causes the discomfort? Have you become close enough yet in any relationship to express and discuss your fears with the other person? When you go out with a man, do you expect to feel comfortable or uncomfortable? This could be a self-fulfilling prophecy. I can understand your wanting to be cautious. There is no easy way; expect risk and face the discomfort. Not every man will be similar to your former spouse.

Recommended Reading:

Burns, Bob, and Whiteman, Tom. *The Fresh Start Divorce Recovery Workbook.* Nashville, TN: Thomas Nelson Publishers, 1992.

Conway, Jim. *Adult Children of Legal or Emotional Divorce.* Downers Grove, IL: InterVarsity Press, 1990.

Fassel, Diane. *Growing Up Divorced—A Road to Healing for Adult Children of Divorce.* New York: Pocket Books, 1991.

Johnson, Laurene, and Rosenfeld, Georglyn. *Divorced Kids—What You Need to Know to Help Kids Survive a Divorce.* Nashville, TN: Thomas Nelson Publishers, 1992.

Prague, Gary. *Kids Caught in the Middle* (An interactive workbook for teens.) Nashville, TN: Thomas Nelson Publishers, 1993.

Prague, Gary. *Kids Caught in the Middle* (An interactive workbook for children.) Nashville, TN: Thomas Nelson Publishers, 1993.

Richmond, Gary. *The Divorce Decision.* Dallas, TX: WORD Inc., 1988.

Swindoll, Chuck. *Strike the Original Match.* Portland OR: Multnomah Productions, 1980.

Whiteman, Tom. *Innocent Victims—Helping Children Through the Trauma of Divorce.* Wayne, PA: Freshstart, 1991.

Wright, H. Norman. *Recovering from the Losses of Life.* (Chapter 10) Tarrytown, NY: Fleming H. Revell, 1991.

Notes

1. H. Norman Wright, *The Premarital Counseling Handbook* (Chicago, IL: Moody Press, 1992), pp. 257-261, adapted.
2. Ibid., p. 256.
3. Kent McGuire, "Adult Children of Divorce: Curative Factors of Support Group Therapy," a doctoral research paper presented to the faculty of the Rosemead School of Psychology, Biola University, May 1987.

Chapter 27

BLENDED FAMILIES

Blending a Family

Q. HOW DO WE BLEND OUR FAMILIES? WE
DON'T KNOW WHAT TO DO.

A. You are building a new vocabulary—words such as stepmother, stepchild, stepsiblings, reconstituted or blended families. You never dreamed this would be a part of your life. And you have new questions—what do you call your new mother or new father? And how do you handle weekend visitation, sexual feelings between stepbrothers and sisters, custody battles, holidays and so on?

A Package Deal

A remarriage is often called a package deal. You marry a person but his children are part of the package.

You may have been idealistic about your blended family but after a few months reality hits and if you feel as most women do:

    1. You will spend a great deal of time patching the wounds of
       fragmented family members.

2. You will come to dread that part of the holidays when children pass each other in airports.

3. You will have more spare toys, blankets, towels and sleeping bags in your home than you know what to do with.

4. Some days, you will wonder which children belong to which parent on what planet.

5. You will quickly tire of being the "bad guy" stepparent.

6. You will want all children to become wards of the court when it comes to dispensing discipline.

7. You will tire of hearing children say, "My real father (mother) said I could do..."

8. Some days you will be loved and unloved in the same minute.

9. You will expect God to give all stepparents a castle free of kids in heaven.[1]

Yours, Mine and Ours

Q. HOW CAN WE FUNCTION AS A FAMILY? I FEEL LIKE MY KIDS ARE MINE AND HIS ARE HIS.

A. It usually takes five to six years for a blended family to actually blend. "Mine" and "yours" don't become "ours" at the wedding ceremony.

You can expect the unexpected from your new spouse's children during the beginning months and years. Their responses can range from acceptance to withdrawal to attack. Children often come into the new family with fear: fear of more losses; fear of how you will accept them; and fear over losing you, too, if they learn to love you. They are afraid of being disloyal, "Who do I love and just how much?" What if their "real" mom or dad is hurt or angry over their relationship with you? The children may be afraid of losing the love of the parent you are marrying. They may not want to share.

Stepchildren come into the new relationship with a series of questions, which if answered help the process of blending. They wonder: "What should I call my stepparent now and can I call them something different later?" "Who is going to discipline me?" "Why can't I do what I used to do and why do I have to share?" "Am I going to be adopted? Why or why not?" Learn to live with more resentments than you expected. Resentful feelings can come from your new spouse's former wife, your own children, from your husband, from your husband's parents, from you and from the stepchildren.[2]

Being a Stepmother

Q. HOW DO I DEAL WITH MY STEPCHILDREN? HOW DO I ESTABLISH MY RIGHT TO DISCIPLINE HIS CHILDREN?

A. Perhaps one of the biggest challenges is being a parent to a new partner's children. Having guidelines to follow will make it easier. What were your expectations and fantasies for this relationship before you entered into it and what are they now? Were they clear? Are they now? Identify them.

Take it slow—you are strangers having to live as a family. The nonbiological parent needs to function as a friend or an aunt or uncle for the first three to five years if it is going to work. And when the biological parent is absent you must discipline as a baby-sitter would. I have seen many second marriages dissolve because the man (without any children) immediately assumed the role of strict disciplinarian with his new wife's children; naturally, she rushed to her children's rescue. The conflicts escalated and soon the wife and children were polarized against the new husband.

Sometimes a mother wants the new husband to relieve her of the discipline responsibility, but that is an unfair position to put him in. Many discipline struggles need to be dealt with: being too strict or too lenient; being a perfectionist (which limits flexibility and spontaneity); favoring one set of children over the other; or withdrawing if you do not feel accepted by the stepchildren. You need to identify your own fears, concerns and the areas in which you are uncomfortable, and discuss these with your new spouse. Decide together what to do.

Remember, you cannot fulfill the role of the nonresident biological parent but you do have a parenting role. Accept the reality of the former spouse and do not attempt to compete with her. You will lose. Prepare yourself to be an outsider if it is your partner who has the children.

Go Slow, Play Often

Q. HOW DO WE MAKE CHANGES AND ESTABLISH A NEW IDENTITY AS A BLENDED FAMILY?

A. Many things will cause discomfort for you within your new family and you might be tempted to make drastic changes. Do not. Make slow, small changes. Concentrate on building your relationship as a couple. Talk about parenting tasks in terms of what is working and what is not and find support through meeting with other blended families. Keep reminding yourself that instant relationships do not work. They take time.

Develop a parenting coalition between you and your new spouse. Work together and agree on the rules. When you have differences, work them out privately—not in front of the children. I know of some families in which the old and the new parents all meet together to develop a program of being consistent and fair regardless of what household the children stay in. They do not seek revenge through the children. This does not mean the rules will be the same at each home. For instance, in one home the children may be allowed to stay up late or have more say in what they eat. Reinforce your own rules when the children are staying with you.[3]

If you have your own children from a previous marriage and your new spouse has children, do not confuse your stepchildren with your own. The relationship and the responses will be different. You may learn to love your stepchildren and be a good friend to them, but do not think something is wrong with you if you do not feel the same toward them as your own children. You may have to reassure your own children at times that your feelings for your stepchildren do not affect your basic relationship with them.

Developing a New Identity

In a blended family, two distinct families with their own identities come together to form yet another identity. The big question is, "How do we blend?" Do we build a new family identity? How?

1. The first step in the blending process involves learning as much as you can about each new family member in order to achieve mutual acceptance.

2. Establish that the authority system of the family rests with the parents and they will be working together to set rules, limits, freedoms and guidelines for the children.

3. Work toward developing your own new family identity through new vacation sites, favorite activities and unique events.

One newly blended family decided to celebrate Christmas a week early so they could have an entire day together, rather than splitting the day between a complex web of in-laws and assorted relatives. Another eliminated the controversy over which parent made the best birthday cake by having a bakery make a special new shape and flavor of cake each year. This fun ritual became the family's annual tradition.

The home you live in needs to become your new family's home. Start off in a totally new residence that neither family has lived in before. But this, of course, can be unrealistically expensive. If you are living in your partner's former residence, fix it up differently to make it a new home for all of you. Make it a family project, using everyone's ideas. This may mean making some impractical and perhaps expensive decisions, but it will help to exorcise the ghosts of the former marriage and partner from the premises. You do not want to feel like an intruder in your own home and have to conform to your spouse's style and furnishings. Remember, where to live and how to make the home yours is an emotional as well as a logical decision.

The extended family is part of the process in blending a family. New members and existing ones will need to be integrated. Visits, gifts, phone calls, correspondence and tapes will help bridge the gap and keep relationships alive.

Recommended Reading:

Belovitch, Jeanne. *Making Remarriage Work.* New York: Lexington Books, 1987.

Reed, Bobbie. *Merging Families.* St. Louis, MO: Concordia, 1992.

Smoke, Jim. *Growing in Remarriage.* Tarrytown, NY: Fleming H. Revell, 1990.

Notes

1. Jim Smoke, *Growing in Remarriage* (Tarrytown, NY: Fleming H. Revell, 1990), p. 92.
2. Bobbie Reed, *Merging Families* (St. Louis, MO: Concordia Publishing House, 1992), pp. 95,97, adapted.
3. Ibid., pp. 101-120, adapted.

WHEN YOU NEED HELP ...

ALCOHOL ADDICTION

Alcoholics Anonymous
P.O. Box 454
Grand Central Station
New York, NY 10017
(212) 686-1100

Alcoholics for Christ, Inc.
1316 North Campbell Rd.
Royal Oak, MI 48067
(1-800) 441-7877

Alcoholics Victorious
National Headquarters
P.O. Box 10364
Tigard, OR 97210
(503) 245-9629

ACOA (Adult Children of Alcoholics)
P.O. Box 3216
2522 W. Sepulveda Blvd., Suite 200
Torrance, CA 90505
(213) 534-1815

Al-Anon Family Group Headquarters, Inc.
P.O. Box 862
Midtown Station
New York, NY 10018
(212) 302-7240

National Association for Children of Alcoholics
31582 Coast Highway, Suite B
South Laguna, CA 92677
(714) 499-3889

Overcomers Outreach (Alcoholics and Adult Children Claiming
Christ's Promises and Accepting His Healing)
2290 W. Whittier Blvd., Suite D
La Habra, CA 90631
(213) 697-3994

CODEPENDENCY

Co-Dependents Anonymous, Inc.
P.O. Box 33577
Phoenix, AZ 85067-3577
(602) 277-7991

CHILD ABUSE

Child Help USA
P.O. Box 630
Hollywood, CA 90028
(213) 465-4016

National Child Abuse Hotline
(1-800) 422-4453

CULTS

International Cult Education Program
P.O. Box 1232, Gracie Station
New York, NY 10028
(212)439-1550

Spiritual Counterfeits Project
P.O. Box 4308
Berkeley, CA 94705
(415) 540-0300

DRUGS

Cocaine Anonymous
World Service Office
3740 Overland Ave., Suite G
Los Angeles, CA 90034
(213) 559-5833
(1-800) 347-8998 (meeting referrals)

Cocaine Hot Line
1-800-COCAINE

Drugs Anonymous
P.O. Box 473
Ansonia Station
New York, NY 10023
(212) 874-0700

Marijuana Anonymous
1527 North Washington Ave.
Scranton, PA 18509

Nac-Anon (Family Group)
P.O. Box 2562
Palos Verdes, CA 90274
(213) 547-5800

Narcotics Anonymous
P.O. Box 9999
Van Nuys, CA 91409
(818) 780-3951

The National Clearinghouse for Alcohol and Drug Information
P.O. Box 2345
Rockville, MD 20852
(301) 468-2600

National Drug Abuse Information and Referral Line
(1-800) 662-4357

National Federation of Parents for Drug-Free Youth
1423 N. Jefferson
Springfield, MO 65802
(414) 836-3709

Substance Abusers Victorious
One Cascade Plaza
Akron, OH 44308

EATING DISORDERS

BASH—Bulimia Anorexia Self-Help, Inc.
1035 Bellevue Ave., Suite 104
St. Louis, MO 63117
(314) 567-4080 or (314) 991-BASH

Eating Disorders Hotline
(1-800) 382-2832 (U.S.)
(212) 222-2832 (NY)
Overeaters Anonymous
P.O. Box 92870
Los Angeles, CA 90009
(213) 542-8363

O-Anon
General Service Office
P.O. Box 4350
San Pedro, CA 90731

National Association for Anorexia and Associated Disorders
Box 271
Highland Park, IL 60035
(312) 831-3438

EMOTIONAL DISORDERS

Emotions Anonymous
International Services
P.O. Box 4245
St. Paul, MN 55104
(612) 647-9712

Recovery, Inc.
The Association of Nervous and Former Mental Patients
802 North Dearborn St.
Chicago, IL 60610
(312) 337-5661

COMPULSIVE GAMBLING

Gamblers Anonymous
P.O. Box 17173
Los Angeles, CA 90017
(213) 386-8789
Gam-Anon/Gamateen
International Service Office, Inc.
P.O. Box 157
Whitestone, NY 11357
(718) 352-1671

The National Council on Compulsive Gambling, Inc.
445 West 59th St.
New York, NY 10019
(1-800) 522-4700

HOMOSEXUAL ISSUES

Exodus International (For homosexuals and their families; also for sexual addiction)
P.O. Box 2121
San Rafael, CA 94912
(415) 454-1017

Spatula Ministries
(Parents of homosexuals and children with AIDS) Barbara Johnson, founder/director
P.O. Box 444
La Habra, CA 90631
(310) 691-7369

INCEST

Incest Survivors Anonymous
P.O. Box 5613
Long Beach, CA 90805-0613
(213) 428-5599

National Domestic Violence Hotline
(1-800) 333-7233
Survivors United Network
Kempe Foundation
3801 Martin Luther King Blvd.
Denver, CO 80205
(1-800) 456-HOPE

VOICES in Action, Inc.
(Victims of Incest Can Emerge Survivors)
P.O. Box 148309
Chicago, IL 60614
(312) 327-1500

INTERVENTION

For an intervention specialist, write:
Families in Crisis, Inc.
7151 Metro Blvd.
#225, Edina, MN 55435
(612) 893-1883
or contact local support groups or health professionals for further information in your area.

OBSESSIVE-COMPULSIVE DISORDER

The OCD Foundation
P.O. Box 9573
New Haven, CT 06535
(203) 772-0565

SEX ADDICTION

Sex Addicts Anonymous
P.O. Box 3038
Minneapolis, MN 55403
(612) 339-0217

Sex and Love Addicts Anonymous
Augustine Fellowship
P.O. Box 119, Newtown Branch
Boston, MA 02258
(617) 332-1845

Sexaholics Anonymous
P.O. Box 300
Simi Valley, CA 93062
(805) 581-3343

Co-SA
Codependents of Sex Addicts
P.O. Box 14537
Minneapolis, MN 55414
(612) 537-6904

S-Anon International Family Group
P.O. Box 5117
Sherman Oaks, CA 91413
(818) 990-6901

SEXUAL ABUSE

Eleutheros
1298 Minnesota Ave., Suite D
Winter Park, FL 32789
(407) 629-5770

Free to Care Ministries
Jan Frank, Director
P.O. Box 1491
Placentia, CA 92670

The Recovery Partnership
Dale Ryan, Executive Director
P.O. Box 1095
Whittier, CA 90603
(310) 947-2685

Kempe Foundation
3801 Martin Luther King Blvd.
Denver, CO 80205
(1-800) 456-HOPE

SHOPPING/SPENDING

Debtors Anonymous Hotline:
(212) 969-0710

Debtors Anonymous
General Service Board
P.O. Box 20322
New York, NY 10025-9992

SMOKING

The American Cancer Society
19th W. 56th St.
New York, NY 10019
(212) 382-2169

Smokenders
18551 Von Karman Ave.
Irvine, CA 92715
(1-800) 828-HELP

Smokers Anonymous World Services
2118 Greenwich St.
San Francisco, CA 94123
(415) 922-8575

Quit and Stay Quit
Terry A. Rustin, M.D.
9731 Greenwillow
Houston, TX 77096
(713) 728-4473

SUICIDE

T. Mitchel Anthony
The National Suicide Help Center
Teens in Touch
P.O. Box 34,
Rochester, MN 55903
(507) 282-2723

For more information regarding teenage suicide read, *Suicide: Knowing When Your Teen Is at Risk* by T. Mitchel Anthony. Ventura, CA: Regal Books, 1991.

For information write:
American Association of Suicidology
2459 S. Ash
Denver, CO 80222

National Suicide Assistance
24-Hour Hotline
(1-800) 333-4444

For information on the workshop: "Suicide—The Preventable Tragedy" contact:
> John Hipple, Ph.D.
> North Texas State University
> Denton, TX 27603
> (817) 565-2741

WORKAHOLISM

Workaholics Anonymous
Westchester Community College
AAB
75 Grasslands Rd.
Valhalla, NY 10595
(914) 347-3620

OTHER

POST-ABORTION RECOVERY

WEBA
(Women Exploited by Abortion)
Kathy Walker, Director
3553-B N. Perris Blvd., Suite 4
Perris, CA 92370
(714) 657-0334

Post Abortion Counseling Services
Glenda Cervantez
P.O. Box 1134
Billings, MT 59103
(406) 245-6441

Families Anonymous, Inc.
P.O. Box 528
Van Nuys, CA 91408
(818) 989-7841
   For those with a concern about the use of mind-altering substances or related behavioral problems in a relative or friend.

Recovering Couples Anonymous
P.O. Box 27617
Golden Valley, MN 55442
   For couples in recovery together with the desire to remain in a committed relationship.The Spiritual Dimensions in Victims Services (for victims of all types of crimes)

David W. Delaplane, Executive Director
P.O. Box 163304
Sacramento, CA 95816
(916) 446-7202

MINISTRY TO SINGLES
The Tear Catchers
Harold Ivan Smith
P.O. Box 24688
Kansas City, MO 64131
(816) 444-5301

TREATMENT CENTERS
For information about the location of more than 1,600 centers offering various programs and services for recovery write:

Rapha—Christ-centered in-hospital counseling care units, treating psychiatric, substance abuse and other addiction problems for the Christian community. Has numerous locations nationwide.

Rapha
Box 580355
Houston, TX 77258
Nationwide number (1-800) 227-2657
In Texas: (1-800) 445-2657

Hope Community
Located in Culpeper, VA, with other facilities opening nationwide.
(1-800) 333-HOPE
U.S. Journal National Treatment Directory
Customer Services
320 S. W. 15th St.
Deerfield Beach, FL 33442
(1-800) 851-9100

Minirth-Meier Clinic—Comprehensive mental health care services, substance abuse, eating disorders and other addiction treatment. Numerous locations nationwide.

Minirth-Meier Clinic
P.O. Box 1925
Richardson, TX 75085
(1-800) 232-9462

Ephesians 5:18 Life Ministries
16819 New Hampshire Ave.
Silver Spring, MD 20904
(301) 424-9713

OTHER HELPS

Hazelden Educational Materials
Box 11
Center City, MN 55012
(1-800) 328-9000

Tools for Recovery
Recovery Publications, Inc.
1201 Knoxville St.
San Diego, CA 92110-0832
(619) 275-1350

U.S. Journal, Inc.
1721 Blount Rd., Suite 1
Pompano Beach, FL 33069
(1-800) 851-9100
Johnson Institute
7205 Ohms Lane
Minneapolis, MN 55439-2159
(612) 831-1630

CompCare Publications
2415 Annapolis Lane
Minneapolis, MN 55441
(1-800) 328-3330

Lifeworks Communications
20300 Excelsior Blvd.
Minneapolis, MN 55331
(612) 475-4911

If you want more comprehensive information (self-assessment tests, suggested readings and so on) on the compulsive-addiction problem, I refer you to a book by Sandra Simpson LeSourd, *The Compulsive Woman* (Chosen Books, 120 White Plains Rd., Tarrytown, NY 10591).

Appendix 2

SIGNIFICANT QUESTIONS WOMEN ASK IN COUNSELING

The questions answered in this book are only a partial list of those sent in from our survey. Of the more than 3,500 questions we received, there was a significant overlap. The questions were tabulated into the questions listed here. This will give you a fuller idea of the concerns of women in the United States. Compare this list with the men's questions in Appendix 3.

- Am I supposed to do everything my husband wants me to do? The Bible does say "obey" your husband.
- How can I obey, submit to and love my husband when he is taking little or no initiative to assume a spiritual role in our lives?
- How can I be a submissive wife and yet maintain my personal identity at the same time?
- My husband doesn't see me as his equal. Do I just have to put up with it?
- Am I expected (by God) to submit to a man who is wrong and not respectable?
- Do I have to submit to my husband regardless of what he demands or how he relates to me or regardless of his spiritual condition?
- My husband has developed strange ideas about health foods, children's education, not using medication, etc., that I can't agree with. Do I have to follow him in this?
- What do I do if my husband and I don't agree on a particular issue?
- What does biblical submission mean in the '90s?

- How do I love and forgive my husband when he verbally abuses me?
- Why is my husband so cruel to me and the children?
- When we have a problem in our marriage, why does he always shift the problem to me?
- Why is he so defensive when I make suggestions?
- I had the expectation that I would experience a love relationship in marriage. Does everyone put up with awful treatment 90 percent of the time and call that "married love"? At this point I'm thinking, who needs it!
- I'm confused. I don't know what I want, I don't feel anything for my husband. I am tired of being a mother. Can you help me?
- I've felt like a "walking zombie" for several years. I need to know from someone just how bad my problems are. Should I continue to stay in the marriage or should I walk? I'm so weary of hanging onto nothing.
- What can I do to regain my love for my husband—like we had when we were first married?
- Why should I continue to struggle to make my marriage work when I feel I am struggling alone?
- Even though I've gotten right with God and I'm in church, why doesn't God make my husband love me?
- How can I find meaning in life when I am caught in a marriage with a man who does not meet my needs?
- Should I continue in an unsatisfying marriage?
- How do I deal with my lack of love feelings for my husband? It's not that we necessarily are fighting, it's that I feel he has abandoned his role as a husband and is a different person from the man I thought I had dated and married.
- How do I stay "in love" with my husband?
- I don't love my husband anymore, but I don't want a divorce. What should I do?

- I just don't think I love him anymore. Why should I continue to try to work on this marriage? (She didn't understand the nature of the marriage covenant.)
- I'm trying but I can't seem to do anything—mainly because I'm not sufficiently interested. How can I get more interested?
- I no longer feel love for my husband; does God expect me to stay in that relationship, or can I find someone else and be happy?
- Can he ever learn to be sensitive or are most men like that?
- How can I get my husband to pay more attention to me?
- How can I get my husband to relate to me at a more personal level?
- How can I get my husband to relate to me emotionally?
- How can I get my husband to spend more time with me?
- How can I get my husband to talk with me?
- How can I get my husband to treat me in a more sensitive manner?
- How can I get my husband's attention or love?
- Do most men have trouble communicating their inner feelings with their spouse?
- How can I get my husband to share his feelings with me?
- How can I get my husband to understand my feelings?
- How can I improve my marriage?
- How can I save my troubled marriage?
- How can we get romance back into our marriage?
- How can we improve our marriage?
- How can we make our relationship more fulfilling?
- How can I change my husband so that I can live with him?
- How can I change to make my partner happy?
- How can I deal with a specific form of frustrating behavior in my husband?

- How can I get my husband to be more of a disciplinarian, more assertive, be home more?

- My husband is so possessive of my time and won't let me go out and do anything with my friends. I don't understand why?

- Why doesn't my husband understand my needs the way he expects me to understand his? Especially emotionally versus sexually.

- How do I continue to live with a husband who is not changing when I am?

- How do I get my husband to treat me with respect in public?

- Why do I perceive such a problem in our relationship yet my husband says everything is okay?

- Why does my husband ignore our marriage problems? He seems to put them in file 13 thinking that if he ignores them they will go away.

- How do you cope with an unmotivated husband?

- How long do I have to wait for him to get his act together?

- I feel resentment in that he does not take the leadership in our home. I have to do everything!

- I want my marriage to grow, but my husband doesn't seem to be interested. What can I do?

- My husband refuses to take initiative in the home. What should I do?

- My husband shows no affection. He never helps with anything around the house. His temper is bad.

- Why can't he do anything around the house? I work, too!

- Why should I continue to struggle to make my marriage work when I feel I am struggling alone?

- How can I get my husband to agree to counseling when he doesn't feel the marriage is in trouble?

- How can I get my husband to come in for counseling?

- How do I go on growing and caring for myself if my husband refuses to get help?
- How do I handle our marital conflicts? We don't even seem to be on the same "wave length" most of the time.
- We can hardly talk without fighting. What do we do?
- What do I do with a spouse who is never home (addicted to sports/work/etc.) and when he is home, he doesn't communicate and when we do we fight?
- Help us to understand each other better—learn to cope better. Arguments are getting out of control. We never get our problems solved. We quarrel all the time.
- My husband and I keep fighting. What can I do?
- How can I be healthily independent and also healthily in a relationship?
- How can I be fulfilled as a woman in today's society?
- How can I develop more independence in my life?
- How can I establish enough meaningful relationships to meet my inner need for intimacy, friendship and affirmation?
- How can I give to others and still meet my needs?
- After my husband has an affair, how do I trust him or other men again?
- How can I learn to trust and forgive my husband when he has betrayed my trust through an affair?
- How can I get over feelings of love for someone that is not my husband?
- What can I do about my attraction to another man?
- Can I feel good about myself and accept myself?
- How can I accept myself and like myself and even love myself?
- How can I overcome these feelings that I am worthless?
- How can I respect myself when I have sinned so?
- How do I get over feeling like a failure?

- How do I stop comparing myself with other women and feeling inadequate?
- I feel so alone, worthless and used. Will I ever be normal?
- The Scriptures tell me to love others as I love myself. The choices I have made make me have no love for myself. How do I love myself?
- Who am I in today's world of the feminist movement?
- Who am I outside of wife and mother?
- Why do I feel...

  ...like a failure?

  ...sad all the time and have no energy?

  ...so awful about myself?

  ...so bad about myself?

  ...so guilty when I do things for myself?

  ...so lonely, especially at church?

  ...so wasted?

- My self-esteem is so low. How do I build it?
- My son is doing drugs. What can I do?
- How do I know if my children are using drugs?
- As a couple we don't agree on how to manage our children in regard to discipline. I'm too easy maybe, but he's too harsh.
- How can I deal with my kids? My husband is so passive I get no help with the discipline.
- How do I teach my children right from wrong when my husband doesn't set limits and says the opposite of what I do?
- I just don't know how to handle my children's behavior. They're constantly acting out.
- My kids won't obey or respect me. What can I do?
- My teenager is rebelling and acting out. How do I deal with the problems and cope with the verbal abuse?

- What can be done about my child's acting out? If it isn't messing up in school, it's running with the wrong crowd.
- What can I do with my daughter or son who strikes me when he or she gets angry?
- My kids are out of control. How can I control them without beating them?
- What should I do if my son or daughter doesn't come home at night?
- My kids are driving me crazy. Help me improve my parenting skills.
- How do I know if I'm a good mother or not?
- How can I be a more effective parent to my children?
- How do I raise responsible children in a loving manner?
- How do I set limits with my children?
- How can I help my children stay out of trouble without "controlling" them?
- How do I deal with anger with my kids?
- I'm having thoughts of hurting my child. Is this normal?
- Is it normal to get real angry and frustrated with my kids?
- What do I do when I get so frustrated with my children that all I want to do is scream, hit or banish them forever?
- How do I deal with the criticism of others, including my parents and other siblings?
- How can I get my husband to hear me?
- How can I get my husband to listen to me?
- How can I get my husband to spend time talking WITH me and not AT me?
- When my husband comes home from work, I want to talk to him but he wants peace and quiet. We don't seem to talk, let alone communicate. What can I do?
- Why are we (my husband and I) unable to communicate clearly?

- Why does it feel that even though my husband allows me to communicate my feelings (hurts, discouragements, etc.), I still feel he doesn't understand or really hear me?
- Why does my husband act threatened when I confront him about a problem in our home?
- How can I communicate my needs and feelings without being responded to as a nag, bitch or a complainer?
- How can I communicate my needs in a way that the man in my life will hear them?
- How can I communicate without exploding? Or how can I explain my feelings without the other person exploding?
- How can I have my husband be more sensitive to my needs and feelings?
- Why doesn't my husband understand my need for affection, appreciation and communication?
- How can I get my husband to understand me better as a woman?
- How can I cope with or overcome depression? I feel bad being depressed.
- How can I deal with my depression? Will I become suicidal?
- How can I get rid of the depression that I constantly struggle with?
- I am depressed and continuously crying. How do I overcome my depression? How do I deal with a meaningless life?
- I feel trapped and alone. My training was not to be a housewife. Life is passing me by. Can you help me?
- Since I am a Christian, why can't I keep from getting depressed and anxious?
- Is depression chemical or emotional?
- How can I truly hear God's voice so that I don't go off thinking that I'm doing what He wants me to do, but have disastrous results?

- After what I've done, how can God possibly forgive me?
- Does God every truly forgive and forget my past failures? Does God really accept and love me the way I am?
- How can God get glory out of this cruelty? What happened to the "umbrella of God's protection" if I obey?
- How do we see God's love when it seems we are constantly going through trials?
- If I am a Christian I shouldn't be suffering, should I? (Or having problems.)
- My dad never cared about me so isn't God the same way? Or, why is God allowing or letting this to happen to me?
- How does God want to use me? What "gifts" do I have to offer?
- Why does God let me go through all of this hurt and pain?
- Why doesn't God do something? I thought if I tried harder or prayed more, it would get better.
- Why is God allowing this to happen to me and why doesn't He intervene to do something about my problem?
- I feel alienated from God. Has He abandoned me?
- How can I be sure that God loves me?
- How can I have an experience with God? Or, is this experience an experience of God?
- Am I less of a person because I was sexually abused?
- Was I to blame because I was abused?
- I want to have healthy sex. How can I get over my feelings of revulsion? I was sexually abused as a child.
- How do I deal with the effects of childhood sexual abuse?
- How can I get free of the damage from old sexual abuse issues?
- How can I express the anger I feel about experiences in the past—particularly those involving emotional, physical and sexual abuse?

- What shall I do? I've discovered that my husband is molesting our children.
- Do I really have to go back and dig up all the sexual abuse garbage from childhood?
- How can I cope with the memories of the sexual abuse of my childhood?
- Is there any benefit to uncovering stuffed or repressed feelings?
- How can I get over the guilt that I still suffer as a result of early childhood incestuous experiences?
- How can I ever trust men when I've been abused?
- How do I forgive my parents? Do I still have to honor and obey my parents?
- What is forgiveness and how do you do it?
- When I became a Christian, why didn't everything become new, including my past?
- Now that I see how much mothering I missed, how do I get those needs met?
- How do you let go of someone you love?
- Why are there periods in my life I cannot remember?
- How can I change unhealthy patterns so I don't repeat them in my family?
- How do I deal with painful issues in my past (childhood) that are affecting the way I live today?
- Will I ever be able to have a "normal" family life? I think my past has messed me up for good.
- How can I be sexually responsive when he is so insensitive?
- How can I get my mate to be sexually sensitive?
- How can I make my husband recognize the difference between his and my sexuality?
- How do I get my husband to treat me as a woman with different needs during sex and not just as a sex object?

- Why do men only think about sex? Why do men want sexual relationship so frequently?

- Why do men seem to think sex is the focal point of a relationship? I want closeness in other ways, too!

- Why doesn't he understand my need for romance and foreplay in order for sexual intercourse to be OK for me?

- I am not interested in sex with my husband. He doesn't understand. Can you help?

- My husband is not interested in sex. I've talked and talked to him. He always expects me to initiate. I can't go on anymore. What can I do?

- My husband hardly seems to touch me anymore. And when he does, it's only a signal that he wants sex. I'm so angry at him. How do I get my needs met? How do I cope with my anger?

- God doesn't really expect me to live without sex, does He?

- Does intimacy always have to mean, or include, sexual activity?

- How can I get my husband to be more romantic and to realize that I need a secure relationship before I can be sexy?

- How can I get my husband to be more romantic, thoughtful, tender, expressive?

- How can I get my husband to notice me?

- How can we get romance back into our marriage?

- Who sets the standard for normal sexual behavior? Is oral sex all right in marriage?

- How do I get healed from parental divorce so I don't repeat the "failure"?

- Will I, of necessity, have a broken marriage if I am a product of a broken home?

- How much shall I tell my little child as to the reason why his dad left?

- It's been two years since my husband divorced me. Why can't I feel comfortable with men?
- Do I have to stay married to my husband who physically abuses me?
- How can I change my husband's abusive behavior?
- How can I keep from being the victim in relationships with my husband?
- How much physical abuse must I tolerate?
- Why do I stay with a man who is abusive?
- How can I better deal with stress?
- How can I handle the stress of working on the job, working at home, and caring for children and a husband?
- How do I deal with the stress of work and family?
- I feel so overwhelmed. I just want to shut down. How do I cope?
- How can I control worry?
- How can I resist the temptation to spend money?
- How can I deal with my husband's financial irresponsibility?
- How do I get my husband to help plan a budget and stay within it? He says he wants a budget, but then he goes and spends and spends.
- My husband spends money on things he wants and when I question him he says I'm being selfish. Why does he do this?
- What do I say when people ask me why I'm not married yet? I'm happy single.
- How do I deal with my sexual feelings as a single Christian woman?
- What's so wrong with premarital sex?
- What's wrong with just living together? After all, we love each other and we are happier than most married couples we know.
- How do I deal with sexual harassment on the job? I'm getting tired of the pressure.

- As a single parent, how do I cope with all the everyday pressures and still do a good job of parenting?

- How can I handle all the pressures and demands of single parenthood?

- I don't want to be a single mother, and I tend to take out my anger and abandonment issues on my children. What can I do?

- What can I do about my suspicions that my husband is not faithful?

- How can a wife win back her unfaithful spouse?

- After so many years of marriage and so many children, he's now seeing another woman. How did I miss seeing this coming? What's wrong with me?

- Why does my husband seek sexual stimulation elsewhere (pornography, affairs, etc.) when he has me?

- How am I supposed to be patient with my husband's anger?

- How can I handle emotions that erupt for no apparent reason? (These are not PMS related.)

- How do I release the anger that I feel?

- I can't express anger or cry. How can I learn to do this?

- Why can I feel depressed but not angry?

- How can I deal with my alcoholic husband?

- How do I deal with a husband who is an alcoholic?

- How is a Christian wife supposed to live non-codependently with an alcoholic?

- What can I, as a Christian, do about a marriage that doesn't function due to a husband's alcoholism?

- How can I not try to control and yet communicate my concerns about my husband's addictions?

- My parents were alcoholics. How can I understand if this affected me or not?

- Are there any healthy men out there?

- How do I know if this guy is right for me?

- Where can I find a Christian man who is as committed to spiritual values and activities as I strive to be? (Most common question from singles.)

- Why am I attracted to men who don't treat me well?

- Why do I keep falling in love with the same type of man?

- How can I get my husband in church? How long do I have to wait for God to save my husband? I can't take his ungodly habits much more.

- How can I get my husband to be the spiritual head of my family?

- How do I get my husband to share my faith in God and attend church with me and my family?

- Why does my husband have no desire to be the head of the home in spiritual issues?

- Why don't husbands/fathers take spiritual, moral, relational leadership in the marriage and family, especially with the children?

- What is the best way to be a Christian witness to my unsaved husband?

- Do I have to suffer because my husband is not walking with God?

- Do I have to stay with a husband who refuses to accept the Lord as his Savior?

- What is the difference between Christian caring versus enabling? Isn't it good to be a caretaker?

- What is the difference between true biblical caring and codependency?

- What's the balance between healthy giving (between men and women especially) and codependency in a relationship?

- How can I gain release from my codependent patterns of needing to please others in order to feel good about myself?
- How do I handle my "codependent" relationship with my husband and adult children?
- How can I learn to set effective boundaries that will be effective but not controlling?
- If I don't take care of it, who will? I'm the only one who cares how things run in the home!
- Why do I feel so responsible for my husband and grown children?
- Isn't it selfish to set boundaries and nurture myself? Aren't we supposed to sacrifice for others?
- How can I deal with my feelings caused by coming from a dysfunctional family?
- How can I keep from repeating the same mistakes that my parents made? I find myself responding to my children the same frustrating ways my parents responded to me.
- Is it possible to break the chain of family dysfunction?
- How do you develop meaningful, positive relationships with family members?
- How do I deal with the fact that my father was distant and cold and unloving? I have a hard time seeing God as my father and praying to Him!
- How can I let go of that which has caused grief in my life?
- How can I recover from the death of my spouse or child?
- How do I cope with my loved one's death?
- When does the pain of grief go away?
- What do I do when I feel stuck in my grief?
- My adult children are not making it on their own. I moved them out of my house into an apartment. When do I stop having to raise them?

- How can I overcome my guilt when my children fail?

- How can I tell my father that all I want from him is his acceptance for who I am and not for my accomplishments?

- How do I please (or break away from!) a controlling, possessive parent? (In most cases this refers to the mother.)

- How do I separate myself from my controlling mother?

- When your parents still want to control you and you are 35 years old, what do you do?

- What will help me deal with the hurt and rejection I feel from my mother?

- I can't seem to please my mother no matter what I do. How can I get through to her?

- How can I stop letting men control me verbally, emotionally and sexually?

- How do I say no or set limits in a relationship without feeling guilty or being rejected?

- How do I stop letting everyone take advantage of me? How do I stand up for my rights?

- I would like to be assertive without getting so angry or later feeling guilty. What can I do?

- There are so many people in my life who "take from me" but give very little back. How can I get a balance?

- I'm confused. What is the difference between being assertive and being aggressive?

- How can I overcome obsessive behavior? How can I stop overeating and drinking?

- How do I deal with the compulsive behavior in my life? This includes shopping sprees, addictive relationships, etc.

- How can I cope with my barrenness? I don't feel whole as a woman because I cannot bear children.

- I am struggling with a serious medical problem. I have cancer. How do I cope with this?

- My spouse is dying. How can I go on alone after 40 years of marriage?

- Am I bad because I suffer from an anxiety disorder?

- How can I cope with the anxiety and panic attacks I am experiencing?

- How can I handle my relationship with my mother-in-law? She seems to interfere in our lives so much.

- How can I encourage my husband to get along with my parents?

- How can I get my husband to put me before his parents in matters of decision making and time?

- How can I be worthwhile when I'm so dissatisfied with my weight and appearance?

- Why is body image used to define me and what can I do about my anger over it?

- How can I live with the memories of trauma in my life over my abortion? How can I resolve the guilt and shame I feel? How can I forgive myself for this? I know I have to, but I can't.

- Can God forgive me for my abortion?

- Where can I learn about PMS and how do I explain it to my husband?

- Is there a way for my husband to understand my emotions more during that time of the month?

- Is watching or looking at pornographic material for the purposes of stimulation all right?

- Is masturbation a sin? If so, how do I handle sexual urges and feelings?

- I'm divorced now. When will I know when I'm ready for remarriage?

- Is it ever acceptable for a Christian to separate or divorce?
- God says He hates divorce, yet He makes provision for it. If God makes provision for divorce, why do people call divorce a sin? Everyone hates divorce. But is it fair to call divorce a sin? Does God?
- How can I cope with the physical/mental deterioration of my parents?
- What is a Christian's responsibility toward aging parents? I feel guilty. Am I suffering from justified guilt or am I being manipulated?
- How can we function as a family? I feel like my kids are mine and his are his.
- How do I deal with my stepchildren?
- How do I establish my right to discipline his children?
- How do we blend our families together? Everything is chaos. We don't know what to do. There doesn't seem to be a lot of help for the blended family.
- I'm a perfectionist. I'm not sure I like being a perfectionist. But it's all I know. And even if I knew how to change, I wonder if I can let loose of this life-style.

Appendix 3

SIGNIFICANT QUESTIONS
MEN ASK IN COUNSELING

What do *men* ask in counseling? Along with the women's question survey in 1991, we asked that question of 700 professional counselors, ministers, lay counselors and social workers.

Here are some of the most significant questions men ask, which we gleaned from the responses to the survey. These and other questions will be addressed in a future resource from Regal Books.

- I feel a lot of anger and frustration and take it out on my family. What can I do?
- How can I control my anger and rage?
- How can I handle the frequent temptation to be involved with pornography? When I travel, it is always available and there is no one around who prevents me from looking at it.
- I feel tense all the time. How can I get rid of this tension and stress and have peace in my heart?
- When will my wife forget how I hurt her and not use it against me?
- How do I handle compromising situations at work (i.e., being asked to be dishonest; needing to be one of the guys to get promoted)?
- What does it mean to be a man and a father? I never had a good role model in my dad, but now I'm expected to be a good husband and father.
- I can't seem to stop lusting after women. Is there any hope I will ever be free of this?
- I have absolutely no control over my temper. How can I learn to handle it?

- With the national economic situation—I feel trapped! I can't quit...I'm afraid to! What do I do?
- What can I do when I am not satisfied with my present job situation but see no way of switching?
- How can I get my wife to support me as the head of our family instead of undermining my authority?
- I'm just a quiet person—why does my wife always want me to talk?
- Why are women so emotional? Why can't they forgive and forget?
- How can I find meaning and purpose in life when I've lost the job I really liked?
- If God is really a caring God, why doesn't He answer my prayers and deliver me out of this difficulty?
- I work hard...why doesn't my wife believe I love her?
- Why is she giving up on the marriage? I didn't know anything was wrong.
- Why can't she accept me the way I am? Why is she trying so hard to change me?
- I think I am going through mid-life crisis. What does mid-life crisis mean and what are the symptoms?
- How can I ever trust my wife again since she lived a lie and was unfaithful to our marriage vows?
- Why can't my wife just ignore the petty issues and save her crises for the important things?
- Should I tell my wife about an affair (one-time fling)?
- Why is my wife willing to lose weight for her high-school reunion (or any other reason), but not for me?
- How can I maintain consistency in family devotions?
- Why does my wife force religion down my throat?
- How can I deal with continual sexual thoughts and urges?

- How can I deal with flashbacks, combat dreams and other PTSD symptoms?
- Why is it so difficult for me to make and keep a close friend?
- Why can't she think like I do? Why does she have to be so irrational and emotional?
- Why does it seem so many privileges are given to the mother of my kids when she was the one who was "playing around" with other men?
- I struggle with knowing who I am. What makes me tick?
- I don't understand how women think and she won't tell me.
- How can I make my wife understand how important my job is to me?
- Why am I the only one that's expected to dish out the discipline to the children?
- If I cry, people will think I'm a "wimp." How do I express my sorrow?
- How do you show comfort to someone else when you yourself are in great pain?
- How can I get in touch with my feelings?
- Is my child so rebellious because I was not good parent?
- How can I have a valid testimony in the workplace without seeming to be a fanatic?
- Why can't I get my wife to believe I have changed?
- Do I have to go back to the past in order to get well (recover)?
- Why won't my wife meet my sexual needs? Doesn't the Bible say her body is mine?
- Why doesn't my wife respect me, support me, affirm me, admire what I do?
- How can I make her understand that men are different and have different values and needs?

- Why can't she see that I can never feel the same about her children as I do about mine?
- Help my wife to submit to me in everything with no questions asked. Isn't that biblical?
- Why did God give me such a sexual drive? How do I control it?
- Why or how do women think as they do? Explain differences in men and women.
- How do you balance your Christianity and work demands?
- How can I exit the affair I'm in when my feelings are still there?
- No matter what I do, it is never enough for my wife. I'm fed up. What can I do?
- Women are so hard to understand. She just sees everything so differently. How can I relate with her?
- My promiscuous past seems to create a barrier that prevents me from being able to develop an intimate relationship with a woman. I would like to marry and settle down, but how do I deal with the past?
- How does a man understand a woman? I'm constantly getting into trouble because I misinterpret what women are really saying.
- What can be done to soothe relations between my wife and my mother? Both think the other hates her.
- What's wrong with me? I've gradually lost my ability to perform sexually in a way that fulfills my wife...it's embarrassing.
- I know I work too much and neglect my family, but I see no options. Can you help?
- Our daughter is having problems and my wife thinks it's my fault. Can you fix my daughter and set my wife straight?
- How can I gain control over my anger so that I don't use it destructively in either active or passive ways?
- How can I lessen my tendency to interpret relationship issues and events with women as having sexual meaning?

- I've tried to lead a good life, so why has God allowed me/my family to suffer (divorce, death)?

- Why does God allow me to struggle with homosexuality? How can I change?

- How can I keep up financially in these times?

- Why can't my wife accept me as the head of the family?

- How can I help my wife be more responsive sexually?

- How can I be strong and tough, yet gentle and loving?

- I'm so fed up with my controlling wife; can you get her off my back?

- Can you help me to stand up to my parents without my ruining the relationship with them?

- What can I do to ease the frustration and tension at work? My boss always wants more.

- I am not sure I love my wife anymore. What do I do? No, there is no one else at this time.

- My wife and I disagree on disciplining the children. How can we work this out?

- My wife spends and spends. What can I do?

- What can I do; what did I do wrong? My wife is filing for divorce because she wants more excitement in her life. She won't reconsider, and I have the children.

- Can you help me with anxiety attacks? I may be laid off at my job soon, and we'll lose our house; a family member needs medical attention.

- How can I tell a woman I have genital herpes? Who would marry me? Are there support groups?

- Why doesn't my wife like my family?

- Why doesn't my wife keep house like she used to?

- How can I get my wife off my back about not being an adequate husband?

- Why are women turned off of sex after the marriage ceremony?
- Why are women money spenders?
- Why do women want to know everything going on in the marriage?
- How can I build my wife's self-esteem? Why is she so needy?
- Do I really need to pay child support and keep painful ties with an out-of-state ex-wife, or could I just forget the past and move on?
- How can I be financially responsible and still do what I want to do?
- I have worked day and night for my family; why is she still complaining?
- Why do women feel they own you after marriage, giving you no private time?
- Why do most women want to act like liberated people but then turn conservative at sex; the missionary is the only *proper* way?
- Why does my wife think her family has to come first?
- Why does my wife feel her values and religious beliefs are the most important for our children to learn?
- If God is all-powerful why do I need to come see a therapist?
- How can I express interests and characteristics that don't fit the "macho" stereotype without being labeled and/or alienated?
- Why am I so lonely? I don't think I have a problem establishing deep relationships.
- How can I sort through the good and bad or healthy and unhealthy things I have accumulated from my family of origin?

What are SMART WORDS?

Smart Words are frequently used words that are critical to understanding concepts taught in the classroom. The more Smart Words a child knows, the more easily he or she will grasp important curriculum concepts. Smart Words Readers introduce these key words in a fun and motivational format while developing important literacy skills. Each new word is highlighted, defined in context, and reviewed. Engaging activities at the end of each chapter allow readers to practice the words they have learned.

ISBN   978-0-545-33443-3

Packaged by Q2AMedia

Copyright © 2011 by Scholastic Inc.

Picture Credit: t= top, b= bottom, l= left, r= right

Cover Page: Andrew Rich/ Istockphoto.
Title Page: Andrew Rich/Istockphoto.
Content Page: Jose Luis Pelaez Inc/Photolibrary.

4: Stephen Kirklys/Istockphoto; 5: Monkey Business Images/Shutterstock, Aaliya Landholt/Istockphoto; 6: Ralph Hutchings, Visuals Unlimited/Science Photo Library; 8l: Cherick /Shutterstock; 8r: Timmary/Shutterstock; 10t: Marie Schmitt/Photolibrary; 10b: Micropix/Dreamstime; 11t: F D Giddings/Photolibrary; 11b: Dave Berkebile/Istockphoto; 12: Marie Schmitt/Photolibrary; 18: Sebastian Kaulitzki/Shutterstock; 20: Matka Wariatka/Shutterstock; 21: Dennis Kunkel/Photolibrary; 22: Tom Barrick, Chris Clark, Sghms/Science Photo Library; 23: Dr. David E Scott/Photolibrary; 25: Advent/Shutterstock; 26: Annedde/Istockphoto; 27: BanksPhotos/Istockphoto; 29: David Rosenbaum/Photolibrary; 30-31: Sebastian Kaulitzki/Shutterstock.

Q2AMedia Art Bank: Title Page, 7, 9, 14, 15, 16, 15, 24.

12 11 10 9 8 7 6   13 14 15 16/0

Printed in the U.S.A.   40
First printing, January 2011

Table of Contents

Chapter 1

The Amazing Brain

Quick! What street do you live on? Can you catch a ball? All of your memories, thoughts, emotions, and actions are controlled by your **brain**. Your brain is your body's control center. It is involved in everything you do.

A human brain doesn't look all that impressive. But your brain can do more than the best computer ever made. After all, no computer can enjoy a joke or make a friend.

The human brain is very complex. Scientists still don't fully understand the brain and how it works.

The brain doesn't work alone. It needs a way to send and receive messages. These messages travel by way of specialized cells called **neurons**. The brain and neurons work together to control your body's activities and respond to changes in your environment. This is the job of the nervous system.

The nervous system sends and receives messages to and from every part of your body. This is how it regulates body activities such as heart rate and breathing.

SMART WORDS

brain an organ of the nervous system that is the body's control center

neurons specialized cells designed to carry messages to and from the brain

Brain Basics

The average brain weighs about 3 pounds (1.4 kilograms). It looks something like a large, soft, wrinkly walnut.

For the brain to function properly, it needs a constant supply of oxygen and other materials. A network of blood vessels constantly supplies oxygen to the cells of the brain. If the brain goes without oxygen for even a few minutes, it may suffer permanent damage.

The brain sits inside the skull. The skull is a hard, bony covering that protects the brain and prevents damage.

The brain uses up 20 percent of the oxygen your body takes in. As you can see in this photo, many blood vessels make sure the brain receives what it needs!

The brain has three main parts: the **cerebrum**, the **cerebellum**, and the **brain stem**. Each part of the brain is responsible for different body activities.

cerebrum

- The cerebrum is responsible for all voluntary activities, or activities under your control, such as walking.

- The cerebellum controls balance and the actions of muscles.

- The brain stem controls activities that are involuntary, or not under your control, such as walking or thinking.

brain stem

cerebellum

SMART WORDS

skull   bony part of the head that protects the brain

cerebrum   part of the brain responsible for all voluntary activities, or activities under your control

cerebellum   part of the brain that controls balance and the actions of muscles

brain stem   part of the brain that controls activities that are involuntary, or not under your control

The Cerebrum

The largest part of your brain is the cerebrum. You use your cerebrum when you think, feel, remember, or imagine. It also allows you to move however you want.

The cerebrum is divided into two hemispheres, or halves. The *left* half of the cerebrum controls activities on the *right* side of your body and the *right* half controls the *left* side. Fortunately, the two halves are able to communicate by nerves running between them.

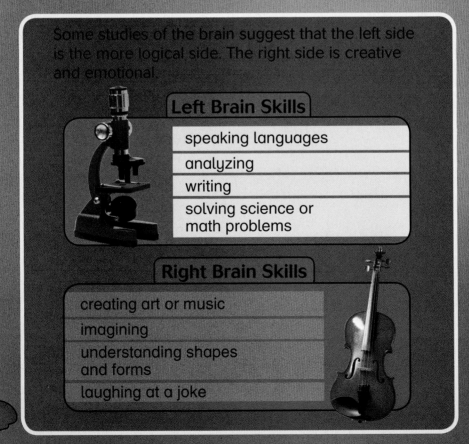

Some studies of the brain suggest that the left side is the more logical side. The right side is creative and emotional.

Left Brain Skills

speaking languages

analyzing

writing

solving science or math problems

Right Brain Skills

creating art or music

imagining

understanding shapes and forms

laughing at a joke

The cerebrum has a deeply folded surface called the **cerebral cortex**. All of the folds give this part of the brain more surface area, making room for billions of brain cells.

The cerebral cortex is where all of the information from your sense organs is received. Special nerve endings in your eyes, ears, nose, tongue, and skin, called **receptors**, respond to changes in the environment. Every message sent by the receptors goes to a specific part of the cerebral cortex, where it is interpreted and acted upon.

motor

touch

vision

speech

hearing

SMART WORDS

cerebral cortex the deeply wrinkled and folded surface of the cerebrum

receptors special nerve endings that respond to changes in the environment

9

The Cerebellum

If you look under the cerebrum, at the back of the brain, you'll find the cerebellum. The name itself means "little brain"— and it looks like a smaller version of the cerebrum!

You learned that the cerebrum controls voluntary movements, such as moving a leg. However, the impulses, or messages, sent from the cerebrum pass through the cerebellum. The cerebellum adjusts the impulses so muscles work together smoothly. It also helps you keep your balance.

cerebellum

Actions like this one require smooth movements and balance. The cerebellum makes such movements possible.

The Brain Stem

The brain stem sits on top of the spine and connects the brain to the rest of the body. It takes care of some really important activities — things you never even think about, such as your heartbeat, breathing, digestion, and blood pressure.

Messages from the brain stem tell your heart to work a little harder when you're climbing up a steep hill or your stomach to get going on the sandwich you just had for lunch.

The brain stem lies right next to the cerebellum. It works all the time just to keep you alive!

Answer each question with the correct Smart Word.

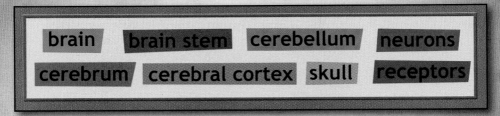

| brain | brain stem | cerebellum | neurons |
| cerebrum | cerebral cortex | skull | receptors |

1. What brain part helps you keep your balance?

2. What are the specialized cells designed to carry messages to and from the brain?

3. What part of the head protects the brain?

4. What do you call the wrinkled outer surface of the brain?

5. What brain part helps you think?

6. What brain part connects the brain to the rest of the body?

7. What is the body's control center?

8. What are special nerve endings that respond to changes in the environment?

Answers on page 32

Talk Like a Scientist

How would you explain the parts of the brain to a student from another class? Use Smart Words in your answer.

SMART FACTS

Did You Know?

Humans may be the smartest of all the animals, but we don't have the biggest brains. Here's how we compare:

Sperm whale	17 pounds (7.8 kilograms)	
Elephant	11 pounds (5 kilograms)	
Dolphin	3 pounds (1.4 kilograms)	
Adult human	3 pounds (1.4 kilograms)	
Dog	2.5 ounces (70.8 grams)	

Why are we smartest?

Compared to other animals, humans have a much bigger cerebrum — the part of the brain we use for thinking. Our cerebrums are cleverly folded and wrinkled to make the most use of the space inside our skulls.

13

Chapter 2

The Nervous System

As amazing as it may be, the brain could do nothing if it had no way to send and receive messages. It is the job of the neurons to form pathways along which messages can be sent. Only when the brain and neurons work together can the nervous system do its job.

The nervous system is divided into two parts — the **central nervous system** and the **peripheral nervous system**. The central nervous system is made up of the brain and **spinal cord**. The spinal cord is a long bundle of nerve tissue. Like the brain, it is protected by a bony cover, the backbone.

The spinal cord is surrounded by 24 interlocking bones called vertebrae.

The spinal cord is the main pathway for communication from the brain to the rest of the body. There are 31 pairs of nerves that connect the spinal cord with the second part of the nervous system, the peripheral nervous system.

brain

brain stem

nerves

spinal cord

The 31 pairs of nerves coming from the spinal cord are part of the central nervous system. They are the connection to the nerves in the rest of the body, or the peripheral nervous system.

SMART WORDS

spinal cord   the long bundle of nerves inside the backbone

central nervous system   the brain and the spinal cord

peripheral nervous system   all of the nerves that are not part of the brain or spinal cord

Messenger Cells

Neurons, or nerve cells, are responsible for carrying signals back and forth from the brain to other parts of your body. They come in many shapes and sizes, but they share common characteristics.

Each neuron cell has three main parts: a body, branching threads called **dendrites**, and a long "tail" called an **axon**. Some cells can have hundreds of dendrites, but only one axon.

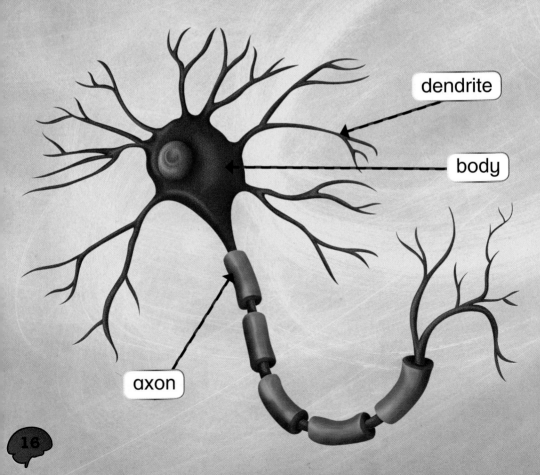

dendrite

body

axon

Neurons are well-designed for their job as messengers. Messages travel through the nervous system using neurons as pathways. These messages travel from one neuron to another as electrical signals, known as impulses.

Dendrites carry impulses toward the neuron's body. Axons carry impulses away from the neuron's body.

Some neurons are specially designed to send signals from sensory receptors to the central nervous system. Others are designed to send signals from the central nervous system out to the rest of the body. Yet another type of neuron acts simply as a connection between other neurons.

SMART WORDS

dendrites   threads branching from the cell body of a neuron

axon   the long tail of a neuron

impulses   electrical signals that carry messages through the nervous system

Sending Signals

So how do signals make their way all around your body? Messages must travel from neuron to neuron. And, actually, neurons don't even touch each other! When the dendrites receive an impulse it travels to the cell body and then down the axon. Remember, at this point the impulse is an electrical signal.

When the impulse reaches the end of an axon, it needs to find a way to get to the next neuron. The place where the signal travels from one neuron to another is called the synapse.

The synapse acts as a bridge from one neuron to the next.

Imagine that you want to lift your leg. Your brain would send a signal down your spine and through the neurons to your leg muscles, telling them to move.

Sometimes, you move without even thinking about it. When you touch something painful, a signal is quickly sent up to your spinal cord. This way, even before the message gets all the way to the brain, a signal is sent back telling your hand to pull away.

These quick, automatic movements are called **reflexes**.

receptor

spinal cord

To protect your body, some messages from your sense organs only have to go as far as your spinal cord to get a response. This could save precious time, preventing injuries.

SMART WORDS

synapse   the gap between neurons that acts as a bridge for impulses

reflexes   quick, automatic movements

Match each clue with the correct Smart Word.

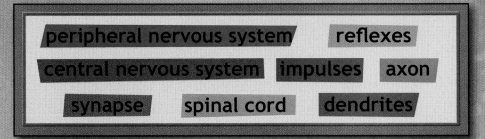

peripheral nervous system   **reflexes**

central nervous system   **impulses**   **axon**

synapse   **spinal cord**   **dendrites**

1. the brain and spinal cord

2. the bridge between neurons

3. quick, automatic movements

4. all of the nerves that are not part of the brain or spinal cord

5. the tail of a neuron

6. the bundle of nerves in the backbone

7. the threads branching from the cell body of a neuron

8. electrical signals that carry messages through the nervous system

Answers on page 32

Talk Like a Scientist

Pick up your pencil. Now explain what happened in your nervous system to make that happen. Use your Smart Words.

SMART FACTS

Did You Know?

If all the nerves in the body were linked together end to end, they would stretch for about 45 miles (72 kilometers).

That's Amazing!

Some neurons have axons that are more than 3 feet (1 meter) long. That makes them the biggest cells in your body.

Wow!

Some high-speed trains shoot along their tracks at more than 220 miles (850 kilometers) per hour. That's fast! But not as fast as the electrical signals that move along the axons of your neurons. They typically go about 250 miles (400 kilometers) per hour!

Chapter 3

The Brain in Action

One of the most important things neurons do is help you learn. The first time you try something new, such as reading a story or riding a bike, signals travel from neuron to neuron along a path. As you practice or repeat the activity, this pathway is used again and again. Pretty soon, things get a lot easier and you can read or ride a bike like a pro.

These colorful lines represent different pathways in the brain.

Nerves in the brain can be "trained" to remember how to do new things, such as learning a different language.

Kids often have an easier time learning new things than older people. There's a good reason for that.

When you are young, new paths are created between neurons every day. As you age, more and more of these paths are used and your knowledge increases. At about age 25, some of your neurons begin to die off. Since new neurons do not grow to replace them, it becomes a little harder to learn new things. Don't worry, though — enough neurons remain to keep you learning through old age!

Making and Storing Memories

Did you ever notice that you can remember some things from years ago, yet forget something you did two hours ago?

The brain divides information it receives into short-term and long-term memory. Your **short-term memory** stores information that happened minutes or hours ago. It has a very limited time span. Your **long-term memory**, however, keeps information for a long time.

MEMORY CHECKER

Look at these images for 45 seconds. Then cover them up and write down as many as you can remember. If you get more than 8 right, that's good. Twelve or more is excellent!

Sleeping may help your memory. You actually sleep in five different stages. During the **REM** stage, your eyes move back and forth under your eyelids and you begin dreaming. REM stands for "rapid eye movement."

Some scientists think the brain uses dreams to sort through the information it has received during the day.

Sleep Stages

1. The brain relaxes your muscles, slows the heartbeat, and lowers body temperature.

2. You go into a light sleep and can be easily woken.

3. Your brain lowers your blood pressure and you go into a deeper sleep.

4. You are in your deepest sleep and may sleepwalk or talk.

5. You begin REM sleep and dreaming.

* Stages 2–5 repeat throughout the night.

SMART WORDS

short-term memory   stores information that happened minutes or hours ago

long-term memory   stores information for a long time

REM   rapid eye movement; the stage of sleep when your eyes move back and forth under your eyelids and you begin dreaming

Studying the Brain

Just like the rest of your body, your brain and nervous system can become damaged or diseased. Doctors have many ways of finding out what's happening in the brain.

One thing that doctors study is **brain waves**. They use a device called an EEG (electroencephalograph) to measure electrical activity in your brain. This activity is displayed as waves that take different shapes depending upon what you are doing.

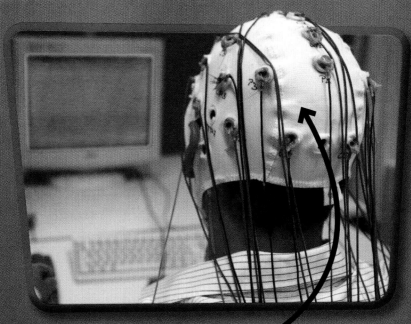

Electrodes placed on the scalp measure electrical signals in the brain. It provides a record of this activity, or an EEG.

Other types of equipment helps doctors see actual images of the brain.

- PET (positron emission tomography) scans show which areas of the brain are stimulated and active.
- CAT (computerized axial tomography) scans look at many layers of brain tissue.
- MRI (magnetic resonance imaging) scans take more detailed pictures of a layer of the brain.

This PET scan shows different levels of activity in a patient's brain. The red areas are most active and the blue areas are the least active.

SMART WORD

brain waves   electrical activity in the brain

Read each clue. Choose the Smart Word it describes.

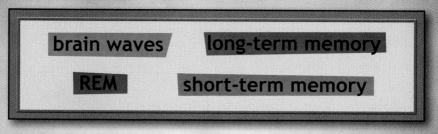

brain waves   long-term memory

REM   short-term memory

1. the stage of sleep when your eyes move back and forth under your eyelids and you begin dreaming

2. where information from long ago is stored

3. electrical activity in the brain

4. where information that happened minutes or hours ago is stored

Answers on page 32

Talk Like a Scientist

Imagine that you are a scientist, and an interviewer asks you about what the brain does to help people learn and remember. What would you tell her? Use Smart Words in your answer.

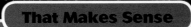

SMART FACTS

That Makes Sense

People tend to remember exciting, scary, or sad events. When you are feeling emotional, chemical changes in your brain make your nerves more active. This process improves your memory-making. That's why many long-term memories are of emotional moments.

Did You Know?

The part of your brain that deals with scents is closely linked to your memory. That explains why certain smells can suddenly make you remember things.

Get Your Rest!

Since your memories are stored while you sleep, a lack of sleep may actually hurt your ability to create new memories.

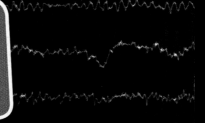

Glossary

axon   the long tail of a neuron

brain   an organ of the nervous system that is the body's control center

brain stem   part of the brain that controls activities that are involuntary, or not under your control

brain waves   electrical activity in the brain

central nervous system   the brain and the spinal cord

cerebellum   the part of the brain that controls balance and the actions of muscles

cerebrum   the part of the brain responsible for all voluntary activities, or activities under your control helps you think, move, and remember

cerebral cortex   the deeply wrinkled and folded surface of the cerebrum

dendrites   threads branching from the cell body of a neuron

impulses   electrical signals that carry messages through the nervous system

long-term memory stores information for a long time

neurons specialized cells designed to carry messages to and from the brain

peripheral nervous system all of the nerves that are not part of the brain or spinal cord

receptors special nerve endings that respond to changes in the environment

reflexes quick, automatic movements

REM rapid eye movement; the stage of sleep when your eyes move back and forth under your eyelids and you begin dreaming

short-term memory stores information that happened minutes or hours ago

skull bony part of the head that protects the brain

spinal cord the long bundle of nerves inside the backbone

synapse the gap between neurons that acts as a bridge for impulses

Index

SMART WORDS Answer Key

Page 12
1. cerebellum, 2. neurons, 3. skull, 4. cerebral cortex,
5. cerebrum, 6. brain stem, 7. brain, 8. receptors

Page 20
1. central nervous system, 2. synapse, 3. reflexes,
4. peripheral nervous system, 5. axon, 6. spinal cord,
7. dendrites, 8. impulses

Page 28
1. REM, 2. long-term memory, 3. brain waves,
4. short-term memory